"Stony the Road" to Change
Black Mississippians and the Culture of Social Relations

This book is the result of an ethnographic study of the impact of Black cultural diversity on social action. The ethnography has three important characteristics. First, it incorporates the multiple perspectives of the ethnographer with the diverse voices of the people through an unusual form of reflexivity that provides additional insight for the descriptions, analyses, and conclusions of the book. This epistemological method is used to challenge traditional structures of ethnographies. Second, it argues for the consideration of nontraditional approaches to studying the Black experience – a focus away from race relations and issues of class and an emphasis on intragroup interaction and diversity. Third, it investigates the processes, social institutions, and structures within the Black community of a small college town that influence social change and social action since the Civil Rights Movement of the 1960s.

Marilyn M. Thomas-Houston is currently interim director of African American Studies and an assistant professor of Anthropology and African American Studies at the University of Florida. She received her PhD in 1997 from New York University in Cultural Anthropology and a graduate certificate in Ethnographic Film during the same year. In addition to an MPhil and MA in Anthropology from NYU, she holds an MA in Southern Studies from the University of Mississippi. She is a member of the American Anthropologist Association, a member of the executive board of the Society for Visual Anthropology (holding the office of treasurer), a member of the Association of Black Anthropologists, and a member of the Society for Cultural Anthropology. Her research interests focus primarily on people of African descent in complex societies, power relations, development, transnational processes, social movements, and identity.

"Stony the Road" to Change

Black Mississippians and the Culture of Social Relations

MARILYN M. THOMAS-HOUSTON

University of Florida

CAMBRIDGE
UNIVERSITY PRESS

PUBLISHED BY THE PRESS SYNDICATE OF THE UNIVERSITY OF CAMBRIDGE
The Pitt Building, Trumpington Street, Cambridge, United Kingdom

CAMBRIDGE UNIVERSITY PRESS
The Edinburgh Building, Cambridge CB2 2RU, UK
40 West 20th Street, New York, NY 10011-4211, USA
477 Williamstown Road, Port Melbourne, VIC 3207, Australia
Ruiz de Alarcón 13, 28014 Madrid, Spain
Dock House, The Waterfront, Cape Town 8001, South Africa

http://www.cambridge.org

First published 2005

Printed in the United States of America

Typeface Sabon 10/13 pt.   *System* LaTeX 2$_\varepsilon$ [TB]

A catalog record for this book is available from the British Library.

Library of Congress Cataloging in Publication Data
Thomas-Houston, Marilyn M.
"Stony the road" to change : Black Mississippians and the culture of social
relations / Marilyn M. Thomas-Houston.
    p. cm.
Based on author's thesis (Ph.D.) – New York University, 1997.
Includes bibliographical references and index.
ISBN 0-521-82909-7 – ISBN 0-521-53598-0 (pbk.)
    1. African Americans – Mississippi – Oxford – Social conditions.   2. African Americans –
Mississippi – Oxford – Politics and government.   3. African Americans – Ethnic identity –
Mississippi – Oxford.   4. Pluralism (Social sciences) – Mississippi – Oxford.
5. Social action – Mississippi – Oxford.   6. Social change – Mississippi – Oxford.
7. Community life – Mississippi – Oxford.   8. Oxford (Miss.) – Social conditions.
I. Title.
F349.O94T47   2004
305.8'96073'076283–dc22   2004044243

ISBN 0 521 82909 7 hardback
ISBN 0 521 53598 0 paperback

Lift Every Voice and Sing
by James Weldon Johnson and J. Rosamond Johnson

Lift ev'ry voice and sing, Till earth and heaven ring,
Ring with the harmonies of liberty;
Let our rejoicing rise, High as the list'ning skies,
Let it resound loud as the rolling sea.

Sing a song full of the faith that the dark past has taught us,
Sing a song full of the hope that the present has brought us;
Facing the rising sun of our new day begun,
Let us march on till victory is won.

Stony the road we trod, Bitter the chast'ning rod,
Felt in the days when hope unborn had died;
Yet with a steady beat, Have not our weary feet,
Come to the place for which our fathers sighed?*

We have come over a way that with tears has been watered,
We have come, treading our path thro' the blood of the
    slaughtered,
Out from the gloomy past, till now we stand at last
Where the white gleam of our bright star is cast.

God of our weary years, God of our silent tears,
Thou Who hast brought us thus far on the way;
Thou Who hast by Thy might, Led us into the light,
Keep us forever in the path, we pray.

Lest our feet stray from the places, our God, where we met Thee.
Lest our hearts, drunk with the wine of the world, we forget Thee.
Shadowed beneath Thy hand, may we forever stand,
True to our God, true to our native land.

*My emphasis.

"Lift Every Voice and Sing" (written by J. Rosamond Johnson and James Weldon Johnson) used by permission of Edward B. Marks Music Company.

Freedmen Town Historical Marker (2004)

The black folks won't hire you, and the white folks won't either. Now that's equal opportunity.

• JD, 1996

For You:
Vivian Edwards Miller
John W. Miller, Sr.
John W. Miller, Jr.
Carl Edward Thomas
Kelvin Thomas
Michael Thomas

Contents

Preface

This study is intended to be useful for several audiences. With hopes of accomplishing this goal, I structured this study for a wide audience readership. As such, the focus is multilayered and the notes are extensive.[1] This method is incorporated as a means of providing students and teachers, activists and politicians, natives and foreigners with a deeper understanding of the Black experience in the United States. Because these various audiences have varying levels of knowledge about the social history of Blacks in the Americas, a great deal of background information (historical, geographical, and social) will be provided in footnotes. This allows the readers an opportunity to gain needed information that may be missing from their particular purview of the Black experience.

In constructing this work, I was influenced by the myths and misunderstandings that shape the thinking of audiences too young or too distant from experiences such as the Civil Rights Movement or slavery or the rural South to have a comprehensive understanding of the relationship between these phenomena and current events. For example, in an essay on the contributions of Martin Luther King, Jr., one student – born almost 20 years after King's assassination – wrote: "King was killed because he fought for equal rights of the slaves." The student was unable to make the distinction between the freedom of the slaves as a result of the Civil War and that of Blacks that resulted from the Civil Rights Movement.

History, tradition, and memory play major roles in the construction of regional culture. In order to provide readers with the most in-depth

---

[1] This design is similar to that of Geertz's (1980) work, which uses endnotes to provide the readers with as much theoretical and historical detail as they wish to pursue.

picture of the community of study, the text depends heavily on historical descriptions from oral histories and folklore. Through these histories,
we are able to trace the connections between current social interactions
and the historical construction of community. The privileging of written
history over oral tradition and memory is a major issue in the interpretive construction, reconstruction, and deconstruction of any moment in
time and space. Since many social scientists, particularly in anthropology,
have abandoned the notion of finding one great "Truth" in favor of documenting and interpreting multiple "truths," the practice of privileging
writing (as a scientific method) is problematic in the study of all cultures
as we work to construct models of the societies we study. The endeavor is
difficult in pluralist complex societies but becomes even more rigorous in
stratified societies. When studying such societies we are often influenced
by the very method (i.e., documentation) we use to accomplish our scientific goals of construction and interpretation, and we often are biased
against new data, particularly if it contests, delegitimates, or disputes previously documented data. In other words, we are often influenced by the
society's level of development.

If we are studying Third World societies that do not have extensively
recorded histories, there appears to be more willingness to accept oral
histories as the legitimate history, particularly when the same stories are
repeated from different sources. However, in complex societies – and here
I am speaking of the colonized societies of the Western Hemisphere – we
often look for confirmation in the written word rather than in oral history.
This is particularly problematic when members of the dominant society
or those educated by institutions of that society document the history or
culture of their colonized selves. The privileging of written history over
oral history also is a problem in raising the consciousness of audiences
who have privileged prerevisionist documentations and accepted them as
"reality." The new interpretations, particularly those based on the oral
aspects of a society, have difficulty displacing those first understandings
and impressions.

This quest for written authentication appears to rest its conclusions on
the belief that a written history of an event or a phenomenon is proof
and consequently Truth. As social scientists, we often give more credit
to the dominant society's perspective than to indigenous interpretations,
and although I caution students on this very issue – Western societies'
tendencies to attach, often unconsciously, the perception of Truth to information in print and just as often to first-printed interpretations – I
sometimes find myself guilty of the same tendency. That is the position

in which one African American organization in my community of study found itself while attempting to validate a section of town as an important historic site for African Americans. A sort of "catch-22" ensued: Written proof was needed, but no written proof was available. For these reasons, the text of this book uses oral histories and memories as its foundation. In addition, my position is that *what*, *how*, and *why* things are remembered matter most in people's negotiation of day-to-day existence. Therefore, the voices of the community are privileged above written documents.

Ethnographic research and publishing protocol require an ethnographer to do everything within her power to protect the identity of the participants in the research project. A part of that protection calls for pseudonyms for places as well as people.[2] The ethical and moral significance of this act is extremely valuable on the one hand and detrimental to the production of knowledge on the other. The value of this research is intricately related to the knowledge of a particular historically documented social event. As such, the recognition of the geographical location in which the event occurred is not only inevitable but also necessary. Therefore, no effort has been made in this work to disguise the area of research. The name of each collaborator is changed through randomly assigned initials in order to conceal identities. This precaution was taken although many said that their identities need not be hidden. While the use of initials instead of names may be difficult in terms of memory and association for the reader, I have chosen this approach for the following reasons. I expect this book to be distributed in the community of study, and the assignment of a name also assigns gender. In a number of cases, the concealment of gender is the primary means for protecting the identity not only of the individual but also of entire families. (Gender is assigned in some cases; however, that assignment is made only to establish social connections.) In most cases, social reprisals would not occur. However, initials provided the best option for constructing identities for the text, given the possibilities of redress, stigma, or negative public scrutiny. Because the specific area of study is identified, it is almost impossible to conceal the identity of public officials.[3] References and descriptions of events regarding these officials are all public knowledge and as such do not violate confidentiality.

---

[2] In spite of the efforts made by ethnographers to disguise their space of investigation, members of the profession always seem to know the exact geographical location and often refer to the actual name rather than the pseudonym.

[3] As anthropologists turn more to studying their own societies and publish there as well, this problem will need to be addressed.

The epistemological structure of this work includes what I believe an ethnography should be – a dialogue between the author and reader that includes not simply the multiple voices of the groups being described but also an understanding of the multiple perspectives of the ethnographer. As such, the work carries a twofold argument. On the one hand, it argues, through examples, that the background assumptions about the world of any ethnographer (native or nonnative, insider or outsider) must be questioned and negotiated; therefore, neither the ethnographer nor the audience to which she communicates can take them for granted. Since "fieldwork is as much a personal journey as it is a method of scientific inquiry" (Jamie Johnson, unpublished conversation), reflexivity is not limited to a small topical area of the introduction but is integrated throughout the chapters in an effort to clarify discussions the author views as being influenced by background assumptions. On the other hand, the work also argues through practice that the authoritative voice of the author/ethnographer should be questioned throughout the work. The researcher's decision to follow one path of questions rather than another is important in understanding the specific depth and breadth of the data provided. What better way than to bring the reader along on the research process by providing an understanding of when, why, and how particular data was viewed as important to the research agenda. It provides the reader the opportunity for discovery along with the researcher and leaves each step open for evaluating and understanding what has been left out of the discussion. Therefore, the research questions addressed in this work are provided in a kind of historical order reflecting the messiness of life as well as the messiness of a "scientific" study of society in which the questions were developed rather than implying through one major question that the research agenda was clearly thought out from its inception.

Finally, in the text, I use "intraracial/intraethnic" to point out that the category of race is predominantly a folk category that connects cultural and social identities to physical features. In daily interaction, the prejudices and discriminations constructed by members of the dominant society are generally carried out based on the assignment of physical features or the knowledge of lineage. Therefore individuals who according to the "one drop of blood" theory would be assigned to the "Black race" but carry no associated physical features may or may not experience discriminatory practices. It is my suggestion that the category "Blacks" should be considered a multicultural ethnic group not identifiable by phenotype or cultural practices but by the assertion of Blackness as identity. In this work, the term designates a politicized unit that shares a particular identity and relationship to the dominant society. From an anthropological perspective, Blacks are "the Other." In the text, I have also attempted to distinguish among "ethnic," "racial," and "cultural" in order to underscore their differences as well as their similarities.

Acknowledgments

This book has grown out of a dissertation submitted to the Department of Anthropology of New York University in May 1997. It has amassed debts to a great number of people. The following are nonhierarchical acknowledgments from my memory of people other than family who have provided intellectual inspiration, friendship, cooperation, and financial assistance that enabled my intellectual pursuits and the completion of this manuscript. Drs. Karen Blu, Constance Sutton, and Ronald W. Bailey have contributed greatly to my intellectual, personal, and professional growth. These contributions will not be forgotten, and I hope they are more than adequately represented here. Praises are due to Dr. Faye V. Harrison, whose intellectual gifts, scholarly successes, and down-to-earth nurturing personality have stood as shining examples and inspiration. Thanks are also due to my other graduate advisors and instructors, Drs. Owen Lynch, Faye Ginsburg, Claudio Lomnitz-Adler, Jeffrey Sammons, and the late Delmos Jones and Annette Weiner, whose suggestions have also contributed greatly to my intellectual development and often operated as lighthouses in a sea of academic distractions. I am grateful for the camaraderie of Ann Kingsolver, Dimitra Doukas, and Maureen Mahon. Our conversations provided a stimulating and reassuring environment in which to flesh out ideas. To Joan Lehn, Michel LaFantano, Larry Schnelle, Margaret Jogner, and my assistant Jamie Johnson whose special organizational and editing skills and unique ability to understand my writing when I could not, at times, understand it myself, I offer an appreciative thanks.

A special thank you goes to the University of South Carolina's and the University of Florida's Anthropology Departments and African American

Studies Programs for providing me with the time and incentive to complete this enormous task. Additional thanks go to the faculty of those departments for keeping me focused and to Deannie Stevens for sharing her computer knowledge during the early formation of this manuscript and Deborah Johnson-Simon for assisting with final proofing.

Many people in the Oxford/Lafayette County area have provided me with inspiration, conversation, suggestions, and consideration. First, I thank those individuals and families who consented to let me into their lives, minds, and hearts and assisted me in understanding their way of life. Without their cooperation, this work could not have been done. I hope and trust that this experience will be of as much value to them as it has and will be for me. They have my undying gratitude. In addition, I appreciate the legwork put in by some very special people, Mrs. Foster Houston, Mrs. Ann Phillippi-Warren, Mr. Ira Lee Morgan, Mrs. Delores Morgan, Mrs. Susie Marshall, Rev. Charles Brewer, and Mr. Leonard Thompson. They have my sincere best wishes. Deepest regards go out to sixteen of my collaborators who will not see the results of their energy and time because they have passed on to a less stony road. Peace!

I am appreciative of the confidence in the value of my manuscript afforded by Cambridge University Press and my manuscript reviews in general and Lew Bateman, Jessica Kuper, and Camilla Knapp, in particular. A special thanks to Daryl Michael Scott for encouraging me to stick with the manuscript to the end.

Finally, the economics must be considered. The National Science Foundation, the Graduate School of Arts and Sciences at New York University, and its Department of Anthropology funded my educational preparation for this work. The research that enlightens this work was funded in part by the Wenner-Gren Foundation for Anthropological Research. The primary funding for transforming the long and drawn-out, dissertation-length manuscript into this book was provided by Drs. Gordon B. Smith, interim dean of the College of Liberal Arts (1998–9), and Joan Hinde Stewart, current dean of the College of Liberal Arts, The University of South Carolina.

If I have forgotten anyone who has contributed to my intellectual growth and completion of this work, I offer my sincere and deepest apologies. But know that within my heart I realize "It takes a whole village to raise a child" and the support of family and friends to grow from student to academic.

Introduction

While traveling west along a beautiful tree-lined street of postbellum homes in Oxford, Mississippi, I observed what I thought to be a disturbing example of the quality of race relations in this quiet university town. A Black man, about 75 years old – driving approximately twenty-five miles per hour – was traveling in front of me along the same side street. Although the light changed from red to green a few seconds or so before the elderly gentleman arrived at the intersection, he stopped. Puzzled by his stopping, I tried to see what was wrong. I saw the vehicle on the cross street come to a stop as well, and knew the problem wasn't traffic. He then beckoned for the car – driven by an elderly White woman, in her late 70s or early 80s – to continue across. My "big city" impatience and "middle-class" self-importance induced me to blast my horn. To my dismay, the "gentleman" waited and the "lady" – after a couple of moments of thought – proceeded across against the light. "We don't have to live like this anymore," I thought while witnessing the unfamiliar show of deference in this Black–White/male–female interaction. "This is 1983," almost twenty years after the Civil Rights Movement (CRM)[1] brought an end to the Jim Crow period in the state and federal troops supported the integration of the University of Mississippi. The year 1983 was nineteen years after the signing of the first Voting Rights Act. Needless to say, the event was traumatic. More importantly, this event and similar ones I witnessed

---

[1] "CRM" and "the Movement" are used (for economy and flow) to refer to the Civil Rights Movement of the 1960s and 1970s.

became driving influences that guided my academic and personal searches for understanding during the next twelve years.

My assumptions about the value of the Civil Rights Movement coincided with perceptions of most Northern and urban dwellers. The Movement was (and to a point still is) viewed as a cohesive effort carried out by Blacks to bring about social change in the United States during the 1950s and 1960s. Along with this view are two major assumptions. The first, greatly influenced by the sheer numbers of people participating and the large regional area of the United States in which its activities were carried out, is the belief that a homogeneous African American community embraced the goals of the Civil Rights Movement.[2] The second assumption focuses on the gains of the movement and is influenced by changes in federal and state laws, the different "interracial" climate, and the large number of Blacks holding public office. This assumption takes for granted that the lives of Blacks in this country have significantly changed. My motivation for embarking on a study that deconstructs these assumptions was not simply my scholarly interest in studying social change but also my interest, as an activist anthropologist, in helping to institute change. My goals were to help facilitate social consciousness on a number of levels and through a number of means.[3] The research questions that influenced the collection of data constituting the body of this work, therefore, are greatly influenced by those interests. Because I, too, held the preceding assumptions, there was a need to understand why the CRM appeared not to have had a significant impact on the lives of Blacks in Lafayette County, Mississippi, so late in the twentieth century.

My journey began in 1983 when I moved to Oxford – five years before conducting organized research as an undergrad in the area and eleven years before completing the anthropological research that informs this work. But my experience at that stoplight on my very first day in town marks the beginning of my inquiry into the differences between the behavior of African Americans in other communities where I previously lived

---

[2] Most discussions of the Civil Rights Movement tend to see the multiple levels and circumstances of mobilization as one coordinated whole, usually spoken of as "under the leadership of Martin Luther King," a perspective that often hides the ideological differences that influenced the various mobilization efforts. There is also a tendency to overlook or gloss over contested spaces of purpose and goals, such as the varied tactics used to raise social consciousness and bring about social change.

[3] Ethnographic Films and Anthropology seemed the perfect venues for carrying out consciousness-raising ventures. I had been influenced by anthropologist Zora Neale Hurston's work and its value in raising the level of appreciation and sympathy for the experiences of ordinary Black folk and their culture.

and worked and the behavior of Oxford's African American residents. My first instinct was to place the reason for differences in behavior on small-town life. However, more interaction with people of the community led me to believe that problems of the region were systemic, and, as such, a particular type of social structure was responsible for influencing the specific levels of interracial relations witnessed. Although I somewhat understood the need for such behavior in the past, reasons for its existence in the present escaped me. Had Blacks in Lafayette County internalized Jim Crow practices to such a degree that they were now unable to abandon the behavior that developed out of their post–Civil War experience? Were they unable to produce new behavior under the new post–CRM social conditions? I anticipated, as most lay people would, that a university town – especially one with a history of social movement activity – would be progressive in terms of cultural production and social consciousness. Additionally, as a person who passed into young adulthood at the beginning of the television generation, I assumed that other African Americans had been enlightened by television and mass communication – Western inventions that I believed were part of a globalization process[4] – in much the same way.

This was not the case in Oxford. Here was a way of "being Black" that did not fit with my understanding of the meaning of being Black in the United States in the 1980s. This "way of being" differed from what I knew about the meaning of the position of being Black in Mississippi. Biographies and autobiographies such as *Coming of Age in Mississippi* (Moody 1968), *For Us the Living* (Evers 1967), and *Fannie Lou Hamer* (Jordan 1972) had introduced me to the significant role Black Mississippians played in the movement. The lives of these activists appeared to have developed and been influenced by a particular social consciousness their fellow Mississippians in Oxford did not share. I wanted to know why.

Having witnessed through my personal relationships the values placed on oral storytelling as opposed to those placed on reading, local friends were asked regularly, "Doesn't everybody have a TV?" I knew that African Americans were major consumers of television and that many of the shows on television had begun to show African Americans living different lifestyles and having different responses to Whites. Television news

---

[4] Read "globalization" as consciousness raising. Communications studies suggest that the bombardment of real life and fictional stories in film and television produce homogeneous cultural practices on national and international levels. Ideas about global markets and consumerism also support theories of homogeneity.

reported stories of successful Blacks in corporate as well as political arenas. These stories, I thought at that time, should have influenced the
residents' understanding of where African Americans stood in today's
society. However, through my eyes, the behavior of Blacks in Lafayette
County did not reflect an understanding of the changes revealed through
television nor an appreciation for the gains of the Movement.

"Culture shock" was the term most often used by the locals as they
tried to help me "adjust" (and perhaps "adapt") to my new environment.
"But I was born and raised in a small town," was my protest against
this accusation of my disconnectedness from the community, although I
realized that Florence, South Carolina, was not as small as Oxford. "I'm
Black [I found myself arguing] and they are Black and we have experienced
the same kinds of problems, but I don't know any people who act like –
this." By the end of this sentence I was struggling to find the right words,
each time trying to avoid such terms as "slave mentality" and "Uncle
Tom." Having heard them for years, I rejected them as inappropriate
terminology for referring to "my people." The negative images such words
conjured up conflicted greatly with my cherished images of the way "we"
actually *are* as a people. I had become convinced that the terminology
originated in the dominant society and its use was "just another way to
keep us divided as a people." Efforts to resolve the conflicting images
guided my subsequent search for who we are as a people and why we are
the way we are.

The major paradox of Oxford is that despite its centrality to radical
civil rights activity widely publicized in the national and international
press, closer inspection reveals a virtual lack of participation by local residents. Understanding how this could occur, why Blacks are so diverse
as a people, why the Civil Rights Movement had such a markedly different impact in African American communities, and the ways in which
this impact influences social action and behavior also became my driving
intellectual and personal goals. These goals eventually led me to the field
of anthropology and the 1994–5 research that informs this ethnographic
study.

As time passed and I pursued my undergraduate studies at Ole Miss,
I developed closer relationships with members of the African American
community. I began to realize that many were good, hard-working people who wanted the same things for themselves and their children that I
wanted – survival without excessive struggle, spiritual peace, and better
lives for our offspring and ourselves. Although these same ideals seemed
to me to be what the Civil Rights Movement was all about, more interaction within the African American community led me to see that many of

its members had different meanings for "survival," "peace," and a "better life." I wanted to understand the local meanings, why they had developed, and the influence they had on the community's seeming reticence to assert its hard-earned rights.

Although my early investigations between 1983 and 1989 revealed the disruptive quality civil rights activities had on communities where activities were initiated from the outside, I continued to believe that the progress of the movement was seen as beneficial and had generated feelings of pride and self-importance. Yet, when asked in 1983 whether the presence of troops in the town gave him a sense of power and pride never felt before, a man who was 11 years old during the integration of Ole Miss said, "The only thing I know [that felt different] was, before the troops came I could ride my bicycle anywhere I wanted to, and after, I couldn't." The troops' presence had completely different meanings based on varying value systems and interpretations of symbols. I viewed the presence as liberating, and he, limiting. In spite of our common history and heritage, there were some significant differences in the worldviews of Oxford's African American population and my own.

What was there about the Oxford experience that made this regional group differ from others in their approach to social problems that affected African Americans as a group? Our ways of viewing the world and, even more important to my personal interests, our ways of dealing with the world after the movement were different. Unwillingly, I began to accept that although almost everyone owns a TV or has access to one, particular historical, social, and cultural factors have an impact on that particular medium's influence. In spite of the belief that the world is "tightly enmeshed in a single global economy, [that is] intertwined by vast networks of telecommunication" (Glick-Shiller 1994:1), exposure through media to the tremendous social changes that have occurred since the Civil Rights Movement has *not* produced or perpetuated either universal cultural practices or ideologies. With these experiences, understandings, and questions, I entered the field in 1994 to explore processes, institutions, and structures that influence intragroup interaction among African Americans in Lafayette County, Mississippi, and their subsequent impact on social change, social action, and mobilization.

BUILDING A NEW PERSPECTIVE

Armed with new analytical tools, research methodologies, and anthropological theories, I returned to Oxford after an absence of four years. The new questions to which I sought answers were better informed by theory and praxis. I was convinced that answers to my earlier questions could be found within the Black community itself, so my primary methodological focus of the ethnographic study was the observation of day-to-day interaction through which the social processes, institutions, and cultural and social problems that influence social action and political participation efforts of grassroots African Americans since the Civil Rights Movement could be examined. My approach to the study differs from earlier movement-focused works because it seeks out the perspective of those who stood on the sidelines. Observations in 1994–5 of social practices similar to that described in the anecdote at the beginning of this introduction and knowledge of the civil rights and race relations history of this small college town led to questions centering on the relationship of contemporary social practices to the lack of participation in the movement. Is there a relationship between standing on the sidelines and reaping the benefits of a social movement? What is there about the structure of this particular community that prevented its members from joining the movement and helping to institute change within its own borders? In what way does this community's particular history have an impact on current practices?

Throughout their presence in the "New World," African Americas have lived under political, economic, and social repression. The institution of slavery, the "class/caste" system of social segregation and "Jim Crow-isms" that replaced it, and racism have been the key structural forces they have struggled to overcome. In spite of these oppressive conditions, African Americans have often contested their subjugated position in society and negotiated social change. Their struggles have taken many forms and have had varying degrees of success and failure. When I first arrived in Lafayette County, I assumed similar struggles occurred there. After all, this was the site of one of the most dramatic and internationally known events to take place in the history of the CRM.[5] But a different dynamic took place in this community, a dynamic clearly unlike those I witnessed and read about. The antebellum and postbellum homes that graced tree-lined streets symbolized more than a former way of life; they appeared to be symbols of the present conditions of servitude that did not reflect the changes brought about by the movement.

An examination of the Civil Rights Movement literature reveals gains in a number of areas of Black life. Perhaps the most significant

---

[5] More than twenty thousand federal troops were sent to assist James Meredith's integration of the University of Mississippi. During this effort, three people were killed.

areas – those that have undergone revolutionary change – are interracial interaction and political participation. A number of important works focusing on the Movement were written since the beginning of the turbulent 1960s. Most of these studies have been structured around the lives of movement participants in their own communities or about civil rights workers who traveled from community to community making the struggle for civil rights a way of life.[6] What is missing from the annals of the Civil Rights Movement is the perspective of those who stood on the sidelines – the varying perspectives of the vast number of nonparticipants whose lives also were affected and often believed to be transformed by the efforts of the movement's participants. Rather than focus primarily on the ways agency manifested itself in Oxford, a significant portion of this work concentrates specifically on intraethnic issues that problematize interracial interaction, political participation, and social change.

From existing literature, we know the ways in which the lives of many of the participants have changed, and we know many assumptions associate perceived changes in quality of life for Blacks as a social group with reported economic advances, such as the right to vote, and institutional corrective measures. The larger numbers of registered Black voters, more Black elected officials, a growing Black middle class, and increased numbers of Blacks in institutions and positions traditionally peopled by Whites bear witness, many believe, to "social progress." But what does this all mean on the level of day-to-day experiences for the masses, particularly those who stood on the sidelines? Have their lives changed? Is there a difference in the ways in which they negotiate their day-to-day struggles? And what are the perceptions affecting that negotiation? In what way, if any, is the "stony road" they travel a construction of the structure of the Black community itself and the intragroup dynamics that occur within that community? By including these questions, this study provides another important layer to our understandings of Black life, social movements, mobilization, and social change.

---

[6] A representative sample of those publications by both Black and White authors include autobiographies such as Moody's *Coming of Age in Mississippi* (1968) and Durr's *Outside the Magic Circle* (1985); historiographies by Barrett, *Integration at Ole Miss* (1965), Holt, *The Summer That Didn't End* (1965), and Silver, *Mississippi: The Closed Society* (1964); and sociological and anthropological studies by Orum, *Black Students in Protest: A Study of the Origins of the Black Student Movement* (1972) and Meier and Rudwick, *CORE: A Study in the Civil Rights Movement, 1942–1968* (1973). Local politicians and newspapers often referred to the workers these studies focused on as "outsiders," an important point for understanding the dynamics of the movement from both White and Black Southern perspectives.

In addition to shedding light on issues related to mobilization, another layer of the study provides a significant look at issues of identity that inform our understanding of such socially constructed categories as race, ethnicity, and class. A contemporary gaze toward the documentation of the study of race has been reinstituted within the field of anthropology with an emphasis on the significance of that social category (e.g., Harrison 1995a, 1998; Gregory and Sanjek 1996). Intraracial social change among Blacks has garnered little attention in the field of anthropology in the past and is an important body of knowledge not only for building theories on the significance of race but also for expanding theories of social change. As the study reveals, perceptions are important to our understanding of the usefulness of such categories as race, ethnicity, and class in explaining the conditions under which social action is likely to occur.

This study differs in a number of ways from other social science studies and specifically the anthropological community studies. Through the analysis of issues that contribute to political participation and to the development of social movements, the study provides ethnographic data for current critical discussions on the defects of the "culture construct" as an analytical tool.[7] In addition, the study provides a look at intraethnic interaction and the ways in which it influences and is influenced by issues of identity particularly in the area of "cultural" boundaries, an area of the African American experience heretofore neglected in anthropology literature. Knowledge gained from this work has major significance for African Americans who, since Emancipation, have consistently struggled against forces of colonialism and the consequences of imperialism to build a "nation within a nation," and for scholars who investigate processes of identity construction and ethnicity.[8]

Since W. E. B. DuBois wrote *The Souls of Black Folk* in 1903, social scientists have struggled to identify the ways in which "two-ness" or "double-consciousness" (i.e., being both of African descent *and* American by birth) influences behavior and efforts toward nationalism among Blacks in America. The investigation of African American participation in the American political system, a system that for more than three hundred years strategically excluded the African American as an "equal-in-power"

[7] See Brightman (1995) for a comprehensive analysis of the culture construct as currently represented in anthropological writing.

[8] Williams' (1991) work investigates the process of identity construction among the Guyanese and vividly describes their efforts "to achieve a consciousness of nationhood" and how particular relations of personal identity reproduce ethnic chauvinism, racial stereotyping, and religious bigotry within this process of nation building.

participant, highlights the depths to which that two-ness contests, sustains, and constructs hegemonic structures. These issues related to two-ness are generally not discussed in formal settings. This work attempts to provide through identity stories an understanding of the divisiveness two-ness creates within the group. Two-ness was a significant factor in the variations in goals among the African American community during the CRM, and those varying goals intersect with processes of social change to produce a complex view of the impact of social movements and the idea of shared experiences as mobilizers and unifiers among participants.[9] The investigation also provides – for critics who contest universal allocation of persons to distinct groups – examples of the conditions under which multiple discourses further divide a community or come together to form larger systemic configurations.[10]

WHY MISSISSIPPI?: METHOD TO THE MADNESS

My personal experiences, no doubt, are important enough reasons for choosing this particular region as my area of study, but there are other historical and social reasons that make this selection important to the study of social change, social movements, and political participation. Because the South was the major arena in which the CRM was staged, the region is an appropriate location for observing the actual long-term impact on people who first felt its influence in their daily lives more than thirty-five years before this study. But what was the social and political climate like in the 1950s and 1960s? On the one hand, the struggle for social change in Mississippi was one of the most brutal struggles during the Civil Rights Movement. Church bombings and burnings, lynchings and assassinations, and the use of armed local and state forces to physically prevent nonviolent demonstrations were regular and expected occurrences.

[9] The CRM simply serves as an ideological and structural point in time from which social change can be examined. To evaluate the quality of the expected change, however, the goals of that movement and areas of contestation must be understood. The purpose of the movement was to institute economic, political, and social change. Although the Movement had a national impact, a number of African American communities and individuals from varied Black communities were reserved in their participation and support. A few nationally outspoken individual African Americans voiced support for the goal of equality but opposition to integration (e.g., Zora Neale Hurston).

[10] The investigation of two-ness provides examples of what Dirks (1994) refers to as varying discourses "coexisting within dynamic fields of interaction and conflict" and what Lomnitz-Adler (1992) refers to as the "culture of social relations" and the lack of cultural coherence, which will be discussed later.

On the other hand, and in spite of the tremendous violence and threats of violence, activism appeared to permeate every corner of Mississippi. Additionally, a great many communities, urban and rural, benefited directly from this insistence on social change. For example, in spite of its reputation as the state with "overwhelming obstacles" and an extremely oppressive social system for Blacks, Mississippi since the 1980s has had the unique distinction of having more elected Black officials than any other state in the union. Many stories about Mississippi detail successful influences of the movement, but areas uninfluenced by the movement remain uncharted courses. Because of these uncharted courses, my research was based in Lafayette County, Mississippi. Lafayette County was a key location in which civil rights activities occurred, and it served as a catalyst for regional and national changes in social policies. Yet unlike most of the other areas of Mississippi that the Civil Rights Movement touched, the town of Oxford and Lafayette County are often referred to, by some of its residents, as "the place the Civil Rights Movement left behind."

Lafayette County, Mississippi, is an excellent location for gaining perspectives from nonparticipants. The economic, social, and political structure of the community and the 1994 perceptions of African American residents regarding their position in that structure provide rich data for understanding the ways in which their lives have and have not changed. The daily routines through which the Black community negotiates the supposed gains of the Movement shed light on intragroup interpretations of what it means to be Black in America, the place of Blacks within the country, and the effect those interpretations have on mobilization. For example, in spite of the stiff competition Mississippi gives Alabama and South Carolina each election year for recognition as having the most Black elected officials, Lafayette County, which has a 26 percent Black population, did not elect a Black to public office until the 1990s, more than twenty-five years after the integration of the University of Mississippi and the passing of the Voting Rights Act.[11]

This investigation also provides a detailed ethnographic description of the spatial, economic, religious, social, political, ideological, and demographic structures of Mississippi's Lafayette County African American community. Ways in which these social phenomena have an impact on concepts of identity and are interconnected in terms of their influence on social change and behavior are emphasized. Identifying the

---

[11] According to the 1990 U.S. Census, Lafayette County has a population of 7,980 African Americans, 23,151 Whites, and 695 "other races."

interconnectedness of these social phenomena is crucial to understanding the ways in which Lafayette County African Americans operate within those social boundaries that shape their worldviews and consequently "the culture of social relations."[12]

The larger ethnographic problem is twofold: First, it is concerned with the relationship of group identity, cultural practices, and perceptions of power relations to mobilization, social change, persistence, and resistance in Oxford, Mississippi. The emphasis, however, is on *African American* resistance to the changes sought by the Civil Rights Movement in the area of their day-to-day living – addressing how we are to make sense of this lack of embracing those changes. Second, it investigates the ways in which history, tradition, and memory interconnect with social and spatial structures to constrain interethnic and interracial interaction. And as such, the social and spatial structures not only contribute to social segregation and increasing gaps of interracial and interethnic socioeconomic disparities but also foster alienation, isolation, and segmentation in intraracial and intraethnic relations.

The primary goals of the Civil Rights Movement were to tear down the walls of segregation and difference, create an appreciation for the humanity of all Americans, and build a more democratic society in which America's diverse population could exercise the political, social, and human rights guaranteed by the Constitution. Thus, a significant portion of this work addresses the interconnectedness of ethnic and racial identity, spatial isolation (de facto housing segregation and the interrelatedness of place), tradition, history, and memory to processes of social change, persisting concepts of stratified difference, and the resistance to meaningful interethnic or interracial interaction. These issues are addressed, not by collecting numerous descriptions of interethnic interaction such as the "first contact" story but rather by focusing on varied intraethnic perceptions of power and the way it is negotiated during a particular point in history. In spite of the numerous changes toward "equality" and "first-class citizenship" created by the movement, current conditions of Black life on a national basis point to the differences in life chances among Blacks rather than to shared experiences and values. Diversity and its impact on social action was the beginning of this investigation. As I researched the original questions the importance of the interconnectedness of nonmovement experience generated additional questions. Therefore,

---

[12] A detailed discussion of this phrase and other terms adopted from Lominitz-Adler will follow in the section that explains the frames guiding data gathering for this project.

an investigation of (1) the influences that produce difference from shared general experiences and (2) those boundaries that define the varying levels of intraethnic social interaction becomes important to any understanding of the impact of cultural diversity on social action.

METHOD FOR THE MAZE

Without a doubt, the development of a method for studying contemporary complex societies is extremely difficult. The complicated maze-like mixture of historical perspectives, forms of stratification, fluctuating boundaries of power relations, and intragroup diversity is so finely blended that the separation and analysis of various parts require highly varied forms of data collection.

Instead of studying race relations, laws, and the structure of social movements, as many earlier twentieth-century ethnographers have done, I sought to define the values, motivations, and ideologies of members of a specific African American community. The traditional categories and processes used to analyze the African American community as one socially organized unit are problematic in several ways: First, the social and economic divisions used in the class/caste models do not necessarily apply to all members of the African American community nor do they represent the most important social divisions that are made by the community and the meanings that are assigned to them. Second, race relations, though an important issue for examining American as well as African American culture, is not the sole factor that defines behavior within the African American community. And third, the diversity within the larger African American community extends beyond ethnic, regional, and cultural differences to a variety of ideological perspectives, even *within* small rural towns such as Oxford. The quality and level of relations within the racialized group provides valuable insight into African American behavior both inside and outside that community.

Such a study must highlight intragroup concepts of self and place, varying ideologies within the African American community, and meanings of social and economic status, processes, and institutions and how they influenced past behavior within the Black community. How and why these same views, processes, and institutions continue to affect interracial and ethnic interaction and complicate ideas about social change in the "heart" of the South are also important areas for investigation. Because of the complexity of such a study, I gathered in-depth detail about the social life of African American members of the larger Oxford/Lafayette County community rather than limit documentation to a description and analysis of voting patterns or the impact of the Black public sphere on public policy.

Since Oxford is a nonurban/semirural community whose social and political borders blend into "the county" areas – in terms of family relations, social institutions, city, county, and community-operated services – I decided to concentrate my data-gathering efforts in both county as well as town areas. I carried out preliminary research between 1987 and 1994. To capture the details of life in Oxford, I collected data primarily through participant observation over an additional period of twelve months and periodic revisits. Out of the twelve families studied intensely, I lived with seven families, completed fifteen extended audio-recorded interviews with other members of the community, attended almost every meeting of Black political and civic organizations (three of which I maintained active memberships in), attended religious services and business meetings of ten of the forty-five Black churches of the county, interacted with young adults as well as senior citizens in a variety of social settings, and secured a job working for the largest employer in the county in order to document specific details that define the varying levels of intragroup/intraethnic interaction and the culture of those social relations. Along with archival research related to the establishment of the town and county and the founding of various churches and community organizations, life histories were taken from each member of the twelve families in order to identify historical factors that contribute to varying degrees of (inter- and intra)ethnic interaction and varying levels of social consciousness and concern. Other interviews specifically related to the Civil Rights Movement and its influence on the practices of local residents born and raised in Oxford were conducted throughout the twelve-month period during group and individual sessions. With the exception of following working family members to their places of employment, all social public activities and most private activities in which family members participated were observed.[13] Two family reunions were videotaped.

I used this method of data gathering to examine African American forms of resistance to and/or compliance with hegemonic structures in

---

[13] Permission, in advance, was sought and received from all family members regarding this intrusive and sometimes harmful process. It was harmful in the sense that notoriety received by some groups or their members can be disruptive to the social structure of that group (i.e., Nisa and the Kung). In another sense, some Whites in Mississippi continue to exercise control over their workers. Because an anthropologist's work in communities is not covert, association with that individual in any form may and often is looked upon with suspicion and fear. During the time this research was conducted, economic reprisals continued to be used in Mississippi to "keep Blacks in their place."

the context of day-to-day social interaction. Such observations provided me with an understanding of the areas in which Blacks asserted rights struggled for and won during the Civil Rights Movement. This method also illuminated the structures and processes developed within the African American community itself that helped to maintain the segregation and/or oppression of African Americans in the southern United States. I paid particular attention to their individual reactions to situations of possible social conflict, focusing primarily on how people as social actors perceived their situation. I also distributed questionnaires specifically related to local elections to members of four different churches and to a specific group of "non-church-going" members of the Black community.

Understanding the small-town atmosphere and the different ways in which the Black community is divided was important to the way I structured my reentry into the community. My preliminary investigations revealed that intragroup interaction was defined by membership in various organizational arenas and each organization is ranked according to value-based criteria (i.e., church and church activities, community organizations, work, neighborhood, family, social activities). While intragroup borders are often crossed, particularly by relatives, as will be discussed in the section on "intimate culture" groups, behavior modification occurs in less prestigious groups most often when the borders of a less prestigious group are crossed by a member of a more prestigious group. In the Oxford/Lafayette County community, the majority of the population accords the regular church-going Christians the highest level of prestige, particularly in terms of deference. With this knowledge, I was able to organize my fieldwork and determine which families I would live with first. To eliminate extremely guarded behavior during the periods of residing in the homes of my collaborators, I began my fieldwork by living with less prestigious families first and the more highly regarded ones after. Economically, the households ranged from recipients of social services to those with multiple working adults. My living arrangements in the homes ranged from sleeping on the floor of the living room in a sleeping bag to displacing the youngest child from her bed to occupying an occasionally inhabited guest room. The occupations of my collaborators ranged from manual laborers to college professors. Social environments varied from drug dens to family reunions. I attended Baptist, Methodist, and Presbyterian churches and one newly established nondenominational house of worship. Other sects such as Jehovah's Witness, Seventh Day Adventist, and Holiness are represented, but I was unable to include visits to these houses of worship.

THE FRAME

The larger more general understanding from the ethnographic data focuses on the impact of identity on social change and movements. To gain this understanding, I used as guideposts theories regarding the influence of the spatial dimensions of cultural production and identity, the interaction of minority groups in cultures of hegemonic domination, and the theory of "placing" as an activity that provides an understanding of where people are ideologically at any given time. And as such, works of Lomnitz-Adler (1991), Ogbu and Gibson (1991), and Kingsolver (1992) have influenced the structure of this research and analysis.

The historical aspect of regional culture construction and its impact on contemporary issues of identity, ideology, and coherence is critical to understanding events and relationships in Oxford/Lafayette County. Southern history and the experiences of Mississippi's African American communities prior to the Civil Rights Movement are unique and profound phenomena that have had an impact on the South as a region of the United States and African Americans as an ethnic group. These historical spatial considerations help us understand – even in the present day – fundamental aspects of the local culture and the way in which space affects cultural production in such key areas as intragroup ideology. This in turn affects mobilization along group and ethnic lines. The interrelatedness of space and place, therefore, becomes a necessary body of knowledge for the understanding of intragroup and intraethnic cultural diversity. Lomnitz-Adler's argument regarding the necessity for locating areas where cultural production differs according to varying levels of interaction within regions provides the foundation for understanding differences in practice that exist among African Americans in Lafayette County, Mississippi.[14] This kind of regional analysis is important for the African American experience

---

[14] Lomnitz-Adler's frame for studying regional culture was developed using a colonial experience different from that of African Americans. However, the development of a caste-like system of stratification in Mexico based on ethnicity presented two poles of exceptionally unequal power, and his idea of "place" for the two social types, in my opinion, is in a number of ways similar to that of race relations in the United States. The dissimilarities between the control of African Americans and the colonization of Mexico's indigenous populations (and the subsequent Fourth World forms of government) are such that modification of his frame for analysis is necessary for dealing with the particular history of the forced immigrants of the United States. ("Forced immigrant" is a term appropriated from Ogbu and Gibson's [1991] *Minority Strategies and Schooling: Immigrant vs. Involuntary Minorities.*) Because of the slave/servant status of the forced immigrants and the plantation system of the Southern agrarian society, the "economic organization of space" that Lomnitz-Adler refers to has different dimensions.

in Mississippi if we are to understand why African American participation in political processes differs within communities around the state.

The connections between the spatial arrangement of power relations and cultural and ideological production are also important aspects of this study. In order to make these connections, the concepts of "culture of social relations," "intimate culture group," "localist ideology," and "co-herence," from Lomnitz-Adler (1991) with slight modification have been extremely helpful. They provide for this interpretation a way of discussing intragroup and regional structures and relationships that have previously been ignored in cultural studies. Because these concepts help to shed more light on behavior among African Americans that would otherwise support earlier – more stereotypical – assumptions about Blacks, their meanings, how they are used, and why these sociological concepts are important to the interpretation are explained.

The "culture of social relations" identifies culturally influenced or so-cially constructed *levels of interaction* and is used in this work to refer to the nature, quality, and intensity of interaction between individuals, or members of groups, or organizations. This term points to the conditions and circumstances under which people interact with each other as well as the quality of that interaction. The term is also used to draw our attention to the fact that power relations play a significant role in constructing that specific interaction we observe. In addition, the term is intended to call the reader's attention to the fact that this specific interaction has its own history, consistently constructs a particular social environment (through behavior and language), and occurs under specific conditions. Because of these parameters, *interaction* is seen as creating a cultural environment that requires deeper levels of understanding than surface descriptions of events that bring about the interaction. Therefore, the culture of social relations, which is constructed by notions of power, place, and group identity, provides a way of identifying regional ideology and competing localist discourses and their impact on interaction and the construction of a larger group identity. Although the culture of social relations (in areas of interracial interaction) tends to favor the dominant society, this study reveals contested configurations of those power relations through the var-ious interpretations of what is actually occurring. The Black community's concept of "getting over," which is discussed later, is one of those inter-pretations that clearly identifies these contested configurations.

"Intimate culture" is a behavioral and ideologically driven phe-nomenon. It is shaped by the needs and beliefs of the individuals drawn into a circle of association. The circle of association forms what is referred to in this work as an "intimate culture group." This group should be distinguished from groups commonly referred to as special interest groups in that all special interest groups are intimate culture groups but all intimate culture groups are not activists involved in politicized activities. However, the activities of these nonactivist intimate culture groups may be highly political. Intimate culture groups also may be known to the general public but involved in personal agendas that do not present a public face. Families are usually intimate culture groups of that fashion. Churches and their associated organizations, however, are intimate culture groups that are known publicly and present a public face. (Black families and churches are most often studied, while other cultural and social configurations of identity and place within the Black community are either ignored or peripheralized.) The structures of the intimate culture groups that present public faces both inside and outside the Black community provide the foundation for examining intragroup interaction in this study. Values of the group give insight into a kind of collective worldview, which has an effect on perception and behavior and provides greater insight into the "messiness" of identity and belonging.

Intimate culture groups are identity categories that provide understandings of the world and experiences of the group members. Their formation and the allegiance of their members become dependent upon the varying combinations of identities of each group member and the need (as perceived by those insiders) the cultural group satisfies. In Lafayette County, intimate culture groups are known by their function as well as by formal and informal names and are judged by their perceived value to the larger intimate culture. In this study, the examination of individuals as members of intimate culture groups helps to place the social histories that affect the culture of social relations between members of various intimate culture groups. For example, divisiveness within "the church" can often be explained and more clearly understood by the identification of competing intimate culture groups.

The culture of social relations between intimate culture groups is shaped by "localist ideologies." These ideologies are formed from perceptions about the value and role of an intimate culture group within the dominant culture (Lomnitz-Adler 1991:205–6). Power is allocated and exerted according to these perceptions. The perceived value of an intimate culture group to the Black community influences and is influenced by localist ideologies. As such, perceptions of intent or how the power obtained is to be used in the selection of a particular aspect of the dominant society practices can and often does generate tension among Black intimate culture groups. The identification of localist ideologies is necessary in any study of the Black community because of the tendency to see coherence where it does not exist. This perception is the result of the influence and at times recognition of one intimate culture group over another. Because localist ideologies, like intimate culture groups, may be formed across class identities, diversity can be masked and as such lead one to mistakenly perceive a particular culture as coherent. Coherence, which is always partial, is a way of gauging "the mutual compatibility of the various major beliefs and institutions in an intimate culture group" (Lominitz-Adler 1991: 208). The identification of the masked competing ideologies within Black society sheds new light on such labels as "self-proclaimed" leader and is invaluable to understanding why some mobilization efforts are effective and others are not. This is particularly so because social consciousness is often envisioned as a class-oriented phenomenon. In an intragroup study such as this, keeping a mindful eye on the coherence and incoherence or degrees thereof in intimate culture helps define contested spaces of group identity and behavior. For example, there was evidence of what West (1996) refers to as a "market mentality" developing among a generation consisting mostly of the children and grandchildren of residents who migrated to other areas of the country. This form of return migration is affecting the culture of social relations. Chapter 5 describes ways in which this phenomenon is becoming important to understanding Black Oxford.

The various responses to the injustices of Jim Crow in Mississippi call attention to the spatial dimensions of cultural production. Identity provides a way to examine differences in cultural characteristics of groups within the same region. This is particularly apparent in systemic processes of cultural variation, the spatial dimension of communication, their impact on identity and practice, and the construction of competing discourses. Attention to spatial issues peels away another layer in understanding both the culture of social relations that exists between African Americans from the Oxford community and residents from other areas of the state and the larger Southern region and the role power relations play in constructing that specific culture. By examining the culture of social relations across geographic boundaries, we are able to see how regional ideology and competing discourses help to construct in some ways and nullify in others the value of shared meanings and identities for mobilization.

While this study has chosen as its historical reference the CRM as the point from which change and behavior are to be examined, others examining the African American experience have chosen the arrival of Blacks in the Americas as a point in time from which to examine such issues. Ogbu and Gibson's study of the way in which identity maintenance has an impact on intergroup interaction maintains that involuntary minorities (those Americans of African descent brought here by force) tend to envision two ways of managing intercultural relations and cross-cultural boundaries; they either play by the rules set up by the hegemonic structure or change the rules (Ogbu and Gibson 1991). This study challenges this assumption and not only helps to define parameters for the establishment of regional diversity but provides examples of other choices for managing intercultural relations and cross-cultural boundaries. The complex manner in which Oxford residents manage intercultural relations and cross-cultural boundaries requires deeper understandings of the intragroup experience that is historically related to but operates often apart from the oppressive system that constructs intercultural relations.

Oxford's African American population's perceptions of the value of the Civil Rights Movement and the values embedded in the Movement are key to understanding the varying degrees of African American participation, the lack thereof, and the resistance to civil rights mobilization and the gains that movement sought. Those values, often articulated through "intimate cultures," can be explored through observation of behavior in two arenas: the "Black public sphere," defined here as that space designated for the presentation of self as a member of a community or group in which issues of concern are brought before those participating in that arena and discussed, and the "Black private sphere," that space designated for performance of individuality where behavior is most often determined and regulated by the individual although it is not completely free of group sanctions.[15] The Black public sphere is where "the group" identity is defined, negotiated, and redefined. Also, the Black public sphere is where political and social issues are expressed or addressed.[16] Group behavior related to those issues is constructed or negotiated and sanctioned by

---

[15] Behavior within one's personal space and uses of private property and capital are at times the object of negative sanctions by intimate culture groups operating in the public sphere. For example, the lack of tithing by officers of the church is often the basis for public discussion, regardless of that individual's financial circumstance.

[16] This sphere is not to be confused with the "public sphere" of the dominant society although they merge from time to time depending on the issues or operative processes.

community members who are influenced in part by the combined regional histories of the intimate culture groups constituting that particular public arena. Value systems, spaces of power, and places of prestige are products of intimate culture formation that are key to understanding the various conditions under which the Black public sphere is constrained as a space of coherence.[17]

National and regional ideologies, their local impact on ethnic and racial identities, and how those variations manifest themselves in the processes of social change are sources for understanding varying degrees of mobilization around particular social issues that affect African Americans as an ethnic group. For example, when considering the changes that have taken place in the larger dominant society over the past thirty or more years (legal integration and an extremely visible Black political participation), the application of such behavior classifications as "White folks' business" and "acting White" shed light on recent events related to political participation played out in the public sphere in greater Oxford, such as the support or lack of support for Black candidates, the emotional responses to an African American running on the Republican ticket, and the small turnout at a "town hall"–type meeting. There appears to be a distinct line that not only divides spaces of behavior but also equates public sphere behavior as White business according to local perceptions of the boundaries of White and Black business.

The details of ethnography derived from participant observation combined with varying degrees of shared understandings obtained by being a native anthropologist provide the foundation from which analysis of the Oxford/Lafayette County African American community can expand and enrich the growing body of literature on identity. Adding to this body of literature is particularly important because it stresses the unifying effects of race, class, gender, and ethnicity (the way in which individuals are influenced to mobilize around these social identities) and the divisive effect of dominant societies' uses of multiculturalism. This study of

---

[17] The 1990s have brought new interest and a flurry of debates and writings under the rubric of the public sphere that build on the insights and critiques of Habermas's work. Two journals have published special issues devoted to this topic, *Social Text: Theory/Culture/Ideology* 8(3)–9(1) 1990, which focuses on contemporary uses of the theory as an analytical tool, and *Public Culture* 7(1) Fall 1994, which focuses on the application of Habermas's theory for analyzing political activism among African Americans. See Gregory (1994) for an interesting counterpoint to the preceding discussion of intimate culture.

a particular Black community gives attention to the ideological diversity within race, class, and ethnicity and tries to make sense of the reason for that diversity. Analyses of the existing ideological diversity suggest that the historical processes involved in separating Blacks by their relationships to production (field and house slave) as well as by the amount of African blood (mulatto, octoroons, etc.) – processes of differentiation that served the needs of the colonial Southeast and was put into use for the domination and subjugation of America's "involuntary minorities" – contribute to the intraethnic diversity that exists. This is particularly important because there is a tendency to see a homogeneous African American community when people write about them. Traditional sociological indicators such as common history and the fact that most African American residents are "Southern" often influence these perceptions of homogeneity. However, closer study, which includes the distinctions people within the South make among themselves, provides important differences that standard sociological analyses do not pick up because they are too broadly gauged. Difference among African Americans in today's society is a direct manifestation of the culture of social relations within that group, the historical processes that constructed its various intimate culture groups, and the impact of localist ideologies on perceptions of place and power.

"FOR MY PEOPLE" – CONCERNS OF NATIVE ANTHROPOLOGY

When I returned to Lafayette County to embark upon my doctoral research in 1994, I struggled with the difference between my desires for what I envisioned as happening in the community and what the evidence presented and worked hard to find alternative answers to my ethnographic questions. After all, these were my people; in my opinion, they should be seen not only "accurately" but also in the best possible light. The burden of my ethnic identity weighed heavily as I struggled to not see myself as "the great Black hope," that person who would right all representative wrongs that have mystified and mythified my people. My desire to present a positive and progressive picture of my people influenced my early perceptions of what was happening in the field. I originally attributed the lack of participation in the changes brought about by the CRM activities of the 1960s to a desire not to buy into "the system" and a resistance to homogeneity that not only made them "more Black" than I, or more importantly representatives of a "core Black culture," but also provided them with more autonomy – a position they were not willing to give up. Thus they resisted many of the changes brought about in the nation as a whole by the CRM. Armed with that notion, the dissertation was tentatively titled, *Quiet Resistance: A Look at Political Participation in an African American Community*. The realizations that follow have been painfully but scientifically drawn despite temptations to build mountains out of molehills and paint the sky rosy. So this work may be painful for some readers and confirming for others.

One of my first realizations was that to be both native and activist is doubly problematic in the field of anthropology. The native side of the problem is much easier to overcome than the activist side. On the one hand, as a native, particularly a "colonized" native, the image of one's own people weighs heavily as we negotiate between what we, the natives, want the world to know about us and the perspective that the tools of anthropology provide for the analysis of that data. To this we add our own personal desire to provide and maintain hope. How much is too much? What anthropological and insider taboos might I break with this writing? To what extent can this data be used against us as a people? In what way can and will what I have to say make a difference? These questions problematize the interpretive aspect of ethnography and the privileged position of the ethnographer when she or he is native.

On the other hand, being an activist has its own problematic boundaries in its integration with the discipline. If, for example, the anthropologist enters into the field with an agenda (such as providing a solution to a perceived problem), the worldviews of both the anthropologist and the members of the culture group being studied play an important part in the culture of social relations that develops between ethnographer and the collaborating group or community. Aside from the expected impact of the unnatural act of being studied and depending upon the specific agenda of the ethnographer, the collaborating group or community could be placed and left in varying states of disorganization.

This research has taught me that my own expectations and desires for my people must take a backseat to the everyday expectations and desires of my collaborators if I am to be both a productive anthropologist and an activist in my own cultural/ethnic group. If, through my activism, I expect to truly serve and aid in the empowerment of my people, before introducing solutions to problems I believe are important, those issues deemed important to the various intimate culture groups must be addressed first. This method of approach was, in fact, somewhat dictated by my collaborators.

The introduction of ideas that appeared on the surface to be foreign to their own established ways of operating were received coolly by some and were strongly attacked by others. Because my approach started out with a personal agenda influenced by my particular perspective of what should be happening (one I am pleased to add I quickly dropped), my activist efforts were less beneficial in the beginning than they were later.

In spite of my training, I realized later that my approach to understanding change within the African American community was informed first by an evolutionary understanding of culture. I suspected that deep within my educationally Europeanized subconscious there existed the beliefs that segments of the African American community had not "evolved" to an appropriate level of social consciousness, that they were stunted by *their* colonial condition, and that all they needed was to be exposed to the knowledge of that condition and they would want to change. This in no way considered the thought that the various groups clearly understood their position and chose to handle their circumstances in the manner they saw best. Any effort to insert my own solutions to their particular circumstances would be as violent and destructive an act as modernization and development are to Third World countries around the globe. The realization that my methods, rather than incorporating rational dialogue, were dictatorial, and that my membership in the community did not mean that my own struggles to understand the problems and find solutions constituted a dialogue was then formed. I came to understand that a people, any group of people (mine included), has the right to decide how much or how little of the innovations of a society they incorporate into their lives and that acceptance of one aspect of cultural change does not in itself require acceptance of all aspects. Indeed, this process guarantees the maintenance of ethnic and cultural distinctiveness and the freedoms cherished by so many in the "United States" of America.

STRUCTURING THE ETHNOGRAPHIC STUDY

The extremely complex interconnection of data has greatly influenced the structure of this book. As such, the somewhat linear narrative structure often expected in ethnographic studies is modified in favor of an event focus of the chapters. The study is divided into three parts. In addition to this introduction, which sets up the ethnographic problems related to social change examined in this study and the methodological and theoretical issues that are explored, Part One focuses on the cultural history of the region. Part Two examines the roles social consciousness and social action play in the history of Oxford's Black community. Finally, Part Three grapples with the problems inherent in the construction of an intraracial identity.

PART ONE

THE CULTURAL HISTORY AND SOCIAL STRUCTURE OF THE REGION

I

Placing the Stones

The Construction of a Region

The problems faced by the African American community of Oxford are the result of a complex integration of historical events, social practices, spatial isolation, and regional ideologies. Each phenomenon contributes to behavior that influences inter- and intraethnic interaction that maintains the social, economic, and political inequities existing in the community. Although these phenomena are described somewhat separately, it is important to remember that the ways in which they have an impact on lives are directly related to the degree to which each phenomenon is integrated into the day-to-day lives of each community member. Historical events may play a greater role in the construction of social practices for some, while spatial isolation may have a greater impact for others, and these combinations may vary according to the specific issues being addressed.

Oxford's social, spatial, economic, and geopolitical histories reflect the racialized domination of the region. Therefore, an understanding of the historical elements that constructed that domination is important to an objective "placing" of the subjugated African American cultural groups, since that process of domination creates and orders classes or castes in a hierarchical political economic space. These historical elements are offered here to make the chapters that follow more meaningful. While Blacks have not been completely written out of the history of Lafayette County, for the most part their perspectives have been situationally limited. Even today, community members struggle against hegemonic structures as they try to tell their stories. Descriptions of the cultural history and social structure of the region are drawn from both written and oral histories in an effort to not simply include the historically marginalized voices but to reveal the important contributions such perspectives make.[1] The inclusion of the oral and informal histories of the Black community is intended to help "outsiders" to be aware of and value what Karen Fields refers to as the "inward and invisible topography" (1994:159) that not only influences the Black community's understanding about its experiences – a perspective often ignored – but also greatly shapes social interaction. Only through the incorporation of both forms of communication, written (formal and informal) historical data and oral histories constructed from memory, are we able to develop a model of any particular cultural environment.[2]

The following accounts are interpretations of both written and oral histories of the Oxford/Lafayette County region. The information used to construct the social, spatial, economic, and geopolitical history of the region is selected from a much larger body of historical data. Facts were selected for their particular relevance to a regional analysis, as well as for their relevance as elements related to change in political participation and social action in Lafayette County, Mississippi, and the struggle of the Black community against domination.

WHERE ON "GOD'S GREEN EARTH" ARE WE?

Oxford has billed itself, unofficially for many years, as "the cultural center" of the Mid-South Region, despite being located merely sixty-eight miles southeast of Memphis, the more likely contender for the title.[3] The University of Mississippi, located just off-center of the town square, boasts that William Faulkner not only made Oxford his home but also worked as the university's postmaster before achieving international fame.

The town's tourism board, which managed an approximately $500,000 budget before 1990, also keeps visitors and the general public aware of the fact that contemporary novelist John Grisham, writer Willie Morris, and the folk painter Theora Hamblett have also made their homes in Oxford. In addition to holding an annual International Faulkner Conference, the

---

[1] See Fields (1994) for a discussion of the importance of not privileging written over oral histories and the value of oral interpretations.

[2] The interpretive historical topography of the region includes the use of published and unpublished life histories.

[3] This local myth has been created and perpetuated by the university and local elites. It is used mostly as a tool of tourism and a draw for national and international conferences produced by the university (e.g., an annual Faulkner Conference and a newly established Elvis Presley Conference). The term "Mid-South" is used similarly to the term "Midwest." Its boundaries are not clear; however, it most often refers to the states of Mississippi, Arkansas, and Louisiana.

university and the town held its first annual Elvis Presley Conference in 1995. Both conferences are excellent examples of the ways in which formerly stigmatized local culture is appropriated and reassigned meaning. William Faulkner's depiction of Lafayette County life through his fictional Yoknapatawpha County does not sit well with many of the area's prominent old families even today. However, his international reputation helps to support the newly constructed cultural image of the area; therefore, the image of Faulkner has been resignified. Even the area's Civil Rights image was resignified by the university through efforts to host a biannual national Conference on Civil Rights.

Oxford has been listed as one of the ten most desirable cities for retirement. The town financed the building of a $2 million baseball stadium for the university from a 2 percent tourism tax (originally instituted for that purpose) and assisted in underwriting a $500,000 block grant for developing an area just outside the city limits that sports a new golf course. Two new hotels and a conference center in the planning stages in 1995 have since been built. The projected image of Oxford/Lafayette County as a service-oriented resort/retirement community by its visionaries greatly affects the increasing disparities between the "haves" and the "have nots." These disparities are based on tradition, ethnic origin, and the racial stratification of the regional society.

A number of Black workers from the university tell a story circulated in the rumor mill about Oprah Winfrey visiting the area to tape a show exploring the reason this particular area is desirable for retirement. One informant had this to say about her visit: "So, you know the White folks. They take her around and show her all the favorite places and all the beautiful houses. And when she asked to see where the Black folks lived, they wouldn't take her. So she packed up her equipment and left." Although the specific details surrounding the departure have not been verified by parties directly involved, it is possible to see that within this oral account is an African American understanding of where they fit – "their place" – in the most recent, postintegration, image of the area. Oxonians of African descent have traditionally occupied the lower rungs of the socioeconomic ladder since the establishment of the county. For them, the elimination of the African American community from the view of the camera constitutes more of the "same ol', same ol'" continuity and maintenance of the culture of social relations between African Americans and the members of the dominant society. The tourism board's focus on the area as a tourist attraction and retirement community confirms Black Oxonian's perception that the town continues to cater to a specific economic and racial population. It signifies for the African Americans that, in spite of the changes sought, fought for, and gained by the Movement, in the eyes of the White residents of the area, they do not count. Oxford/Lafayette County, as is often said about America, was "founded for Whites and you can change the laws but you can't change hearts." The African Americans recognize they are invisible to most and of little importance to others.

Located in the center of the northern quarter of Mississippi, Oxford is the largest municipality in Lafayette (pronounced Le-FAY-et) County (see Map, *http://formypeopleprods.info*). No interstate highway touches the borders of the county, which is the site of two national forest reserves. Because of the ecological layout, Lafayette County has never been a major agricultural producer. This fact is significant for understanding the distribution of enslaved Blacks in this county as compared to the Delta counties west of Lafayette (see Maps, *http://formypeopleprods.info*). At the height of the "King Cotton" era, Lafayette County never reached the economic importance of western counties in Mississippi because it was not solely dependent on cotton. Nonetheless, the county's enslaved population was substantial, averaging as much as 44 percent of the total population in the three decades prior to the Civil War (see Appendix A). These figures become more important when one considers that the majority of the enslavers maintained two to fifteen Blacks, although, reportedly "five owned between one hundred and two hundred slaves" (Sobotka 1976:32). Allowing for 150 enslaved Blacks for each of the five largest plantations and estimating household size as three, figures indicate that 2,994.33 possible households potentially "owned" 2.1 Blacks in Lafayette County. These figures translate socially into an elitist standard of living for Whites immediately before the beginning of the Civil War. The small number of African Americans enslaved per household strongly suggests that the opportunity for developing an autonomous way of life, as an African American cultural community, was limited. Much of the limitation was caused by the local Black churches' relationship to the White institution from which it separated and the patronage system that constricted autonomous development. The spatial distribution of the enslaved African Americans per household likely had a tremendous impact on communication between Black members of the community as well as an influence on their ability to organize.

Today, Oxford's economic structure is mostly service oriented, and there are only a handful of manufacturing companies whose products include electric motors, clothing, wood products, and appliances. The

FIGURE 1 The University of Mississippi Lyceum (1997)

largest employers are the university, the private medical center, and the electric-motor plant. The sprinkling of a significant number of fast-food restaurants (a total of 103 places that serve food, according to the County Business Patterns Report [U.S. Department of Commerce 1993], employed 1,897 people) and the local mall employ a significant number of part-time workers, most of whom are African American. The town's most recent interest in the tourism industry has produced development in areas that provide few additional jobs. A third golf course and two additional motels will require very few full-time workers in management positions and a small number of part-time workers for housekeeping and maintenance.

The lack of industrial or technological growth is by design as the city of Oxford works to maintain its quiet small-town image. Capitalizing on its most recent acclaim as one of the outstanding retirement communities in America and building on its pre–Civil War elitist status, both the town and the university campus strive to maintain a quaint appearance by continuing to build in the traditional architectural style or by adding columns and other early "Southern" veneers to existing structures. (See Figures 1–6.) The influx of large numbers of older citizens of means (many from the Midwest), the conversion of the county's state-supported hospital into a privately run medical center, the expanded motel industry, and university faculty all help to maintain African Americans as service workers in

FIGURE 2 Fraternity house on university's campus (1997)

FIGURE 3 Guyton Hall (ROTC building) (1997)

FIGURE 4 Sorority house on university's campus (1997)

FIGURE 5 Farley Hall (1997)

FIGURE 6 Oxford Downtown Square intersection (1997)

grounds and building maintenance both on campus and at the hospital
and as housekeepers and handymen for motels and private homes.

After its charter in 1844, the University of Mississippi, known nation-
wide as "Ole Miss," was Mississippi's only public institution of higher
learning for twenty-three years and the state's only comprehensive university for 110 years. During its sesquicentennial celebrations throughout
the 1994–95 school year, the university boasted on Internet Web pages
and radio public service announcements about a number of "firsts" it had
attained on regional and national levels: the first in the nation to offer en-
gineering education (1854), the first in the South to admit women (1882),
and the first to hire a female faculty member (1885). According to the
announcements, its Medical Center surgeons performed the world's first
lung (1963) and heart (1964) transplants in humans.

The university maintains its own police department and public post
office and is located in an area of the town officially named University,
Mississippi, although one of its three main entrances is only five blocks
from the town square, four blocks from the post office, and two, albeit exceptionally long, blocks from the Oxford Police Department. The university continues to acquire prime real estate from bordering neighborhoods
for its own development and invests a tremendous amount of money in
maintaining an antebellum look to its campus. Most fraternity and sorority houses would be fit settings for Miss Scarlet and Rhett Butler.

The university's Conference on Civil Rights is of particular interest as it relates to the university's resignified image, and it is of particular significance since before 2003 the university displayed no visual evidence in the form of markers, plaques, or photographs of the university's role or the role of James Meredith in the Civil Rights Movement in 1962. Before a 1989 effort to document the history of the African American Studies Program, there was no organized record of the tumultuous demonstrations that occurred before the establishment of the university's Black Studies Program. Ninety-seven African American students were arrested for having raised their voices in protest over the need to hire Black faculty, to establish a Black Studies Program, and to expose racist treatment by faculty and students. This number represented, according to one of the demonstrators, "practically the entire Black student population." The arrest manifests indicate that nearly half of the students were jailed for at least one night in Parchman State Prison located approximately eighty miles away. One of the students sent to Parchman states that a few were there almost a week. The rest were jailed in the local city/county facility. The university's second response (the first being the arrests) was to suspend eight of the students, one of whom graduated before the suspension could be carried out. The final outcome of this matter was the hiring of the university's first Black faculty member, a female in the Department of Social Work, and the establishment of the Black Studies Program – both over the summer of 1970. The first African American administrator was hired in 1972 as director of the program, which then took on the name Afro-American Studies. An important recent historical addendum to that event is the fact that one of the student protestors returned as a graduate student and served as coordinator for the Afro-American Studies Program. At the time this research was conducted that same former student was the associate dean of the Graduate School.

After the integration of the university, a small group of White part-time Law School faculty and local lawyers formed the Lafayette County Legal Services, which originally began as an Office of Economic Opportunity (OEO)-funded program on the university's campus. The program had as its objective the integration of the Law School curriculum with legal problems of the poor and racial minorities. The lawyers with the agency began to take on class action cases involving school desegregation and the constitutionality of some state laws. This made members of the state government very uncomfortable, and, as a result, legislators moved to kill the program. Ole Miss abandoned the program, but the staff was determined to keep it alive. The program was moved to the local community and eventually became North Mississippi Rural Legal Services (NMRLS). There is irony in the fact that this is the same program that launched the 1975 Ayers case. This landmark case, which lasted twenty years, challenged the disparities in the allocations of funds to state universities, including the University of Mississippi.[4]

In an effort to make a significant change at the university during its sesquicentennial celebrations, the Afro-American Studies Program sought support from the university to place a plaque in the student union honoring the ninety-seven student protestors. (For a comparison of proposed acknowledgments by the Afro-American Studies Program and the university's administration see Appendixes B and C. The letter from the chancellor was submitted on plain bond stationary, no letterhead. It should also be noted that without official university approval, university seals and letterheads could not be used.) Ironically, the 1990 effort spearheaded by the Afro-American Studies Program was unsuccessful while a later 1996 effort by a White student majoring in Southern Studies received both moral and financial support for the establishment of a civil rights marker.[5]

Religious Foundations

Oral histories collected during my 1994–5 fieldwork indicate that in the antebellum period, underground churches, those "invisible institutions" that provided during slavery the opportunity for self-expression, self-management, and the evolution of a Black social consciousness, did not develop in Oxford/Lafayette County. History suggests the first sign of religious autonomy was somewhat slow in arriving. "After freedom," Blacks continued to worship "as they had in their days of bondage, in the White churches" (Sansing unpublished manuscript, Marshall unpublished manuscript). Church markers and oral histories reveal that the first independent church established by Blacks was a Methodist church built in 1869 and the second was a Baptist church built four years later. Local lore

---

[4] This class action suit, which was brought before the U.S. Supreme Court, was instituted against the governor of Mississippi, the board of trustees of State Institutions of Higher Learning of the State of Mississippi, the commissioner of higher education, other state officials, and the five historically White universities in the state. The class was defined by the court as all Black citizens residing in Mississippi whether students, former students, parents, or taxpayers who have been, are, or will be discriminated against on account of race in the universities operated by the board (Mississippi State University 1999).

[5] The memorial marker has been placed in an active area of the campus – between the Lyceum and the library (Molpus 2002).

reveals freed Blacks built each of these churches after receiving permission to establish the new facilities from the churches of their former masters. The need for Whites to sanction the establishment of the Black churches speaks to the degree of dependency created by post-Emancipation paternalistic structures of this Southern society.

The hard-won battle for the establishment of the first Black Baptist church makes a recent phenomenon quite interesting. The current pastor of the Black Baptist church that broke away from its mother church in 1873 has developed a ministerial exchange with a White church with the aim of reconnecting spiritually across racialized barriers. Although I did not observe these services, conversations suggest that the exchange may be more a cosmetic cover than a realistic breaking down of barriers.[6] Other efforts are being made to build connections on the religious level. A predominantly White church on the edge of town has become the church unofficially sanctioned by the university for its Black faculty to attend. Invitations by the church and individual members have been extended to new university faculty. No nonuniversity residents reported being invited to attend. However, the majority of Lafayette County's 106 churches, sixty-one White and forty-five Black, remain glaringly segregated.[7]

The Educational System

Prior to 1968, Oxford/Lafayette County's school systems were separate and unequal in every way. When the schools integrated, the public schools followed the process in practice over most of the South. Instead of keeping all the schools open, the Black high schools were eliminated from the system, and Blacks began attending the formerly all-White schools. The total restructuring of the public school system in spite of the goal of integration presented new problems for African Americans in the system.

White students in large numbers were sent to private academies established in response to desegregation laws, a practice that continues to a lesser degree today. In addition, the integration of the schools provided for only a small number of African American teachers to be incorporated

---

[6] Priest (1998) is an important study of the ideological and cultural differences that prevent a Black and White church merger in South Carolina. It provides an understanding of the complexity of race in the integration of worship practices.

[7] Four of the Black churches were observed to have White members and or visitors on various occasions. On one occasion, the visitor at one of the Baptist churches was an investigative reporter doing a story on the Ayers court case. The nondenominational Black church had a minimum of four Whites who were members.

into the new structure. After integration, hundreds of students and their teachers who had rarely, if ever, interacted on any meaningful level were suddenly supposed to produce a cultural environment conducive to learning. The fruit of that social relationship, which is a cosmetic form of integration, is evident in the number of African Americans who drop out of school to this day. The problems generated by integration are also evident in the large number of students labeled "learning disabled" and the number of complaints, both formal and informal, of White faculty's and administrators' racist practices. Physical segregation was exchanged for psychological and intellectual alienation.

Lafayette County now has two school systems. The county school, servicing only residents of the county, is located where the majority of African Americans live, and the city schools, which primarily service city residents, are located near the town square[8] (see Maps, *http://formypeopleprods.info*). In the county system, all grade levels are housed at one facility located east of town close to the city line. A few buses travel the county area to pick up most of the 2,100 students – some scheduled for pickup as early as 6:45 A.M. The Oxford School District services about 2,696 students who live within the corporate limits of Oxford and some additional areas of the county. These areas are west and north of town and include the predominantly White subdivisions that have developed over the past fifteen years. The city district consists of four schools (two elementary schools, one middle school, and one high school) and two learning centers. The teacher-pupil ratio is 1:16. Reportedly, over 80 percent of the district's graduates pursue postsecondary training, an interesting phenomenon when you consider that the majority of the area's African American workforce earns less than $10,000 per year.

In addition to the primary and secondary schools, the county supports a division of Northwest Mississippi Community College (NMCC) and the University of Mississippi. NMCC has an average yearly enrollment of 384 day students and 304 night students. Although the division offers programs in cosmetology and business technology, the majority of its programs are directed toward the medical profession (i.e., nursing, technicians). The University of Mississippi has an enrollment of approximately 12,500 graduate and undergraduate students, of whom fewer than 10 percent are African American. Close to 10,000 students are on the main Oxford campus. Although the university is the largest single employer in the county and a significant number of those employed are

---

[8] The entire K–12 levels are located in one set of buildings in the county.

African American, the hiring and promotion policies, according to an administrator knowledgeable about the university's affirmative action practices, keep African Americans in low-paying, dead-end jobs. The wife of a faculty member related the following story to me.

Deciding to go back to school, AB, who is White, wanted to have a part-time job to offset the cost of books, clothes, and childcare. She explained to personnel that she did not want a position with responsibilities. She wanted something that she would not have to think about outside of the job. She was sent to a service department that hires mostly Blacks and work-study students. The supervisor conducting the interview, speaking in a confidential-type manner, suggested that she didn't really want the job she was sent to interview for, and that if she waited a week a better position, one "more fitting" for her, would be open. The supervisor went on to explain that they usually tried to keep the type of position for which she was applying "for our Blacks."

Political History of Region

After freedom, as Lafayette County and Oxford worked to reconstruct their society from the "ravages of war," both oral and written history suggests that little had changed in terms of social and political structure (Sobotka 1976, Sansing unpublished manuscript). This conclusion is not surprising in spite of the November 27, 1869, issue of the Oxford *Falcon* indicating that the number of freedmen registered to vote outnumbered Whites – 355 to 315 – (Sansing unpublished manuscript:2) and the fact that the board of supervisors had "several Black members" (Sobotka 1976:56). (This is a fact of written history that is not a part of the oral history or mythology of the African American community.) The major change in party control occurred in Oxford in 1871. However, "the scalawags" elected into office walked a thin line between compliance with federal laws and administering punishment (Sobotka 1976). The party system in Oxford resembled that of most of the South – a one-party system (cf. Bass 1986).

According to Sansing, Lafayette County's little-known slave rebellion that took place during the Civil War had little impact on alienating the races. He attributes "the amicable relations between Whites and freedmen" to a lack of "political turmoil and racial tension during Reconstruction" and to the belief that the "Freedmen's Bureau functioned very well in Oxford and did not excite the anger of local Whites" (unpublished manuscript:1).

In practice, political control remained in the hands of the Democratic Party, although the party did not officially gain control until 1871. Party leaders maintained control through negative sanctions. Sobotka reports the use of public slander of freedmen and radicals by the press. "Some election officials felt conservative pressures to such an extent that several Republican officeholders relinquished their commissions rather than risk further association with the Radicals"(1976:53–54). In order to control the Black vote, *The Falcon*, according to Sobotka, "published a list of Blacks voting for and against the [ratified state] constitution, placing the names of the voters who cast negative ballots in boldface type" (1976:54), presumably as a positive sanction given the fact that the paper vehemently spoke out against the document. (This story has made its way into the local African American lore.) In his treatment of the history of Oxford's Freedmen Town, Sansing states that after the election of 1871 in which the Democratic Party regained political control, "the process of rebuilding and *restoration* (my emphasis)" occurred as Mississippi was being readmitted to the Union. The operative word for examining the status of Blacks during this time may well prove to be "restoration," which indicates that a reconstruction of the political, economic, and social atmosphere never occurred in Oxford. The following Fourth of July speech given by Jim Nelson, a freedman who was about 35 years old – published in the *Falcon* on July 13, 1867, and recounted in an unpublished speech written by Marshall to commemorate the placing of a marker at Freedman Town – reflects a stark difference between the attitude of a prominent local African American and that of Frederick Douglass:[9]

My colored friends, we are all free now, as the White folks are. I don't know why I am free, nor who made me free. The Yankees said they did and I suppose it's so. (But the White folks are our friends.) We have known them all our lives. But who ever made us free, I thank them. And we all thank them for it. Although it made many of us a heap worse off than we were before, but we all love to be free. And I hope some day it will make us a heap better off than we ever were before. (Marshall 1996:1)

Politics and Community Borders

In 1990, according to the twentieth anniversary edition of the Joint Center for Political and Economic Studies Press publication *Black Elected*

---

[9] Frederick Douglass's 1852 Fourth of July speech (delivered in New York state) contrasts starkly in tone and temperament from that of Jim Nelson. This tone provides insight into the culture of interracial social relations at that time in both regions.

TABLE 1.1 *Comparison of 1990 Black Elected Officials*

	Alabama	Mississippi
Total population	4,052,000	2,625,000
Total Black population	1,053,000	919,000
% of total population	26	35
Total voting age population	2,962,000	1,805,000
Total Black voting age population	652,000	596,000
Total registered voters	2,162,000	1,408,000
Total Black registered voters	443,000	441,000
% of total registered voters	20.5	31.3
Total elected positions	4,015	4,263
Total Black elected positons	705	669
% of total elected positions	18	15

Source: Black Elected Officials for the year cited.

TABLE 1.2 *Percentage of Black Residents in 1990 by Congressional Districts*

Districts	Alabama	Mississippi
1	31	25
2	31	58
3	28	32
4	—[a]	42
5	—[a]	19
6	34	—[b]
7	33	—[b]

[a] No figures provided.
[b] Mississippi has only five congressional districts.
Source: Black Elected Officials for the year cited.

Officials, Mississippi had 669 Black elected officials and 441,000 Black registered voters, which is approximately 31 percent of the total number of registered voters. Ranking second to Alabama in total number of Black elected officials, the Mississippi total number represents 15 percent of the approximately 4,263 elected official positions. (See Tables 1.1 and 1.2 for a comparison between Mississippi and Alabama.)

The formal political structure of Lafayette County and Oxford resembles that of most of the other eighty-two counties in Mississippi. Five elected district (formerly called beat) supervisors run county government. This board is the chief policy-making and administrative body of the county. Other county government officials include a five-member county board of education, sheriff, tax assessor-collector, chancery clerk, chancery court judge, circuit clerk, circuit court judge, county court judge, district and county attorneys, justice court judge, constable, and the co-operative extension service staff appointed by the board of supervisors. In 1990, Lafayette County had one elected Black official holding a seat on the county school board. Prior to his election, no African American had held an elected position in the county since the period of Reconstruction.

An elected board of aldermen governs Oxford. The board consists of seven members who represent six wards (one at-large) and the mayor, who, until his most recent election in 1993, served part-time. The alderman for Ward IV, which includes the area formerly known as Freedmen Town, is an African American who was first appointed by the mayor to his position and then was elected by the residents in a later 1992 election in which he ran unopposed.

Since the integration of the public school system in Oxford, every four years, for almost twenty years, at least two African American males ran unsuccessfully for county supervisor. According to one Democratic Party representative, they were "expected fixtures," and little attention was given to their efforts for the last couple of elections. The distribution of Blacks over the county area, however, makes a difference in the area of political power. There is no county district that is predominantly African American, although the majority of Oxford/Lafayette County African Americans live in the rural areas of the county. This spatial problem of dispersal is compounded by the way the boundaries of each district cut across social communities and dilute Black voting power.

The November 1995 election is the first election in which African Americans who were not handpicked by the dominant White society won seats in the political structure of Oxford/Lafayette County. For the first time in its 153-year history, Oxford/Lafayette County has African Americans in the positions of constable and justice court judge.[10] And for the first time since Reconstruction a Black supervisor and alderman were elected to office. The election of these officials constitutes a change in the operation of local government and African American political participation. Later I will discuss whether that change has significance for the African American community in areas other than prestige.

[10] Often referred to as the "people's court," the justice court hears common cases involving mostly civil disputes and various misdemeanor offenses. The judge of this court serves as a notary public and can also marry people. The constable helps the justice court judge, the sheriff, and other officials preserve the peace. The primary duty of the constable is serving court papers.

Space and the Demographics of De Facto Segregation

The geopolitical layout of the region plays a large part in defining the social structure and economic growth of the different areas of Lafayette County. It is bordered by seven of Mississippi's eighty-two counties and, like each of Mississippi's other counties, is divided into five wards informally referred to as beats.

The residents of the county are dependent upon state highways and county and federal roads for travel. These public transportation routes range from four-lane structures to gravel and dirt roads. The two state highways, 6 and 7, which border the southeastern lines of the city limits, run east–west and north–south, respectively, and are the main roads traveled when residents journey from one side of the county and town to the other.

The physical infrastructure of the city of Oxford that lies, for the most part, northwest of the intersection of the two state highways connecting Oxford to the major areas of northern Mississippi (Tupelo and Batesville) is unconventional because it does not follow the general grid layout of streets. The layout of the city greatly resembles that of the county with its series of enclaves that consist of cul de sacs. (See *http://formypeopleprods.info* for comparison of county and town layouts.) There are no thoroughfares within the city limits connecting the east side to the west and only one street connecting the north side to the south. Interestingly enough, even this north–south street is forced to detour briefly to go around the court house in the center of the town square. It both literally and figuratively provides a break in the street, which at one time was referred to as North Street on the northern end of town and South Street on the opposite end.[11] Just as the court house, a symbol of power and authority, divides the north from the south, the university's campus and its Lyceum (the building that houses the top university administrators) interrupts the main streets that connect the east to the west.

With the exception of the stores on the square in town that consist mostly of specialty and boutique shops that cater to the purses of the area's elite, convenience is not a part of the layout of the area. Supermarkets operate at the west, east, and northern ends of the city limits. The "small mall," which has had difficulty supporting shops other than Wal-Mart and J. C. Penney, is located on the west side of town and across

---

[11] This street is currently named after a former university professor who served as an associate justice of the U.S. Supreme Court (1888–1893) and whose reputation was that he associated with Ku Klux Klan officials.

from the west entrance to the university.[12] The industries of the area are located north and south of the city line. The hospital and doctors' offices are located in the southern end of the town. Transportation is a necessity of life, yet the economics of the area that boasts having the lowest unemployment rate in the state is such that, according to the 1990 U.S. Census Report, 594 Black households out of a total of 2,566 have no vehicles for transportation. The 960 total households without transportation constitute a significant number of workers who walk or are dependent upon others for transportation to work.

The layout of the town and county presents a number of transportation and travel-related problems, particularly since the area does not have a public transportation system and the one-car taxi service's minimum fare for a ride is four dollars. Because of the distances residents must travel for work, services, shopping, and visiting other neighborhoods, automobile accessibility is practically mandatory, particularly in the area of public safety. This is one problem that blatantly exposes the connectedness of economics, spatial constructions, and race. A significant number of African Americans are without access to automobiles altogether or own vehicles that are often unreliable. Therefore, instead of walking into the heart of the city for safer sidewalk access to another area, some residents walk the highways and then cut through wooded areas for the more direct route to the places they need to go.[13] As a result, African Americans constitute the majority of highway pedestrian injuries and deaths that occur.

The spatial divisions in terms of use of space also have a significant impact on communication among the African American population. African Americans constitute 38 percent of the total county population and are scattered among the enclaves of this varied and isolated rural area. As a result of the spatial isolation, the communication of information ranging from public and private events to social problems depends heavily on ritualized and regularized social occasions such as church services and functions and lunch hours on the job. This need to communicate does

---

[12] A visit in 2004 revealed significant growth in the service sector – an increased number of hotels and fast food restaurants, new campus buildings, further encroachment into Black residential neighborhoods by commercial properties, and the now almost dead mall. The death of the mall is attributed to Wal-Mart's building a supercenter further west.

[13] Because of the exceptional number of young, inexperienced, and often reckless, university students who travel the major and often narrow streets of the town and highways, the only safe place to walk is on sidewalks and the only places with sidewalks are the center of town and the heart of the university.

not ignore the use of the telephone for communication; rather it places a heavy burden on telephone communication for such important social action needs as instant or speedy mobilization. A local primary elections meeting organized by the National Association for the Advancement of Colored People (NAACP) is one example. A regular meeting of the organization was held on the fourth Sunday of a month that included a fifth Sunday. The decision was made to hold a meeting on the first Wednesday after the fifth Sunday at a church located in a county area where complaints related to road maintenance had been filed with the organization. Because most churches do not hold services at their own facility on the fifth Sunday, prayer meeting services held the Wednesday before were counted on as key avenues for getting the word out to the residents of that community. Association members who lived in the area were expected to call community residents who attended prayer meetings irregularly or not at all. At the time of the scheduled meeting, while waiting for the arrival of community members, we learned from passersby and those who arrived from thirty minutes to an hour and fifteen minutes late that they thought or had been told that the time of the meeting was actually one hour later than scheduled. This misunderstanding was the result of speculation about conflict with prayer meeting services at the church where the meeting was being held. The meeting opened with fewer than ten people, including the four association representatives who were to conduct the meeting. Although the business of the meeting was broadly discussed, the attendees unanimously agreed to postpone the decision until the meeting could be rescheduled. The repercussions of that failed attempt will be evident in the description of the local social movement in practice.[14]

The physical structure of Lafayette County and the use of space affect local social consciousness and action, Black political participation, and group identity formation. The irregularly drawn boundaries of the county, district, and city limits physically and ideologically segment the Black community. As such, these markers rarely facilitate group consciousness or lead to mobilization. There appear to be direct relationships not only between spatial arrangements and mobilization but also between spatial configurations and their sense of identity. For example, during the latter part of the 1980s, a White fraternity on the Ole Miss campus incorporated

---

[14] Another example, the first meeting of a civic organization I attempted to attend, will be discussed in Chapter 3. Both examples point to the degree to which intimate culture perceptions of the problems within the Black community are appropriately identified.

a ritual as a part of its initiation that required pledges to travel to a small Black college in another county on the northern border of Lafayette County. The pledges ran through the grounds naked and wrote racist epithets on buildings. Most Black Oxford residents were appalled by the incident, as were residents of the neighboring county. Both believed that something should be done about it, but a coalition between organizations in the two counties never developed. Immediate mobilization was impossible because of communication limitations and the impact of spatial divisions on their sense of community.

Another example relates to the political borders within the county. County services such as police protection, garbage pickup, and fire departments are poor in African American neighborhoods, including those neighborhoods that sit right on the city–county line. In 1995, a fire occurred not more than one hundred feet from the city line. Although the closest unit (a city unit not engaged at the time) was less than five minutes away, it was reported they did not respond because the residence was technically in the county. The one county unit of reserve firemen, which was much further away, did not arrive in time to save the residence or the life of the man living in the home. African Americans in town and in the county areas were aware of the incident, and it was the topic of conversation among intimate culture groups for weeks. However, efforts by the NAACP to mobilize residents of the five-county beats and those of the city were unsuccessful. Although this is a problem that exists at most municipal borders, African American residents of this community are well aware of the mixing of city and county services that occurs in predominantly White neighborhoods, such as city collectors making garbage pickups in the county, city schools being attended by county residents, and city police patrolling subdivisions in the county.

In the latter examples, the distancing of Blacks from the incidents was evident in comments such as the following: "They ought to be ashamed of themselves going over *there* and doing that." "That's a shame how they treat Black people." "They need to do something about the way Black folks are treated in this town." Connections were rarely made between the victims and the individuals speaking. Conversations indicated that there was an awareness of systemic problems that affected Blacks, but at the moment of the conversation, the speakers had no racial or ethnic ties or sense of community and shared relations and experiences. The references to "over *there*," "Black people," and "Black folks" in these conversations juxtaposed against the "they" of each sentence do not imply "we" but rather "stranger," "those people," or "them folks."[15] This type of dissociation or lack of identity formation that occurs among the community's African American neighborhoods often prevents the formation of a "they/we" or "them/us" dichotomy that can give birth to coalition or mobilization. The ideological roots of these identity formation problems are explored in Part Three, which discusses the construction of an intraracial identity. It is important, however, to remember the role psycho-spatialized distancing plays in that formation. Concepts like "the other side of the tracks," "White folks' business," and "them folks" all have historical foundations that were shaped by physical and ideological boundaries.

WHO ARE THESE PEOPLE AND WHY ARE THEY HERE?: ORIGINS OF THE REGIONAL AFRICAN PRESENCE

The first African Americans to inhabit the Lafayette County region were brought to the area by the county's founding mothers and fathers. These settlers migrated mostly from South and North Carolina. In the early half of the nineteenth century when the north central area of Mississippi was being settled, the foreparents of most of Lafayette County's African American population were brought enslaved to this western border of what has often been referred to as both the Bible Belt and the Black Belt. Their ethnic identities perhaps were already redefined and convoluted because of categorization systems in place in the areas of the country from which they migrated. However, there are definite categories used by White residents of the county as late as 1866 to distinguish Blacks. A board of police record dated 1866 makes reference to "Freedmen, Free Negroes and mulattoes" (Sobotka 1976:47). This record indicates that definite external distinctions in terms of intraethnic categorization existed.

Although certain census reports refer to "Free Coloreds" and "Mulattos," there is no official record of who Oxford's Free Blacks were. The report makes a distinction between "Free Coloreds" and "Whites" and combines them in a column labeled "Total Free," while the larger category "Slave" is subdivided by the classifications "Mulatto" and "Black." An assumption is made here that the term "Mulatto" refers to a category deemed important given the handful of people who occupied that position

---

[15] The same distancing occurred in conversations about the class action Ayers case and their response to Meredith's move to integrate the University of Mississippi, which will be discussed in Chapters 2 and 3.

in society. One can only speculate, but there is no doubt that this difference in categorization plays a significant role in the interracial and intraracial structure of the county in its early years. The 1860 census report shows a few households that maintained slave parents with a mulatto child. It is assumed here that this was the recorders' way of accounting for "master/slave" offspring. The recognition of these relationships is important to our understanding of property ownership and how in some cases it changed from White ownership to Black. In addition, those relationships can be seen as continuing to have an impact on the social structure of the enslaved African American and postslavery family composition. The intraethnic/racial distinctions appear in contemporary society in the ways in which residents reckon kinship. Members of certain families that share the same progenitor make distinctions in the heritage of its members by using different spellings of family names. In some cases, family groups that share the same spelling of the family name do not claim relations to one family group while maintaining relations to another. For example, the brown-skinned cousin in family XYZ claims and is claimed by both dark-skinned cousins and extremely fair-skinned cousins in the family named XYZ. However, members of the dark-skinned family group XYZ claim no relations to fair-skinned family group XYZ. In a few of these families, two differences are noted. The first is ownership of prime real estate and the other is educational level. There are no formal records that support the reason for these differences. However, local mythology tells of one exchange of prime real estate that supports an idea of favoritism for the mixed offspring of Black and White informal unions.

The story tells of a White man who owned much of the real estate around the town square and who was in love with one of his enslaved Blacks. Even after freedom, it is told, she stayed with him, and they had many children. Some stories say that the man wanted to marry the mother of his children but local law prohibited it. The significance of his intentions toward the woman and their children was revealed at his death when he willed all his property to the offspring of this "illicit affair."

Social Structure of the African American Neighborhoods

Until the 1960s, African Americans owned considerable land in the county areas as well as those areas that constituted a significant portion of the east and west sides of town. African American neighborhoods in the rural areas of the county are physically structured like those in the town, but the neighborhoods/cul de sacs in remote areas of the county have social structures quite different from those neighborhoods in town or on the borders.

Although Lafayette County does not depend upon agriculture as an economic base and there are few viable farms in the county, the majority of the county's African American population lives in the rural areas owing to land ownership. Most of the enclaves in the county area consist of extended family groupings. The closer these groupings are to town, the closer physically they are together. In some areas, members of the same family occupy several enclaves within a five-mile area. There are usually one or two major houses that belong to the older family members and trailers that belong to the younger members who eventually will build their own homes on the property or will inherit the older family members' houses and live in them. Although some of the enclaves sit immediately off a county road, others require traveling a private dirt road that leads to the heart of the family property. The different enclaves form what is usually referred to as a community. Each community's name is derived from the community's church, which is usually located close to a county-maintained road and often between that community and town. The number of African American churches in Lafayette County symbolizes the significance of religion in this region. Of the forty-five churches, all but five are scattered throughout the rural area of the county. Because a large proportion of the rural Black population owns the land on which they live, the mostly Missionary Baptist churches in varying communities represent the initiative of particular families to establish places of worship within their communities.

Nearly all Black county residents use the land for subsistence farming (greens, string beans, tomatoes, corn, a handful of livestock such as cows, goats, and chickens) rather than for commercial purposes, although a few family members may occasionally sell some of their crops at markets and to other community members or allow the cutting of trees by pulp-wood dealers. Therefore, the considerable amount of land owned by African Americans in the area is not significant in terms of actual income.

After slavery, many of the Black families that moved from the rural areas to the city settled in an area they called Freedmen Town. They migrated to town to take advantage of the schools set up at the first Black Baptist church (Marshall 1995, Sansing 1996). The area they settled in is the largest of only four sections of the city that are African American neighborhoods. Freedmen Town is the only one bordered by main streets and the only one near the town square. Life histories of some residents reveal that many of the original settlers of this neighborhood were poor but industrious. They maintained small gardens and raised chickens and occasionally a cow or a goat. In addition, they hired themselves out for day labor, particularly after the Civil War, when Oxford rebuilt itself from the ravages of the war.

Although extended families may reside in individual homes, this community does not consist of related families. The current community is a mixture of middle- and upper-lower income families who were able to take advantage of the modestly built brick homes, which are the result of an urban renewal grant. Only a few are relatives of the original settlers to the area. Occupations run from housekeepers to schoolteachers. Two of the other neighborhoods are variously mixed in terms of income and the fourth neighborhood consists of mostly factory workers. Although some of the members of these neighborhoods interact with other members of their neighborhood, the majority forms intimate culture groups outside of the neighborhood. Those that do interact with each other are usually members of the same church or organization. This is a stark contrast to the interaction in the rural communities where, because of family relations, they interact with each other on more occasions than church or organizational meetings.

During my stay in the home of one of the town residents, I became aware of a particular problem endured by the community. While sitting in the living room watching television one Thursday evening, I became extremely distracted by music from outside. At first I thought perhaps it was some youth in his automobile with his sound "pumped up," but the music continued and appeared to become louder and louder. I opened the front door to see where the sound was coming from and concluded that the sound was a band practice or performance at the local high school located near the other end of the square. After closing the door, I commented on the loudness of the sound considering it was coming from so far away. My host informed me that the sounds were coming from the town square. Just at that moment I began to recognize the strains of an elaborately orchestrated version of "Dixie."

"That's the song 'Dixie.'"

"Oh, yeah. They play it every Thursday. They are winding down now."

"They who?"

"The kids from the university. You know. They having ... [aside to a relative in the room] what they call that thing?" The relative, who works at the university, responds with "Pep rally."

"That music is coming from a pep rally? This late in the evening and on a Thursday? Have you all complained?"

"What can we do about it? Them folks gon' do what they want to."

"I can't believe that the university band is playing that song. Don't they have Black musicians in that band?" The relative nods yes, as she flashes a look that says, "Isn't that something?"

The residents of Freedmen Town who live on streets named after the famous civil rights leader Martin Luther King, Jr., are reminded every Thursday night during football season that "the old time days" in the land of cotton have not been forgotten.

In the city of Oxford, the percentage of African Americans, approximately 12 percent, is much smaller than that of the county. The African American population of Oxford/Lafayette County in contrast to the White population consists mostly of families who were born and raised in that county. With the exception of trips to Memphis, Tennessee, and church-related conventions and congresses, a significant number of the residents have not traveled out of the state. Many of the property owners in the rural areas own land not far from the location where their foreparents worked as "slaves." Many of them tell stories of their relatives purchasing the land after freedom, suggesting that as early as Emancipation, Lafayette County Blacks did not venture too far from home. Nor did the former enslaved Blacks migrate in great numbers north after freedom. However, around the turn of the century during "the great migration" period and World War I, some residents from the county did migrate to such areas as Chicago, St. Louis, Omaha, Memphis, Atlanta, Dallas, and Los Angeles seeking better opportunities for themselves or their children and for some to avoid violence at the hands of White vigilantes.

Evidence of these migrations is most prominent around the weekends of Memorial Day, the Fourth of July, and Labor Day – historically family reunion weekends – and during the month of August when most churches have their homecomings. License plates from the previously mentioned areas of the country are seen on cars that fill the lots of the local motels and crowd the yards of members of the families who are holding reunions. Family reunions are major social events that occupy a tremendous amount of time for the family members chosen as the committee responsible for organizing them. On these occasions, the family history and myths are passed on. During this time distant cousins and great-great-grands, children of family members who left the area, meet for the first time those family members who stayed. One family, whose reunion I was allowed to attend, has family scattered to the extreme eastern, northern, and western states, and the majority of the reunion is spent on keeping up with new births and events that relate to family life away from the Oxford/Lafayette

County area. Current audio-visual technology contributes greatly to documenting these events as video cameras run for the entire length of the typical three days of activities, and family historians have begun to use computer programs to document family trees.

The Black Contribution

Few oral history stories are told that discuss the Black contribution to the development of Oxford/Lafayette County without specifically relating to the formation of Black churches and schools. More recent history mythologizes individual community leaders who helped establish the older Black organizations. The contributions documented in the local American Revolution Bicentennial Celebration commemorative book, "A History of Lafayette County, Mississippi" (Sobotka 1976), are fairly unknown to African American residents. The story of Blind Jim Ivy is one story told in both African American and White circles. This story symbolizes the desired image both Whites and a certain segment of the Black population prefer to project about the state of race relations that have existed in the community since the Civil War. (See Appendix D for a version of Jim Ivy's life history and the story of his bridging the racial gap.) From my own interpretive perspective, however, the story reveals a few things about interracial and interethnic interaction that become important to the remainder of this study. The adoption of the story and mythologizing of Ivy's life by both Whites and Blacks reveals the way in which symbols shared by dominant and subordinate groups may be used to create histories that redefine relations between those groups. These stories form oral histories that present a counterpoint to published histories.

Community Churches

Black churches are located in Black communities, and the majority of the county's Black churches manifest the scope of that segregation in their physical appearance and resources. Of the forty-five Black churches that exist in Lafayette County, only four have pastors who reside in the Lafayette County community. This becomes a significant fact when we analyze the role of leadership, or lack thereof, in mobilization and in the development of a community social consciousness.

Economic disparities in this segregated society contribute to another social structure phenomenon distinctive to the African American community. A number of churches share the same pastor. These churches, often referred to as "sister" churches, meet twice a month – alternating first and third and second and fourth Sundays. A few of the members of these sister churches may attend both churches, but most use the off Sundays to visit other churches that are not in competition for the pastor's time. Some ministers pastor two churches because no single church wholly supports a minister. In spite of the low economic compensation, many Black residents choose to become ministers. The prestige gained in both the Black and White communities seems to offset the lack of financial gains. The educational level of pastors, with the exception of a few, is high school or less. Five preachers are known to have some college education. However, the vocational preparation for most is local or regional nonaccredited seminary study. In the majority of cases, the ministers were "called" into the profession. The combination of educational level, preparatory training, and being "called" lends itself to the development of what West (1996) refers to as an "after-life theology" rather than a "liberation theology." This tendency has significance for social consciousness and political participation because any emphasis given to social issues relates directly to preparation for life after death. Therefore, the primary leadership of the African American community rarely makes connections between social conditions on Earth and economic, political, and social structures but rather refers to the trials and tribulations one must bear in order to get into heaven.

The social and cultural histories included in this chapter provide a foundation for understanding the diverse actions and reactions of Oxford/ Lafayette County's African American community. The influence of the culture of social, economic, and political life over the more than 150 years can be observed in the following chapters that focus on intraethnic social relations and efforts to organize around those very issues.

2

Getting Around the Stones

The Civil Rights Movement

The 1960s was a trying time for the United States' system of democracy and especially so in Mississippi. Cornel West (1996), reiterating conclusions drawn by DuBois, Myrdal, and others, states that the problem of the twentieth century is the problem of the color line, which has contributed to the "arrested development" of democracy and undermined the power of everyday people to determine their destiny. This arrested development manifested itself in numerous ways that affected the quality of life for most Blacks in the United States. The intent of the Civil Rights Movement of the 1960s was to change those deprived conditions. The extremely oppressive conditions in Mississippi made it a targeted area for concentrated efforts to improve the quality of life of its Black citizens. As a result, Mississippi tops the list in numbers of slain civil rights workers. The reign of bombings and burnings occurring throughout its countryside during the 1960s and 1970s gave testimony to the potentially revolutionary activities being born within its borders. The efforts at directed change in Mississippi during the 1960s make the period of the CRM an ideal temporal marker from which to begin an analysis of social change issues in Black communities.

To understand the behavior of Black residents in Lafayette County, Mississippi, during a mobilization effort in the 1990s, it is necessary to situate the history of the movement in Lafayette County within the history of the larger Civil Rights Movement. After the 1954 *Brown v. Board of Education* decision struck down the 1896 *Plessy v. Ferguson*, "separate but equal" doctrine, African Americans throughout the country saw opportunities for career development, economic progress, and social advancement within the guidelines of this decision. Written and unwritten policies set up before and after the *Brown* decision, however, continued to perpetuate segregation in all areas of Black participation in American society. Despite this resistance, Blacks in Mississippi, from all walks of life, began to challenge Jim Crow in almost every avenue of social interaction through boycotts, sit-ins, and demonstrations. The spirit of the movement gained in momentum as each wall was knocked down. Each area of the South had its own particular battle; Mississippi was no different.

In Mississippi's capital, Jackson, the battle was over racial discrimination in employment practices and access to public facilities. In most of Mississippi's rural areas – through which the Civil Rights Movement passed – the ability to secure a voice in the political system became a primary grassroots goal. The general pattern of the movement in areas outside of Lafayette County was that boycotts, sit-ins, or demonstrations were followed by voter registration drives. Voter registration drives eventually led to African Americans running for local public offices, and those attempts eventually brought about the election of Black officials. Today, as a result of this intense effort to institute social change, Mississippi leads the nation in the number of Black elected officials with a total of 669.

JAMES MEREDITH AND THE MOVEMENT COME TO TOWN

The events in Lafayette County differ greatly from those in other areas of the state. The part of the national movement that touched Lafayette County and Oxford, Mississippi, was James Meredith's efforts and subsequent enrollment at the previously all-White University of Mississippi, an institution that even in the 1990s continues to revel in its commitment and participation in the Civil War.[1] Evidence of the sense of pride associated with the university's role in the war is symbolically shown by the statue of a young Confederate soldier standing at the heart of the main entrance to the university, supporters of the athletic teams insisting on waving the rebel flag, and the university band playing "Dixie" at football games.

The university (and its surrounding area) was the site of one of the most dramatic displays of contemporary White American resistance to social change. A statewide public and political effort to prevent Meredith from integrating Mississippi's most prestigious symbol of White Southern culture resulted in the deployment of federal troops to enforce the Supreme Court judgment and protect Meredith. The local African American

---

[1] September 1993 marked the thirtieth anniversary of the integration of the University of Mississippi.

community, however, remained distant from this national drama being played out in their town. The reason for the reticence is the area's complicated social order and organization reaching back in time to the initial construction of institutions, processes, and worldviews that continue to support the past practices of the dominant society.

In spite of the presence of more than twenty-three thousand troops (many of whom were African Americans) and the decline in random and orchestrated acts of violence by angered Whites who had converged on the town from all over Mississippi, no sigh of relief exhaled from the mouths of Oxford's African American residents the day James Meredith was successfully enrolled at the University of Mississippi. The same man mentioned in the introduction who was 11 years old at the time the troops entered Oxford remembers vividly going to bed in relative peace, only to "wake up the next morning to soldiers coming out of the sky and tents in front yards." When asked again in 1994 whether he believed that he benefited from their presence, his answer was basically the same as before. "All I know is that before they came, I could ride my bicycle anywhere I wanted to, and after, I couldn't." He referred to the fact that race relations became more strained in the community, and even those Black families who formerly enjoyed a little privilege from the White community had to watch their steps thereafter. Black teachers from the period recall the fear they felt as they passed through roadblocks. Domestics who worked for many of the prominent White families discuss the fear and suspicion of strangers they carried with them as they performed errands in town. Others talk about the tension that developed between them and shop owners and that often resulted in verbal confrontations. Middle-aged men and women remember being taunted in their adolescence by White college students when walking from one neighborhood to another. African American residents of Lafayette County do agree though that the presence of troops during the integration of Ole Miss prevented Klan members and other staunch segregationists from carrying out further violence on campus. An older African American male said: "Oh, they would have killed that boy [Meredith]." Another resident who lives on the eastern county line described how hundreds of rebellious Whites gathered in cars and trucks and camped in yards waiting for an opportunity to get past the troops.

When asked why local Black residents did not embrace Meredith, the overall consensus was, "I guess we were afraid." Further inquiry into the presence of troops as possibly providing strength and a sense of power as motivation to escalate civil rights activity evoked a most memorable response from a leading member of the Black community: "We figured this way. If it took *all that* to get *one* Black boy into the university, what would it take if we tried to do more?"

Meredith, in *Three Years in Mississippi*, an account of his struggle to integrate the University of Mississippi, relates the story of the fear his presence generated within the Black community. He discusses how a local teacher – an ex-classmate from Jackson State College – invited him "not to visit him" (1966:248). Indeed, the former classmate's wife refused him entrance when he stopped by their house to visit. According to Meredith, later that day the former classmate offered him the following explanation: "he'd been informed by his principal [who was also Black]...that any teacher who had anything to do with me would lose his job" (1966:248). Meredith adds, the high school Social Science teacher offered an additional explanation; he was afraid that his father-in-law, who worked as a street cleaner in Oxford might lose his job (1966:248).

During the year that Meredith attended the university, local leaders of the African American community did not attempt to make him feel at home in the community. One community activist's conclusions about the role fear played in the distant culture of social relations between Meredith and the Black community coincide with Meredith's. This African American woman of modest means who was an immigrant to the area relates one of the stories that traveled the Oxford grapevine but was not documented in Meredith's book. She tells of Meredith approaching the principal of the local Black high school in search of room and board at his home. The principal refused Meredith a place to stay in spite of the difficulties the townspeople knew he faced living in a dorm by himself. Meredith's own account of the townspeople's response included covert communication between himself and a groundskeeper, and Meredith's relationship with an older unidentified resident who introduced him to members of the community. Of the many prominent and not-so-prominent families that I interviewed or observed who lived in the area during that period, I did not meet nor know of any who were willing to say they actually formed a relationship with James Meredith. One cannot determine from the data the exact level of interaction that existed between Meredith and the Black community. However, it is clear that whatever the level, the culture of social relations between Blacks and Whites had a significant impact on that interaction.

Although reports by newspapers and scholars describe race relations on the local level in Lafayette County as being historically amicable, new interpretations and findings contest such relationships. In fact, the show of force by federal troops in 1963 very much resembles the presence of federal troops in the county almost a hundred years before when their presence was used to aid in the reduction of violence and to ensure the maintenance of order during initial voting on the post–Civil War Constitution of 1868. Sobotka (1976) suggests that the presence of troops helped to curb violence in the county, where there were four dens, or chapters, of the Ku Klux Klan. Also, Nathan Bedford Forrest (founder of the KKK) made a point of coming to the county for organizational purposes (Sobotka 1976:50–3). His presence is one indication that relations between African Americans and Whites were not as "amicable" as some may have believed, and the memories and mythology that describe such negative relations (as that with the KKK) underpinned the Black interaction with Meredith. Another indication of the culture of social relations between Blacks and Whites comes from members of the community. One of the local leaders has taken on the responsibility of rewriting the county history from an African American perspective "because things that people were writing [referring to university faculty, students, and local town historians] painted a rosy picture about race relations that did not exist." He points out that residents more than fifty years of age often reported fears of economic reprisal and physical violence as the primary factors determining the culture of race relations in the area as long as they could remember.

Through the eyes of the Black residents of Lafayette County, the benefits of the movement coming to their community were ambiguous at the most and nonexistent at the very least. Access to previously uncontested areas of the city was now contested. People not only had to watch who they talked to but where they went as they negotiated their way through checkpoints coming and going to work, church, stores, and the like. To some of the older residents, these inconveniences seemed not worth the reward. Others indicated, however, that access to other public facilities came as a result of the presence of Meredith and the troops. The changes occurred mostly in the elimination of segregated entrances to certain businesses. There are mixed feelings among older members of the community as to whether this was a significant change and who benefited most from it. For example, many of the stores that prevented Blacks from trying on clothes before purchasing them changed their policies, but their treatment of Blacks grew even more despicable.

One elderly African American resident who continues to hold a favored spot within the Oxford White community tells of the time she purchased a piece of costume jewelry from a local merchant who ran a dress shop. This occurred after one of her children became one of the first local Black residents to study at the university and had most recently tried to integrate the lunch counter of the local drug store. The merchant, a known racist, who showed displeasure with her Black customer, did not wrap the jewelry. She took the money and threw the pendant at the customer while reportedly yelling, "Get out nigger." "I'm praying for you," was the customer's response. The owner's daughter came from the back of the shop to join the confrontation. "Get out, nigger, before I call the police on you." "I'll be right here when the police come," the customer said. As the epithets escalated, the customer asked for a bag. When the owner refused to put the jewelry in a bag, the customer picked up the pendant, left the store, and walked around the square to the police department to tell them what had occurred. She made the report not to have legal recourse for the abuse but to counter anticipated accusations of her stealing the merchandise.

Although there were no identifiable civil rights events born or "homegrown" in the area during Meredith's stay, his legacy for Oxford revealed itself in 1969 when the first students from Lafayette County enrolled in the University of Mississippi. Although Oxford did not jump on the movement as a community, some individuals initiated efforts directed at change and had varying degrees of success. These efforts are an important part of the history and mythology of Oxford's African American experience, and they reveal the role social consciousness plays in mobilization. The following accounts are by individuals or family members of Blacks who have tried to institute social action in Oxford/Lafayette County. Each account gives a local-personal perspective of the problems that have an impact on mobilization in their community.

FROM THE MOUTHS OF THOSE WHO WOULD BE KING

Snapshots of the small number of people who have consistently continued to work for social justice and a better way of life for their Black brothers and sisters of Lafayette County, Mississippi, follow. Their comments provide insight into the difficulties involved in local organizing and speak to their commitment to an ideal. Through their voices, we witness the fragile and, at times, antagonistic culture of social relations between local Black leadership and their constituents. "King" here (in the head above) refers to Martin Luther King and reflects the willingness of these individuals to sacrifice their future, family, finances, and friends for a greater cause. They are members of the community who in spite of potential reprisals initiated efforts to bring about social change for Blacks in the community.

Although efforts have been made to somewhat disguise their identities because of the specific activities described herein, they may be identifiable by other members of the local community. As a result of that possibility, each story included in this section is included because the individuals do not mind being identifiable or directly connected with the stories told.

MDJ. Coming from a Mississippi community that supported a number of civil rights organizations, MDJ graduated from high school in a nearby county and entered a local, traditionally Black institution during the same year James Meredith won his battle and entered Ole Miss. During this time, MDJ set a goal to aid poor Blacks of Mississippi. In 1968, at 25, MDJ helped a group of lawyers from Ole Miss establish legal services for the poor. He turned his attention toward this group after trying to lead students in a march against the destructive aspects of the town's urban renewal plans. This effort landed him in jail for two days.

According to MDJ, soon after his arrival in Oxford, he learned that in this place he was to call home for the next twenty-six years he was viewed as an outsider and that garnering cooperation from local African American leaders would be difficult if not impossible. "I knew when the minister of a prominent Black church said, 'How are you going to come here and tell us how to run things?' that the Black people here were not too much different than the Whites." Because of this belief, he attempted the housing movement with youth rather than adults, but his efforts still failed. He concedes that a few local Blacks have tried to help "the race," such as the woman whose children were the first to integrate the public schools; the family who tried to lend a hand in getting food stamps, clothes, and other benefits for needy Black families; and the young woman who tried to raise the consciousness of members of various Lafayette County communities about the need for church involvement in the social problems of the community. Nevertheless, he also points out there has never been a successful, mass movement born or carried out in the town. He went on to explain that in 1968 it was difficult to conduct a movement because African Americans in the community felt conditions were better there than in other places. As an example, he points to the fact that the local movie theater did not have physical barriers dividing the races, although Whites and Blacks didn't sit with each other. MDJ mentions both the instability of the NAACP as evidence of the difficulties of mobilization and the firing of the head attorney for the plaintiffs in the Ayers case from his federally funded position with the NMRLS as examples of Oxford's Black elite/professionals who are concerned only with family and self and have no concern for the problems of poor Blacks in the area. "The agency," he said, "is doing just enough work to keep their funding," and those subverters of social action who are employees of the agency work in concert with the dominant society to maintain structures that have been most comfortable for that society because such allegiances are rewarded through patronage.

In speaking of his efforts to obtain employment since being fired (he believes) for his activist role in the community, MDJ makes the comment, which appears as a caption for the frontispiece of this work, "The Black folks won't hire you and the White folks won't either. Now *that's* equal opportunity."

ALB. Born into a poor farming family in central Mississippi, ALB, now 77 years old, is the mother of twelve children. Growing up she was always strong willed and cared about those around her. While still an adolescent, ALB began helping those who were in worse condition than her own family. "I said one day to myself, why is it we're always giving food to the ministers and deacons? So I asked my mother for a plate of food for a family living on a farm nearby who barely had anything to eat. She set a plate aside for them. And ever since then, I have been trying to help people."

This mostly self-taught public servant has spent more than twenty-eight years working for a community service organization. In a recent evaluation of her contribution to the community, she discovered that she had raised more than $35,000 to assist poor families in the community. These were monies she was able to secure after plowing her way through the legal system of hearings and appeals in order to help those needy families. She has worked diligently to make poor African Americans of the community aware of their rights and the resources that are available to them.

When asked what she thought about Meredith, she said: "The Lord put him there to break the chain." In her response to a comment about the community's lack of outward support for him, she advised that even today in her area in Lafayette County in particular, "you need to know where you're going, who to be with, and what to say." She explained that many people involved others in conversation about various controversial subjects not for enlightenment but in order to carry information back to those people who are working to keep things as they are. Often, not knowing whom you are talking to could mean the difference between life and death. But she quickly adds, "I never was afraid. They can't do nothing but kill me. Somebody have to go. I love to help people do things they can't do." ALB was one of the few adults living in the community who joined MDJ in his housing march, and she and her husband were the only ones who bailed him out of jail.

ALB, who is very aware of national events, indicated that a Christian education, an understanding of "what things were like for us during slavery," and "people getting together" were the things the community most needed. "It seem like we got more freedom, we just don't have the love. Since they (referring to some of the more privileged Black who have begun to focus on their individual needs at the expense of the larger community) see we making money, got beautiful churches ... we don't care about one another. And we ain't got no love for nobody."

JWR. Born to sharecropping parents in the Oxford community, JWR went to college in Alabama after graduating from the all-Black high school. Later when he finished theological school in Atlanta and returned to Oxford, his public service work in the community and on campus made him the local folk hero. A day care center and a public housing project are named in his honor.

In 1969, he became the first campus minister for African American students at the university and provided guidance and counseling. Black students and faculty pay tribute to his tremendous efforts to make a difference. He founded a co-op store, a day care school, a credit union, a civic organization, a local Boy Scout troop, the community newsletter *Soul Force*, and a tutorial program. His small frame was no indication of his courage, and people still praise him as "a man that stood his ground" and "a man they couldn't arrest." JWR died at the early age of 46. His wife sums up the problems that he faced in organizing the community by stating that people were fearful of repercussions – losing their jobs, being denied credit, and being victims of violence.

ALD. Born into a military family, ALD traveled a lot and lived in different areas of the world. Her early impressions of Mississippi, formed from summer vacation visits to relatives in the central part of the state, were that the state was "a place where Blacks weren't treated right ... [were] always afraid." With family roots in Mississippi, however, she later joined her family when they returned to the state. She received her undergraduate degree from one of the state's traditionally Black institutions, joined the Military Police Corp for five and a half years, and in 1988 entered the University of Mississippi's Law School.

Hired by the university as their Equal Employment Opportunity Commission (EEOC) officer, she comments that she was confused by the pressure exerted by fellow employees for her to apply for the position, particularly since she had no experience in that specific area. Although she "survived" law school at the university and secured a position after graduation in the school, she had no idea why certain White administrative staff kept insisting that "they would love [her] over in the Lyceum." In retrospect, she believes they assumed she would be ineffective in the position, which she concludes was what they actually wanted. According to ALD, the administrators wanted someone to continue the hiring and promotional practices instituted in 1970, the year African American students successfully protested, demonstrated, and secured the hiring of the university's first African American instructor. She believes they wanted someone who would allow them to ignore creatively EEOC guidelines regarding hiring practices. She, also with hindsight, believes they thought that her inexperience would help dissipate the power of that office. Determined to do a good job, she attended numerous conferences and seminars in her field to prepare herself for what she believed would be a difficult but doable task.

Although she was successful at obtaining some concessions by bulldozing, cajoling, and threatening the top administrators of the institution during her two years in the position, she concluded that she was fighting a losing battle. As she prepares to leave the university (her decision), she concludes that change of any structural significance is impossible there.

ALD also tried to use her university position to help the African American community at large. She convinced the chancellor to fund a weekend workshop to advise Black small business owners of resources available to them, an endeavor that might be expected from the Small Business Development Center but one never addressed by the center prior to her intervention. She also became an active member of the NAACP. She perceives the principle problems of Black community organization in Lafayette to be the lack of cohesion in the community and sees that lack as a direct result of the excessive number of churches and community leaders.

CTL. Born and raised in the Oxford community, CTL is one of the fortunate few with a college education who was able to secure a "good job" in his hometown. CTL's father worked as a manual laborer for one of the prominent White families of the community and as such enjoyed a certain amount of respect from both Blacks and Whites. After a stint in the military service during the late 1950s, he returned with a new wife and a desire to make things better in the community. One of the first incidents that inspired him to work toward community development occurred when he wanted to build a home for his family. Desiring to give his family the best that he could, CTL wanted to build a brick home for his family. After he applied for a loan to build the house, his father was advised to convince him that he could have the loan if he would build a *wood-framed* house and if his father put up the family property for security. Although his father was willing, CTL refused the offer. Determined to accomplish his goal, CTL tells of buying the materials for his house a little bit at a time in order to keep Whites from knowing what he was doing. Before they knew what was happening, his house was built with no mortgage to pay, and it was the first *brick* home to be owned by an African American in the community. CTL tells a humorous story of how during the months when Meredith worked to integrate the university, many of the rabble-rousers who were stopped at the county line camped on his property because they thought the substantial brick house belonged to a White family.

A highly intelligent and sensitive man, CTL was disturbed by the duplication of efforts on the part of the various organizations and social clubs to improve existing conditions. He successfully organized a coalition to coordinate the efforts of the various organizations. The coalition operated for a little more than two years and then fell prey to the factionalism that plagues many of the efforts of organizers in the community. A respected member of the community in his own right, CTL is also one of the few leaders (who is not a minister) appointed to a position of prestige by the White community. This position, which will be discussed in Part Three, is problematic at times for the work he tries to accomplish in the African American community.

The actions of White officials and members of the White community who abuse their positions of privilege often disturb CTL who is an integrationist ideologically. A part of his worldview is religiously based, and so he believes that "all men are brothers." Connected to this belief is a strong commitment to reciprocity. He believes that one should get out of something as much as he or she puts in. A recent incident has begun to influence his integrationist ideals. CTL's mother-in-law, with whom he was exceptionally close, died. She had dedicated her life to serving a particular White family, at times to the neglect of her own family. CTL is deeply disturbed that members of the household to whom his mother-in-law had given lifelong service did not attend the funeral nor even send a card or flowers. CTL believes this was a statement being made to him regarding his most recent social activist position in the African American community – the efforts to elect a Black sheriff.

As a longtime resident and activist in the community, he has definite ideas about the problems that plague the Black community. "Fear. Most people are afraid. That fear makes people not always act in their best interest." He goes on to describe how not enough people in the community are willing to get involved because of that fear, and that this places a tremendous burden on the few people who are willing. The fear CTL speaks of is a fear of the myriad negative sanctions White society has the ability to carry out. Those members of the community who mention fear believe that the thought alone of antagonizing Whites in any way is frightening because of their dependency on the patronage system.[2] CTL has lost his zest for community-related social action and has decided to focus on himself and his family and turn the reins over to someone else. When asked to whom, he responded: "Whoever is going to take them, but I've done my part."

These stories of social activism reveal the ways in which fear of bodily harm and social sanctions have an impact on Black participation in social movement activities. They also reveal a form of social consciousness that does not automatically mobilize. Although fear has a place in understanding why the majority of the community avoided involvement in social movement activities, it is also clear that something else is afoot. Because Oxford is a small town, a deeper look at the historical, cultural, and social roots of social inaction is possible.

---

[2] These thoughts exist in spite of the fact that many of the residents who are dependent on some form of patronage are at times very outspoken on the level of individual interaction with Whites.

PART TWO

SOCIAL CONSCIOUSNESS, SOCIAL ACTION

3

Social Consciousness and Black Public Culture

Social consciousness often becomes the focus of organizers and organizations looking to create social change. Organizers frequently assume that simply bringing the issue to the attention of community members will provide the impetus for mobilization, and as such those who do not join the effort do not understand the need for action. That assumption, I believe, is the primary reason that studies of social movements focus on the consciousness-raising aspect of mobilization. Sometimes, however, this model does not hold true. In this chapter, I present examples where consciousness exists but social action does not occur.

African Americans as a diasporic group have struggled throughout their existence against their subordinate state. On the individual or group grassroots level, their particular struggles have historical, regional, and ideological roots. After slavery, African Americans formed a tremendous number of organizations to address their social, political, and economic problems. These associations, societies, clubs, and religious and political groups formed the body of the Black public sphere. This vast effort to organize demonstrates that African Americans do not lack social consciousness, but rather that there exists a complex mix of ideological diversity, social relations, intimate culture groups, and power relations that influence efforts to mobilize around issues important from an objective perspective on the community level.

The social and civic organizations (public and exclusionary) that constitute the structure of Black society are both helpful and harmful (often simultaneously) to both identification of the problem and the subsequent actions that follow. Understandings of this phenomenon are not new; however, most studies of the organization of Black society focus on high-profile structures such as national/international associations and societies, the church, and the family separately. No doubt these structures are important symbols alone, but these larger studies often mask the myriad ways in which Black communities divide themselves thus leaving out important cultural and social identities that affect group dynamics. In addition, such studies rarely integrate these various institutional structures to form a larger picture of the Black public sphere. Oxford, because of its size and significant number of organizations, is an excellent community for addressing the interconnectedness of intraethnic social group interaction and its impact on perceptions of social issues, social action, and mobilization.

The significance of varying perceptions of numerous social problems in Oxford/Lafayette County and the responses to those problems are the primary concerns of this chapter. When we focus specifically on the behavior within a number of intimate culture groups, through which these various perceptions and reactions are manifested, we are able to understand why certain changes have not occurred and to identify the stones on the road to social activism and mobilization. The following descriptions are intended to highlight the culture of a selected number of intimate culture groups as well as provide a partial view of the variety of intimate culture groups within the community; in no way is this chapter meant to imply that they constitute the total number of groups in Oxford. Nor do I suggest that these descriptions are exhaustive of the culture of any one group discussed. The specific descriptions included were chosen because of my own particular understanding, as an anthropologist and member of the community, of their significance to social action and because they are representative of various social categories of intimate culture groups.

The first day of my return to Oxford in 1994 I went to court to take care of a traffic ticket left unpaid from my last visit. While I was waiting to speak to the clerk, a number of people recognized me from my previous work with the university before. Eager to get started with my research, I commented on the considerable number of physical changes that had occurred since I left four years earlier and asked about the changes I couldn't see. "Nothing's changed," was the comment from the husband of a former co-worker.

"Nothing?"

"Nothing."

"That's hard to believe."

"That's the trouble."

"What do you mean?"

"You can't believe what you see. Everything ain't what it appears to be."

"How do you mean?"

"You know how they say, you can't judge a book by the cover? Don't let Oxford fool you."

"Can you give me an example?"

"All these pretty things make you think everything is nice and quiet and peaceful. But it ain't."

"You mean crime?"

"You don't know who to trust. That thing [referring to crack cocaine] will make you do anything to get it. Including killing."

"It's that bad here?"

"Worse than that."

"I'm sorry to hear that. So how are you doing?"

"Trying to make it. Staying to myself. You back at the university?"

"Not now but I will be. I'm here to finish my dissertation. That's why I've come back. I want to study Oxford – especially the Black people here. See why they do what they do."

"Well, good luck. Just watch your back. Remember what I told you. Things ain't the way they seem to be." These words would return to haunt me throughout my fieldwork.

The construction in and around Oxford of new middle- and upper-class subdivisions, an additional golf course (bringing the total to three), more than a handful of new apartment complexes, and the widening of county highways most certainly, I thought to myself, had created changes in the behavior of both Blacks and Whites. As for the issue of drugs, I knew that drug trafficking and drug use had become problematic before I left, and I wondered, "Could this be the social issue that will unite the Black community into social action?" Or, the question became, "Is this a symptom of a greater problem around which the larger African American community would or could rally?" If neither proved a strong enough rallying point, I wondered if there was another issue that a significant number of African Americans in Lafayette County face that would bring about mobilization.[1]

---

[1] The following community or ethnic studies reveal a variety of social issues around which various social groups in America have mobilized: Public services for a Queens African American community in Gregory's (1992) "The Changing Significance of Race and Class in an African-American Community"; West Indian political power in Brooklyn in Kasinitz's (1991) *Caribbean New York: Black Immigrants and the Politics of Race*; the abortion debate

PERCEPTION OF THE PROBLEM IS THE PROBLEM OF PERCEPTION

A number of social categories construct group identities in Lafayette County. Often the constructed identities conflict with each other, with the goals of the Civil Rights Movement, and with the process of community social action. Just as the collective judgments of the intimate culture group shape group expectations that can be rationalized when threatened, the collective judgment of the intimate culture group has been shaped by selective perceptions of the group members. In the area of political participation, the categories of religion, social standing, organizational affiliation, lifestyle, and levels of intraethnic interaction (or "the culture of social relations") provided a greater understanding of political social action and attitudes toward participation in social movements than class and gender. People in each of these categories had developed distinct understandings of what problems exist in the African American community and what the necessary solutions, if any, must be.

Each intimate culture group in Oxford has its own collective take on what is wrong and what needs to be done in order to improve the quality of life of the members of the Black community. The level of collective social consciousness, however, is not a great determiner of action. Instead, it is the importance placed on particular social issues by each intimate culture group that greatly affects the kinds of activities with which that group becomes associated. If we simply focus on the level of social consciousness of each group, a great deal of the intragroup dynamics that influences collective perceptions and judgment would be left out, and we would still wonder why social action did not occur. Therefore, a picture of the culture of social relations within intimate culture groups in Oxford is where we focus our attention in order to explain why community members do or do not respond to mobilization efforts or become involved in social issues.

The Religious View

Observation of seven Sunday School classes at five Black churches and three Sunday School teachers' meetings revealed that, in spite of the differences in denominations, the emphasis in each class was on preparation for the afterlife. Examples used as things that prevented one from "entering the kingdom of heaven" became important for identifying varying

in Ginsburg's (1989) *Contested Lives: The Abortion Debate in an American Community*; and elderly care in a Jewish community in Myerhoff's (1980) *Number Our Days*.

perceptions of the problems faced by Oxford residents. When asked directly to identify the most pressing problems among Blacks in the area, the standard answer by Sunday School teachers and many members of most of Lafayette County's forty-five Black churches was, "They need to stop running from God" or "They need to get out of the street and come to church."

The majority of the community's Sunday School teachers are not teachers by profession. Most have less than a high school education, and very little abstract discussion occurs in the classes. Often in the classes, both teachers and students pull from personal experiences in order to discuss the complicated lessons in the Bible and Sunday School book. Pregnancy, drugs, theft, teens with nothing to do, disrespect, and people who just don't care were subjects that formed the basis for most examples used to explain the need for Christian missionary work. Discussions of problems that were educationally or economically based only related to Christian obligations: "People were not educated enough in knowledge of the Bible." "They need to stop throwing their money away and pay their 'tides' [tithes]." Any mention of problems by the participant–observer, which questioned the role or contribution of discrimination or racist practices, was met with the solutions of "prayer" and "leaving it in God's hand" and responses that implied that the offenders will answer for their offense on judgment day. When asked if people had an obligation to help themselves and each other "to find solutions for their problems," most often the response was, "Christians need to be more Christian-hearted to each other. Feed our neighbors if they are hungry. Clothe them if they are naked."

The discussion of approaching solutions to social problems with direct action within the church setting was difficult if not impossible in most cases. Human intervention was considered almost sacrilegious. If human action were to take place, it had to be through divine guidance. This way of thinking perhaps explains why most accepted civic leaders are men of the cloth who were "called" to lead through divine intervention.[2] In spite of the separation of religious and secular concerns, the Baptist church I attended announced during regular service that the NAACP was conducting a membership drive in order to reestablish the local county chapter

---

[2] Most tell their stories of conversion in the sermons they give. Each story reveals revolutionary change. During my years of association with this community, I have never met a minister who planned to become a preacher *before* a dramatic conversion. Perhaps church members are looking for this dramatic moment of insight as guidance for social action.

(which had been inactive for more than five years). Ironically, given the aversion to the mixing of "the religious" and "the profane," the meeting was to be held in one of the local churches. Even more ironic was what I would witness later after the association was reconstituted. The minister of the church in which the meeting was held would be observed during devotional prayers at a meeting of a Black civic organization praying for the Black community to be grateful for and content with what they have.

The largest Black civic organization, the Oxford Development Association (ODA), also has its monthly meetings at churches on the last Monday of the month. The use of churches for meetings is the result of both the economic and religious structure of the African American community. Few buildings that are not church facilities exist for public use because African Americans in the community are unable to secure loans or raise money to build facilities that are not churches or social clubs. The social clubs, however, have such negative reputations that "respectable" members of the community do not patronize them; therefore, civic meetings are scheduled at churches or the city-run community center.

The Political Organization View

I believed that the efforts to reinstate the Lafayette County chapter of the NAACP would prove valuable to gaining an understanding of the development of social consciousness and implementation of social action. Therefore, I spent a tremendous amount of time participating in its activities and observing the dynamics of the group's efforts. The first meeting I attended was the association's third organizational meeting after reinstatement efforts had begun. The meeting was brought to order by the acting president, an assistant pastor of one of the churches in the county. This minister, a graduate of the University of Mississippi, had a history of activism. (As the first African American to hold the esteemed position of Colonel Reb at Ole Miss, he refused to carry the Rebel flag, which had unofficially become the school flag.)[3] However, a month of Sunday visits to his church never revealed a hint of his activist side in his sermons. To all appearances, he was another "fire and brimstone" preacher whose calling was to get his members ready for "the afterlife."

The spirit of the secular meeting was infused with the dynamics and energy of church services. However, the topic was no longer "the afterlife" but "daily struggle and survival," and from all appearances, it seemed

---

[3] Colonel Reb (Reb stands for Rebel) is the university's mascot.

that action was the focus of the fifteen (out of fifty-one) members present. Typed agendas were passed out prior to the meeting, which was opened with a song and a prayer after being called to order. Still maintaining what I would later learn is his "minister" mode and voice, the president proclaimed his disappointment with the lack of support being shown by the local population for the plaintiffs and particularly the legal representatives in *Ayers v. Fordice*, a prominent class action case which will be discussed later.[4] The president complained that although he could understand and excuse those people who worked, there was no excuse for those who didn't, and they should be at court everyday. "If I can come down there in my work clothes during lunch hour,[5] surely ya'll can make it down there some time during the day. We need to support [LSA] and what he's trying to do. Them White folks are down there."[6] A number of "amens" were voiced by the members who ranged in age from late twenties to late seventies and whose occupations ran the spectrum from professionals to manual laborers to the self-employed and from unemployed to part-time employed to retired.

The next order of business was the coming organizational election of officers. Judging from the reaction of a number of executive board members, few people wanted the leadership positions. The acting first vice president preferred to serve only as an advisor, and a number of committee chairpersons asked not to be reassigned. The impact of this avoidance of leadership positions will become much clearer in the chapters to follow. At present it is important to note that while people were willing to dedicate time and money to the organization, they shied away from leadership.

A special presentation related to voter registration, and the primary elections revealed an intention by the association to play an active part in local and state primary and general elections. The presenter said that owing to the extremely poor turnout at the last election (less than 30 percent of registered African American voters), the number of ballots ordered had been significantly decreased and various district polls were scheduled to

---

4 The long-term legal representative for the Ayers case was an attorney for the North Mississippi Rural Legal Services, a more than twenty-three-year resident of Lafayette County well known for being outspoken particularly about interracial problems.

5 All ministers from the African American community maintain jobs in order to support themselves and their families. Who the employers of these ministers are has import for the amount of power and prestige acknowledged by the dominant society.

6 It should be noted that one White male who is married to a Black female was an active member when I began attending meetings, and a White female, the wife of a university professor, joined later.

merge with others thus making it more difficult for residents in various county areas to get to those stations at election time. Nods and groans provided evidence that members understood the importance of the announcement.

Other business, related to membership dues both past and current, dominated the remainder of the meeting. The meeting became emotionally charged when several individuals expressed their suspicions about the association's reorganization and the legitimacy of the new leadership as representative of the people. (The acting president was not born in Oxford/Lafayette County.) A couple of members implied that other members were not present because they thought that the current reorganization was a political move designed to bestow individual power, prestige, and recognition. Another reason for the tension was the accusation that membership money had been collected from residents during a period when the organization was not active on the state and national rolls. Those members unaware of this at the time wanted to know what had happened to the money. This problem was also given as one of the reasons the membership drive was not going well. The president vowed to provide answers to the questions before the next (monthly) meeting. Most of the discussions overlapped each other and a great many side conversations were taking place regarding these complaints. This appeared to be a very important moment in the meeting when everyone who had something to say said it, whether to the entire group or just to the people sitting nearby.

A Civic Organization View

The first meeting of the ODA that I participated in and observed was held in a meeting room at one of the motels in town. It is important to note that this was not the first meeting I had attempted to attend. The first meeting held after my arrival was to take place the last Monday of the first month of my fieldwork. The events surrounding my efforts to attend that meeting speak to the communication problems organizers have in the community. The announcement for that first meeting was read on the Sunday prior to its scheduled date at the church I was attending. Uncertain of the location of the church where the meeting was to be held, I requested a ride to the meeting with one of the long-standing committee-chairperson members of the organization. We arrived approximately five minutes after the scheduled meeting time and discovered we were the only ones there. My guide suggested that we wait a few minutes because another program sponsored by one of the local churches may have caused the delay in arrival of the other members. After a fifteen-minute wait, my guide wondering if we had the right location checked the church bulletin in her purse and confirmed that we were at the right location. When an additional fifteen minutes had passed, she decided that the meeting had been canceled, so we left. We discovered later that week that the meeting had been moved to another location because official permission to hold the meeting at the church had not been obtained prior to the scheduled time.

The ODA meeting at the local motel was attended by approximately twenty of the nearly five hundred members of the organization.[7] Like the NAACP, membership ranges through all walks of life, but unlike those in the political organization, all members of the ODA are also active church-goers. Presided over by a female president who had held the office for more than twenty years, the meeting began about ten minutes late and was opened with its usual religious devotion. As in other secular and religious organizations' meetings, there is an attempt to conduct the meetings according to Robert's Rules of Order. The rules rarely hold for long because of the conversation styles of the African American membership that consist of a number of small conversations and cross talking.

The meeting's agenda was divided into a large number of committee reports, old and new business, a pitch given by an African American minister from another county for a White candidate for state senator, and announcements. The representative for the senatorial candidate was not present at the opening of the meeting and upon his arrival the order of business was interrupted to accommodate him.

An important point in understanding "the culture of social relations" is that the day before the ODA meeting, the White candidate himself had spoken before the NAACP, distributing very little background material and approaching the interaction as a concerned citizen operating at the same advantage or disadvantage as the organization's members. The representative at the ODA meeting, on the other hand, preached an appeal to the members – mostly senior citizens were in attendance – and solicited a multitude of "amens" from his audience, particularly at times when the topics were related to controversial issues. During the question and answer segment of his presentation, the general questions that were asked by the group were not related to the issues discussed but to logistical

---

7 Most members are not active participants, and a considerable number live in other states. The one-dollar membership fee provides them with an inexpensive moral support connection to home.

information such as the date of the primary and the availability of help at the polls for those unfamiliar with the newly structured ballot.

Having learned at the earlier NAACP meeting the problematic areas of the candidate's platform and past record of race relations, I mentioned to his representative a number of issues I viewed as questionable. The questions not only sparked fidgeting from the candidate's representative but an uneasy quiet from many of the elders of the organization. Each answer the representative provided was an attempt to prey on the fears of the uninformed elderly members of the association. He twisted relationships between such things as the "weapons in school code,"[8] welfare and social security taxes, and the vulnerability of elderly citizens. Young people with weapons in schools were connected to elderly people being victims of crime, which he reasoned the elderly couldn't afford given their meager resources and fixed incomes. He then conflated these ideas with those of the candidate's on Christian beliefs and religious lifestyle. He frequently invoked religious vocalizations and emotionalism in order to solicit "amens" and at the same time confuse the issues. Another member, in her mid-thirties who recognized both the uneasy air and the point I was attempting to address, joined in the questioning of those issues, in particular the newly adopted weapons in school laws and the "three times you're out" ruling. The concern over the weapons ruling was related not just to the expulsion of a student for possession of a weapon on the school campus but also to the student's mandatory arrest and the recommendation that the student be tried as an adult with felony possession of a firearm. Another point raised was concern over the disproportionate number of African American youths who would be affected by the "three times you're out" ruling because of their inability to bargain felony charges down to misdemeanors owing to inadequate legal representation.

Another member, the only "Caucasian" member of the organization, also sought clarification on the same issues, which the representative was unable to provide. Sensing that the questions would continue, and slightly

---

[8] The weapons in school code was the local school board's rule that prohibits students from bringing deadly weapons on campus. The code gives the schoolteacher or administrator the authority to seize the weapon and call the police. The questionable aspects of the code were in the interpretation of what items fell into the category of "deadly weapon." Race entered the debate in a couple of ways. Were hunting knives and chains, traditionally carried by young Whites to be considered deadly weapons or were handguns, weapons more commonly associated with Black youths the only items that fit the category? Shouldn't the discipline of the infraction remain in the jurisdiction of the school, unless some greater crime was intended or being committed? A great discussion arose around the possibilities of this code as another means of discriminating against Black youths under the disguise of law and order.

embarrassed by the bombardment of questions, the president interceded on behalf of the representative, giving him an excuse to leave by suggesting that he had other obligations to which he had to attend. At that moment, the party representative who had escorted the candidate's representative to the meeting and who is a nonactive member of the organization stood up without solicitation and stated in a chastising tone: "There was no reason for people to complain if they didn't get out and vote." He added further that, "[the representative] could not be held accountable for the particular point of view of the candidate." He ended his speech of approximately ten minutes with a warning that we needed less discussion and more action and that, rather than complain, we should vote.

After the "guests" (both of whom were African American) left, the minister, who is recognized as a local Black leader by both Blacks and Whites, stated that the party representative was right; as a people we complain too much. "If God wanted things to be different, he would have made it that way. He has given us what we need to have. We should be grateful. Stop complaining all the time or he'll take what we have away." My efforts from the position of researcher to tie the varying social problems to other social conditions that relate to public policy and practice fell on mostly unsympathetic ears, and no group discussion was initiated.

As the meeting returned to its regular order of business, the topics turned to the projects considered central by the organization. The most important was the drive to secure property on which to build an office for the organization. The discussion revealed that the current property in question, which was not their first choice, had a number of problems associated with it in addition to the continually escalating asking price. One of the problems was a city ordinance related to the number of parking spaces for the size of the building. The number of parking spaces required by the city allowed very little space for the construction of a one-story building. Another problem (even larger in my eyes) was the plan for raising the money to purchase the property and build the facility. The plan resembled the problematic methods most often used by local African American organizations and churches.

Always eager to assert independence from the larger White community, the expectation in most fund-raising projects is to raise the money among the organization's members or among local African American allies. This method of fund raising was observed at church functions and civic organization functions and was documented through an historical account of the building of the T.O.M.B. church, otherwise known as the project building. The description that follows symbolizes economic strategies most often used by the Black community.

The idea for building a larger facility that the smaller Missionary Baptist Churches of Tallahatchie and Oxford Baptist Congress Districts (referred to as the T.O.M.B.) could use as a seminary school, district meeting place, and location for all the district churches to conduct a joint Fifth-Sunday service was conceived at the turn of the twentieth century. Members of the district constructed a temporary one-room wooden struc-ture on the land just east of the city limits as they waited for the building fund to grow. Over the years, the first structure became inadequate and in dire need of repair. Thus, a second temporary building, a concrete block structure, was built over a period of time around the middle of the cen-tury. This facility was used and maintained until the current structure was initiated in 1985 and completed in 1986. The funds for building the facility were raised entirely from the contributions of district member churches. The length of time it took to raise the money was influenced by three major circumstances: (1) the poverty-level economic base of the church members; (2) the limited range of fund-raising venues (church sup-pers, bingo, and other forms of secular-type events were never used); and (3) the desire to shelter this venture from White input or control.

The building fund project of ODA, however, was not constrained by the second circumstance. As a result, the members were open to the suggestion of conducting an auction, which they anticipated would raise a great deal of money toward the purchase of the property.[9] PAM, the one White active member of the organization, introduced this idea. She suggested that each member of ODA donate an item of value that could be sold in a public auction during the month of October. Given the tremendously large membership, this would provide a great number of items, which reasonably could raise a large sum of money. PAM's understanding of auction and items of value varied tremendously from the other members. The picture of "auction" for most of the members resembled that of a "garage sale" and PAM's "items of value" were translated by the African American members as items no longer useful to the donor but perhaps useful to someone else, items you would basically find at low-income yard sales. This is an excellent example of what Lomnitz-Adler refers to as regional "intimate cultures" variation in the interpretation of signs.[10] The

---

[9] Bingo, however, would be considered gambling and as such would not be deemed ap-propriate.

[10] It is perhaps important to mention here that this grassroots population maintains a great deal of the "found" cultural aspects of Black life; therefore, all items that are not worn-out (and at times even broken items) are considered valuable because a resourceful person can always invent a use for the items. For example, one of my collaborators collects milk

divergent understandings greatly affected which intimate cultures would attend the auction and in turn affected the amount of money raised. PAM expected to have an auction where both Whites and Blacks attended, but the majority of the Black members of the group envisioned other Blacks – mostly their church members. The auction grossed only a few hundred dollars and the organization incurred expenses in excess of $100.

Aside from the coming primary election, the only other issue discussed that related to the improvement of the African American condition in the county occurred during the report of the organization's scholarship fund. This is a fund from which a local African American high school student is awarded a scholarship to attend medical school with the hope that the future doctor will return to the community to practice. To this date, the extremely small gift given each year has not produced a medical doctor. There is hope that the daughter of one of the members, who is also deeply rooted in the community, will complete her internship and return to the area. There was no discussion of the Ayers case or of the case of a nine-year-old being detained for possessing an unloaded gun at school.

During the refreshment portion of the evening, the two women who eventually joined the questioning of the candidate's representative approached me to introduce themselves and to voice their understanding of the points around which I was attempting to garner a discussion. The African American also mentioned that it was time for the older members to take a back seat, but she realized that would never happen. PAM, in a later conversation, commented that she believed that the high turnout at the monthly meetings was primarily to show respect for the president, a retired school principal who was a well-regarded community leader in both Black and White intimate cultures, rather than to support the progress or civic contributions of the organization.

A Socio-Civic Organization View

The Oxford Sewing and Savings Club was established by a group of retired teachers to help young males learn how to save and to give its members opportunities to display their handicrafts. They are also involved in providing scholarships to local high school graduates. The first meeting I attended of this organization provided a clear example of the

and juice cartons. These items are used during canning season in the place of freezer bags, which are too expensive for her social security income.

problems connected to intra-African American community development.
The meeting opened with a religious devotion, as had all the other meetings I attended. The order of business was formal as committee chairs or
members made reports. The two major topics of discussion were the annual awards and scholarship fund dinner and the request for support from
another organization's scholarship fund. The discussion about supporting
the other organization's fundraiser went as follows:

President: This comes at a really bad time for us because we are trying to put
                on our own event.
Member #1:   Yes, but, they contributed fifty dollars to our fund last year.
Member #2:   Well we have to give them something.
President: All those in favor of giving a donation to [the requesting organi-
                zation] signify by saying aye. Opposers nay. The aye's have it.
Secretary: How much are we going to give them?
President: Well, if they gave us fifty dollars last year we'll give them fifty. We
                may have to call on them again for something we are doing.
Ethnographer: Excuse me for butting in, but have any of the organizations ever
                tried getting assistance for some of your projects through grants?
                There are a number of ways to raise money for non-profit organi-
                zations. Have you considered it?
Member #3:   No. Those things take a lot of knowledge, and we don't know
                where to go anyway. You could do it for us. That could be some-
                thing you could do.
Ethnographer: Well, yeah, I could. But it would be better if one of you helped so
                that when I'm gone you can continue.

Member #3, a retired schoolteacher and vice president of the organization and my sponsor at the meeting, laughed and indicated that she
had too many other community responsibilities. The order of business
continued with no further discussion of the suggestion.[11]

There was no discussion of the Ayers case or of the incident involving
the 9-year-old with the gun. By the time I attended this meeting, the
general public had become aware that an African American for the first
time had entered the race for the position of county sheriff. Yet there was
no mention before, during, or after the meeting neither of this historical
event nor of the election in general.[12]

---

[11] Although it is not discussed later, it is important to mention that Member #3 and I
continued a discussion of proposal writing at her home and with only a little additional
prodding she has written three small grant proposals that have been funded.
[12] An important part of this organization's gathering of its members is the considerable
amount of time devoted to eating. The meeting is usually adjourned after forty minutes,
and the remainder of the time is devoted to socializing and eating elaborately prepared
meals by the hosting member – three or four meats, five or six vegetables, a variety of

During the meal portion of the meeting, I approached the president and suggested that the various organizational scholarship efforts might best be benefited if they joined forces and created a large fund that could be used as an endowment. I was informed that the effort had been tried before but was not very successful. I then suggested that the way the fund raising and contributing was structured, no organization was actually getting anywhere. They were actually shifting the same fifty dollars back and forth from one year to the next and therefore the treasury was not experiencing an increase. After thinking about it for a minute, she commented that she never looked at it in that way but didn't see what could be done about it.

A Public Culture View

Oxford/Lafayette County has a number of public locations where socializing intimate culture groups congregate. I refer to this as "public culture" because they are the most consistent group formations viewed by the general public that influence external perceptions of Black culture. Unlike the organizations previously discussed, these localized gatherings consist of the smallest group of people who share the most symbols and who interact most often within the same setting for the same individual purposes. They maintain a group identity status because they share the same activities on a regular basis; however, group membership changes. Although beauty parlors and barbershops are not as homogeneous as other locations, the people who congregate there also create, through their conversations, a space for public culture.

The daytime intimate culture gatherings are distinct from the nighttime ones mostly by age and income. Daytime congregators are mostly over thirty, and although the groups are predominantly males who are regularly unemployed or seasonal workers, the groups are dotted with females from time to time. These groups are the most difficult in which to conduct participant-observer research even with a member as an entree. My presence, as a female, made observation of the general day-to-day interaction extremely difficult. Most of the conversation was directed toward me and much of it became a game of one-upmanship as each member competed for the position of most impressive. The observation of these groups was limited to observing reactions to my very pointed questions.

homemade and bought breads, a table full of desserts, and a variety of nonalcoholic beverages. As pointed out earlier, during this time of communion, none of the previously discussed issues were mentioned.

As a result, it is difficult to know what the general topics of conversation would be within these groups. The introduction of my topics might never have been of importance to this group had they not tried to impress me with their wit, worldliness, and intelligence.

The following is an example of a conversation with a group of men who congregate daily on a side street under some extremely overgrown hedges. Many of the men are seasonal or part-time employees at the University of Mississippi. The size of the group varies, and from time to time a female and a couple of teenagers have been observed as part of the group. Because I knew no one who could introduce me to this particular group, I made a habit of taking walks in the area at different times of day for approximately two weeks before approaching the group. The approach was easily facilitated because almost every day that I passed, greetings, comments, or some sort of solicitation was sent my way. The day of the following conversation, one of the teenage boys who hangs out in the area and periodically joins the group was present with five older men.

Member #1:	[Some sort of greeting and an inaudible comment.]
Ethnographer:	Hi! You guys trying to stay out of the sun?
Members:	Yeah. Trying.
Ethnographer:	[To #1] What was it you asked me?
Member #1:	Who me?
Ethnographer:	Yeah. You said something; I couldn't understand what you said.
Member #1:	Nah, nah. Not me.
Member #2:	[Interrupting.] Don't I know you?
Ethnographer:	Maybe? What do you do? [Group members laugh.]
Member #2:	A lot of things. There ain't too much I can't do. [Group laugh.] What can, I mean, what do *you* do?
Ethnographer:	Well, I do a lot of things, too. But right now, I'm working on my dissertation – [#3 interrupts].
Member #3:	You out there on the campus?
Ethnographer:	Yeah. But that is not connected to what I am doing. I don't go to school there; I teach there. I go to school at NYU in New York.
Member #2:	I knew I knew you. I work on campus too. I'm just on vacation now.
Ethnographer:	Vacation? What do you do?
Member #2:	I work at one of the houses. [Referring to the university's fraternity and sorority houses, which actually close during the summer. I learned from this group and another collaborator that the housekeeping staff members for these houses are unemployed without unemployment benefits for that period of time.] I knew I knew you. You used to work over there with that stuff about Black people.
Ethnographer:	Afro-American Studies.

Member #2:   I knew I knew you. Yeah, you married. . . . Yeah. You ain't from
               here.

During the entire conversation, Member #4 had been walking around
me as if carrying on an inspection. Member #5 sat quietly attempting to
send messages to me through stares. The teenager found a lot to snicker
about. I explained what I was doing and let them know I was interested in
hanging out with them for the purpose of finding out what they thought
about certain subjects.

Member #1:   You don't want to know what I think.
Ethnographer: Why?
Member #1:   Cause you can't write about what I think.
Ethnographer: Why not?
Member #1:   Because I know too much about what's going on around here.
Ethnographer: Well you're just the person I need to talk to then. What about
               you? [Pointing to the other congregates. They laugh.] What
               about you? [Indicating the teenager.]
Teenager: Who me? I ain't gon' be here. I'm going back home.
Ethnographer: Oh, you're visiting for the summer.
Teenager: Kind of.
Member #5:   Boy, stop your lying. [They laugh.]
Ethnographer: Is he not telling the truth? Are you visiting or what?

He explains that he was sent to live with his grandparents in order to
finish school because he had gang affiliations back home. When asked if
he had graduated, his remark was that he didn't need to graduate to do
what he wanted to do, which was going to be his own boss. I made an
effort to explain the value of education even for those people who want
to be their own boss and received encouraging comments from the rest of
the congregators, particularly from #5, who I later learned was the young
man's uncle. The topic of conversation danced between young people not
knowing what it takes to make it in the world today and whether I would
be doing private interviews with various members so that they could show
me everything that they knew. The needs of this intimate culture group
(to turn a position of powerlessness and unemployment into a position
of power, the objectification of women from one perspective, and the
position of knowledgeable authority from another) determined the culture
of social relations and far outweighed my efforts to influence the direction
of a conversation to social issues I perceived as important to this group.

A second intimate culture daytime group consisting of almost as many
women as men gathered in the afternoons at a small restaurant in the

county to play cards. Depending upon who the players were, the stakes could be for money or food or both. Because of the nature of the game, quiet and contemplative at one moment and boisterous, offensive, and argumentative at the next, my presence was often forgotten. The conversations in this setting focused mainly on other people's problems, such as who was having family, mate, or employer problems. The conversations bordered much of the time on gossip; few testimonies were the result of direct knowledge. The introduction of such topics as the Black running for sheriff and the drug den no more than five hundred feet up the road sparked reactions of the futility of trying to have something decent and the fact that one sheriff is no different than another even if there is a difference in skin color. The activities of this group are also influenced by economic conditions, but unlike the hedge group, they have exercised a degree of autonomy by finding alternate methods for satisfying economic/subsistence needs (playing cards for food or money). The culture generated by both the existence of the need and the solutions practiced set the stage for pessimism and hopelessness (i.e., West 1994).

I *observed* rather than participated in two nighttime intimate culture gatherings. It is important to note that of all the intimate culture groups I observed, participation was problematic here because of the culture of social relations for both groups. Illegal activities were the catalyst for the construction of the groups. The same contact provided my access to both groups, although he was only a regular member of one. One group gathered on the front porch and front yard of the home of the owner of a now-closed pool hall and juke joint that stood next door and the other was the inner courtyard of a trailer park. One must make a distinction here between a trailer park and a mobile home park. In most mobile home parks, a significant number of residents are trying to purchase their homes and, as such, they try to make the surroundings as pleasant as their finances can afford. Vegetable and flower gardens decorate the yards, signs of children are evident, laundry hangs on lines, and neighbors look out for each other's property. Trailer parks are empty shells that are rented to extremely low-income residents or single parent households on public assistance. There is no pretense of a wholesome lifestyle at trailer parks. Individuals coexist by minding their own business.

The majority of the congregants at the trailer park – most often referred to as The Hole – are not residents of the park but people who come from all over that side of the city and county line. Drugs and gambling are the attraction. The gambling is conducted on the bed of a truck that arrives at first dark with its own generator to provide light for a small area that is confined to a few feet around the truck. The congregators of this intimate culture group are divided into clusters. It was difficult to determine if the boundaries of the clusters were determined by age, type of drug use, or something else. I was able to determine, however, that within each cluster a great deal of posturing occurred, and one individual appeared to determine the nature of the behavior of the others. In one mostly teenage group, a young man was trying to impress his cohorts by handling and firing a gun. In another group ranging in age from 20 to 35, sexual exploits were the topic of conversation. Bits and pieces of conversations about who can outdo the other in various feats were picked up from some of the other more than seven separate clusters. Every observation of this intimate culture group was interrupted either by gunshots or the police. Therefore, I abandoned further effort to define this group.

The Yard presented a somewhat safer environment, perhaps because it is open to county highway traffic. At dusk, members of the household sit on the porch at The Yard, which communicates to the regulars that it is okay to congregate. On any particular "meeting day," the congregants begin to gather on the porch, parking their cars in what they consider a choice spot for the evening. (The length of time individuals intend to stay determines how close they park to the house.) As the evening wears on, clusters also form around various vehicles that are parked in the yard. All members of the congregation in this intimate culture space practice a certain identifiable protocol that was not observable at The Hole. All who enter the yard come to the porch to pay their respects to the household and to introduce any visitor they may bring with them who joins the congregation.

A first-time visitor or new member is placed during the initial introduction by the sponsor or through direct questions by members present at the time, and the subject is not ended until they are satisfied as to exactly who the new arrival is and in what capacity the new member will interact with the others. For example, my initial introduction to the group by my sponsor occurred in the following manner: Before getting out of my car, which I had been advised to park on the perimeter of the yard, my sponsor/collaborator suggested that these were "common" folk and that I needed to let him do the talking. He said that I should follow his lead, and that when he indicated it was time to go, I should not delay. As we walked up to the house, my sponsor/collaborator said that I should go up on the porch. "How ya'll doing this evening?" he inquired. Various people responded and nodded greetings. Speaking to a young lady about 17 or 18 years old, my sponsor/collaborator said, "Girl, get up and give my big sister a seat." The young lady got up, and I sat on the crate she offered. Although I was sitting on the porch, it was difficult to distinguish the features of anyone else on the porch. However, under the dim yard light I was able to identify faces of those who stood on the porch steps or in the yard. Calling the man of the house by name, my sponsor continued:

"You never met my sister before have you?"

"Your sister? That ain't Sistagal is it?"

"Nahhh, nah."

"Is that the one from St. Louis?"

"Nah, this is the one from New York. She's a student, working on writing a book."

"New York? I didn't know you had no sisters in New York."

"That's 'cause she from my father's side of the family. She don't come down here too often. Just every now and then to see Big, I mean, Little Brother."

"A book huh? Well I guess she ain't related to this side of the family cause she got brains."

"Oh yeah, plenty of that. But you know, I went to college too. Anyway, she's writing a book about us common folk. She gon' let the folks know how it is. That's why she came down here this time. To study us and make us famous."

There was laughter from all who were present indicating that in spite of the side conversations taking place at that time, attention was being paid to placing me. After a few questions by other members, my presence was accepted and conversations turned to other things.

The members of this intimate culture group are both males and females whose average age ranges between 28 and 35 years. The females tended to be ten to fifteen years younger than the males. Although illegal alcohol sales and consumption and the sale of lighter weight drugs are a part of this intimate culture, entertaining conversation is the impetus for congregating as evidenced by the small percentage of congregants who actually drink or use drugs while there. Many people visit The Yard just to get these products after hours, but for the majority it is a place to "socialize" and "talk trash."[13] Because traffic is heavy in The Yard, much of the conversation is of a "shoot-the-breeze" nature with various

---

[13] There is a corner store less than five hundred feet from The Yard where individuals purchase beer as well. An additional point important to understanding this intimate

members making fun of each other. A good deal of courting also takes place at The Yard, but sprinkled between are conversations that range from discussions about racist foremen at the major factory to being tired of working hard for little pay. There are also conversations about legitimate and illegal business deals. Because this is an informal social intimate culture, the serious topics are discussed in a joking manner. The only topic discussed with a solemn tone was a short discussion about the need for an OSHA investigation into the death of a young employee at a local factory who had been assigned to drive a forklift without adequate training or a license. As the evening wore on and the clusters merged around the remaining vehicles that still had cold beer and members became more intoxicated or high, the conversations were playful discussions about each other's personal relationships and the need to go home to get ready for work.

The Local Talented Tenth View

The voices of African Americans as an intimate culture group on the campus of Ole Miss were exceptionally quiet during the entire length of my fieldwork. The analytical voices of scholars, educators, and administrators, however, often commented in private conversations and periodically in meetings of the Black Faculty and Staff Organization (BFSO) about social issues that affected Blacks in both the college community and the larger Oxford/Lafayette County community. However, the organization's main purpose, to address campus issues, dominated their actions. During the 1980s, it had been somewhat successful in getting university administrators to establish certain changes in institutional (written and unwritten) policies that affected African American employees. During these earlier years, the makeup of the organization was more representative of the various occupations of Blacks on campus. In the 1990s, the membership became more class oriented (white-collar workers) – drawing more from the pool of faculty and departmental administrative staff than from such areas as building and grounds maintenance and housekeeping. This phenomenon is not the result of intentional alienation of blue-collar workers by the administrative staff and faculty members, but rather it is an intentional disassociation by buildings and grounds personnel. This disassociation has occurred as a consequence of perceived differences in goals

culture formation is the fact that the county is a "dry" county, so beer drinkers usually carry stocked ice chests in their vehicles.

and power, a perception that often makes the blue-collar workers uncomfortable in this specific intimate culture setting. These differences in
perceptions of goals and power will be discussed later.

Throughout the year of sporadic meetings, the organization put a
tremendous amount of time into discussing plans for the major social
functions it sponsors yearly – a welcome-back gathering, which includes
welcoming new faculty, and the Christmas party, which traditionally
is given for the Black students. Membership fees and a contribution
from the vice chancellor's budget help to sponsor university-sanctioned
events, while meals for other events are paid for mostly through ticket
purchases.[14]

During my year of observing the organization, a number of problems
were brought before the membership for discussion of appropriate action. One was an ongoing problem, of at least two years, related to the
university administration's inattention to the evaluation and recommendations of a consultant firm hired to study minority personnel issues and
practices. Letters were drafted from the organization to the appropriate administrators with little fanfare or public awareness and even fewer
results.

A second concern arose over a more recent event. After an important
administrative position was vacated, the supervisor of that department
publicly announced that MM, a Black, would be promoted to the position.
A higher-level university official, however, rescinded the appointment.
The Black administrator, who also happened to be a key member of the
Black faculty and staff organization at that time, was embarrassed, hurt,
and angered by the affair. During the regular organization meeting that
occurred only a day after the withdrawal of the offer, some members of
the organization expressed their concerns and suggested that the incident
required action. MM offered to leave the room during the discussion that
occurred in order to allow members to speak freely and not feel pressure to
respond in her/his favor. Some members argued for drafting a letter that
both lent support for MM and at the same time questioned university
policies and procedures in handling such matters. Those members who
opposed writing the letter recommended that the organization ask MM
what she/he wanted done. It was argued by those in favor of a letter that
asking for a suggestion would put MM on the spot. The opposers of

---

[14] Each member of the organization must commit to providing either a food dish or some
   other item needed for the Christmas dinner.

independent action prevailed; MM was asked; and she/he diplomatically tried not to influence the decision, and this action was taken as sanctioning noninvolvement by the organization. The matter was cause for much discussion and gossip in various campus circles, and the organization was ridiculed for its weak handling of the issue.[15]

EFFECTS OF SHARED EXPERIENCES ON INTIMATE CULTURE BEHAVIOR

Members of the intimate culture groups discussed previously generally prioritize their personal and intimate culture group needs above those of African Americans as a whole. One key reason for that prioritization is that the shared experiences, goals, and views of that group become the primary focus for behavior during the times they come together as a group. The degree to which that specific group is marginalized or incorporated into the larger African American community greatly influences what value they place on the experiences, goals, and views they share with the larger African American group. Those members of the community who belong to a number of different intimate culture groups have become experts at managing the different identities and roles played in the various groups. Later we will see how the maintenance of those intimate culture boundaries limits public sphere discussions and, as such, affects mass movement efforts.

RALLY ROUND THE FLAG: LOCAL CAUSES FOR SOCIAL ACTION

In the following incidents, various members of the community attempted to gather support from the broader African American community for some form of social action. The various intimate culture groups in Oxford responded to the efforts in several ways. The descriptions include my interpretations of the events and the Black communities' responses (both on and off campus) and their efforts to organize around them.

The Ayers Case

In May of 1994 when I formally began my fieldwork in Lafayette County, the remnants of Mississippi's attempt at "interposition and nullification"

---

[15] Later this appointment was confirmed but only after the position had been announced and opened to the public for applications.

of the *Brown v. Board of Education* ruling were being contested by the Ayers case (*Ayers v. Fordice*) in the District Court. Jake Ayers, Sr., initiated the case in 1975 on behalf of his son and twenty-one other students attending historically Black institutions. The suit accused the state of Mississippi of maintaining a dual system of higher education. Ayers, who died in 1986 of a heart attack at 66, sued because the two systems, one for Whites and a separate and unequal one for Blacks, in essence violated the *Brown* decision, particularly in its funding.

To my surprise the courtroom was glaringly empty, and, on most days, the few who observed the proceedings were disproportionately White. This peculiarity existed in spite of the following: a local African American lawyer, who has resided in the community for more than twenty-three years, represented the plaintiffs; the team of lawyers representing the Justice Department had a Black female lawyer; and the Institute for Higher Learning was proposing closing some of the state-supported institutions, mostly the traditionally Black ones. Given the magnitude of this case, which had been argued before the Supreme Court of the United States and kicked back to the district court for remedies, I expected to have difficulty getting a seat, but that was never a problem during the nine remaining weeks of the hearing. Although this extremely important case, which affected the educational and, therefore, economic future of African Americans from every part of Mississippi, was taking place in Oxford, I was in town four days before I heard that the case was being reviewed.[16] Later I was to discover that open discussions about the case occurred at the meetings of the newly revived NAACP. In most of its meetings, discussions centered on the lack of support from the local African American population. Comments were made about universities from other states bringing in people to observe the proceedings, but the locals, who also had a stake in the outcome, couldn't organize a steady group of viewers to show their support.

During those nine weeks (I rarely missed a day), three ministers from the community sat in on the case from time to time. Although the minister of the largest Missionary Baptist church in the city was the clerk for the

---

[16] The case also has significance for African Americans in other southern and border states. After the Supreme Court ordered Mississippi to further desegregate its public higher education system, the Southern Education Foundation, an Atlanta based nonprofit organization that promotes education equity, began a month-long study that concluded that Alabama, Florida, Mississippi, Louisiana, Maryland, North Carolina, Tennessee, Kentucky, Texas, Virginia, and Pennsylvania could not demonstrate "an acceptable level of success in desegregating [their] higher education systems" (Hawkins 1995:12).

case, I did not observe any members of his church present during my entire period of observation. A Black Nationalist family and an elder of one of the largest Black Missionary Baptist churches in the county were the most consistent Black observers other than myself.[17] African American observers from various areas of the state accompanied different African American scholars and experts during the days of their testimonies, and a couple of African American lawyers from a prominent law firm in central Mississippi observed the case for a couple of days. I had not arrived in Oxford when a Black professor from the University of Mississippi testified for the plaintiffs, but no African Americans from the university attended as spectators or witnesses during my period of observation.

My observations were of interracial, interregional, and intraethnic interaction. On days when the courtroom was sparsely populated, people sat in groups made up of friends and business associates. Family members sat together; members of the same churches or organizations may not have been seated together, but there was usually pretrial and recess conversation among them. For the most part, Blacks sat with Blacks, and Whites, with Whites. From time to time, cordial nods of heads occurred between these latter groups, and during short recesses those Whites who sat near me usually asked if I was a reporter or a student. During exceptionally dramatic moments in the courtroom – usually when a particularly negative or telling remark was made by a witness – African Americans would generally look to catch the eye of another African American in order to pass on a knowing or amused glance, which they shared for a moment before turning their attention back to the questioning that was taking place. There were many of these moments, but there were also moments when the glance was a shared expression of disgust or anger. Those moments became topics of conversation during short breaks and recesses.

Outside the court house in the local community, there was a different air. Rarely, as has been described earlier, did an unsolicited comment about

---

[17] An interesting side point about the Black Nationalist family is that the children of this family were given temporary names and as a result of their Afrocentric "home school" education were allowed to choose their own names – all of whom chose African names whose meanings they understood. These brothers and sisters, seventeen in total, are in a home school program taught by their parents and are perhaps the most socially conscious young people in the Black community. All members of the household old enough to work maintain some form of employment with the exception of the mother. This income allows them to sustain their large family unit.

the case occur at meetings of civic or religious organizations and never in my presence at social gatherings or in private settings. When the topic was brought up among the unorganized grassroots population, who appeared to be more open and heartfelt in their expression, comments included a wide range of views. "They [the Whites involved] know they are wrong; they ought to go on and give that man what he wants." "They [White people] still trying to find a way to keep us down." "They [the White defendants] gon' have to do what's right." "Ain' nothing gonna change." "That man [the attorney for the plaintiffs] must be crazy if he think those folks gon' let them run anything that belongs to them." The responses from university faculty and administrators were more often directed toward the suggested remedies. One professor stated: "Moving programs will not solve the problem of inequality. If they put the only program in the state in a particular area at an historically Black institution, it simply means that those [White] students who want that major will go out of state to get it, rather than attend one of the Black colleges." The response of the Black community as a whole reflects the spatialized distancing that helps to rationalize the lack of aggressive mobilization efforts called for by the president of the NAACP.

The Black Bid for Sheriff

One evening as I left a meeting of one of the community organizations, Oxford's only Black police detective approached me and in a confidential tone told me that he was considering running for the office of sheriff. Shocked and elated, I thought to myself: "I am here at the right time. I will get to see mobilization around the election of Oxford's first Black sheriff." I also thought that perhaps my original title *Quiet Resistance* . . . would be appropriate after all.

Ethnographer:	I heard somebody mention it, but I haven't seen any signs or anything up so I didn't think much of it. I'm glad you're running.
Potential Candidate:	Well I haven't officially said that I would. I'm trying to see how people feel about it.
Ethnographer:	I don't think too many people know. Do you have a committee helping you?
Potential Candidate:	Yeah, I have a lot of people wanting to help me. But you know I could use somebody like you to help me out with some ideas.

Ethnographer: Well, that's a lot of work and I'm trying to do the research
                           for my dissertation, which keeps me busy day and night.
                           But, if some ideas pop into my head, I'll give you a call,
                           and we can meet and talk about them.
Potential Candidate: That's good.
Ethnographer: But you know you can't wait too late to let the public
                           know you're running.

The next time this historical event was brought to my attention in public space was about a month and a half after that first private conversation.
At the NAACP meeting, it was brought to the members' attention that
the board of aldermen and the mayor had dealt the potential candidate
a low blow. They called a special meeting and, without discussion of the
matter on the floor, unanimously voted that employees of the city could
not run for public office while maintaining employment with the city.
Anyone running for office would be required to take a leave of absence
during that time, and the candidate was not guaranteed a return to his
or her former position. Members of the association were incensed. Since
the city elections had taken place the year before, the only city employee the ordinance affected was this African American who chose to
challenge the White sheriff who had held the position for more than
twenty-three years. Angered by the threat of economic reprisal and the
"secretive underhanded" way the board went about the matter, members –
inspired by the president – vowed something needed to be done. They
wanted to address this issue before the board and voted to send a letter in
the form of a petition stating their discontent and challenging the timing
of the ordinance.

Block Grant Funds/Annexation

Events related to block grant funds and annexation were strong circumstances to rally around. For many years, various African American
neighborhoods within Oxford/Lafayette County have suffered from deprived quality of life conditions such as poor and overflowing sewage
systems and poor or no garbage collection, street lighting, or road maintenance. The securing of a grant of $500,000 for development within
these neighborhoods would go a long way toward improving conditions
and hence the quality of life for the residents.

In 1994 the city of Oxford secured $500,000 in block grant funds
from the state of Mississippi. Under the Federal Block Grant Act, block

grant funds are designated for the improvement of conditions that affect the quality of life in low- and middle-income communities. The funds must, according to the act, directly benefit members of those communities in jobs, social services, and community improvements. The funds, originally designated to improve urban centers, cities, and incorporated communities, are not designed for rural development. However, the city of Oxford secured the funds for the development of an area of the county that lies just south of the city limits. The area designated to benefit from the funds consisted of a partially developed upper-class White subdivision and golf course and an area designated as the location for a new (Marriott) motel. The funds were needed to purchase and install a very expensive, state-of-the-art sewer system and to complete the building of streets. The benefit to the lower- and middle-class communities (according to rumor and confirmed later by a meeting with the mayor) was to come in the form of jobs that would be generated once the community was developed and the Pro Shop at the golf course and the hotel were open for business.

Various activists in the community challenged the planned usage as a misappropriation of federal and state funds. Efforts by the NAACP were made to get broad community support.

Legal Problems of Weapons in School Rules

The move to bring a 9-year-old boy to trial for felony possession of a gun in school was another issue of concern. The local school board adopted within its guidelines of student conduct a rule that allowed them to call in the police for any violation of its no-weapons-on-school-premises policy. The loosely structured policy allowed the decision regarding the need for such an extreme measure to be made by school officials and staff. Frightened by the idea of a gun on campus, a school official called the police and a 9-year-old was detained by juvenile services. Later it was learned that the gun had no bullets or firing pin and that the youngster brought the gun to school to trade for a knife that another classmate brought. In spite of the uselessness of the weapon and the fact that the child did not have a previous juvenile record, the district attorney's office wanted to take the case out of the hands of the juvenile courts and charge the child with a felony as an adult.

The child's parents called on the NAACP for assistance. The issue was brought before the membership, and they unanimously agreed that the general public needed to be made aware of the problems connected to the weapons ruling.

Voter Registration

The office of sheriff was not the only position of interest to African Americans. New life was being breathed into the NAACP, and members and nonmembers were becoming excited about the possibilities ahead. Members from all economic levels had made the association aware of problems they faced that had potential for class action suits or organized protest. The fact that the next year was an election year for some important county and district offices fueled the fire of political interest.

During the summer, suggestions were put before the members of the NAACP that the organization needed to assist communities to get political representation. After concluding from the charter that the association could not support any particular candidate, the organization decided to start a voter registration drive that not only would get people registered to vote but also would educate those who were registered about the importance of exercising their vote. In addition, they wanted to hold workshops where members of the different county districts would discuss the kind of candidate they needed and decide who they would back. There were two positions where the Democratic incumbent would not seek reelection, and, given the past overall voting patterns, if African Americans turned out in record numbers, an African American could be elected. Members of the association agreed that this was the best election opportunity African Americans had in the area in a very long time.

The Ayers case, the Black bid for sheriff, the block grant funds/ annexation issue, the weapons in schools rule, and the voter registration drive constitute the majority of the issues that affected African Americans in the community brought into public view. As mentioned earlier, the various intimate culture groups responded to the problems in various ways. Some of these issues continued to be ongoing throughout the period of research for this project; however, the voter registration drive and election are the only issues that received continuous concentrated broad community support.

The discussion in this chapter is intended to provide an understanding of the public issues that the Black community recognized as problematic or important for Blacks as a whole. Additionally, it not only provides a snapshot view of the social structure of the Black community but also

presents a context for understanding why tensions exist periodically between these various intimate culture groups. It also establishes a foundation for understanding the difficulties involved in creating a Black public
sphere that is representative of the concerns of the various public culture
groups that exist. The discussion on space later in this work will help to
connect the difficulties of communication for the larger community as a
whole as well as between intimate culture groups specifically.

4

Social Action:

A Social Movement in Practice

In the previous chapter, a number of social issues around which a social movement within the African American community could evolve were described. Of those, only two proved strong enough to bring the community together. The two issues, voter registration and the bid to elect a Black sheriff, are so interconnected and interdependent that this chapter describes the two movements as one larger movement. I describe this social action by incorporating three perspectives: the organization spearheading the movement, the candidate, and the wider African American community. The chapter also discusses the failed attempt to rally the community around the block grant controversy.

As mentioned in Chapter 3, soon after my arrival in Oxford, I became aware of two potentially significant actions being undertaken by African Americans – an effort to reestablish the local branch of the NAACP and an attempt by the first African American police investigator in Oxford to be elected Lafayette County sheriff. Plans to achieve these two goals were developed along two very different lines. The young leader of the NAACP believed that the best route to increased membership was to jump right into the middle of any social issue that was currently being addressed by the dominant White society and that had a significant visible impact on the African American segment of that society. By contrast, the police investigator who was running for sheriff was cautious and guardedly tested each political move. These two approaches served as the sparks needed to start the fire under efforts to elect a Black official.

Through word of mouth, the NAACP made it known to the general African American public that it was interested in helping or advising members of the community who had problems with the larger society. As a result of this open invitation, myriad complaints came from varied segments of the African American community regarding a multitude of problems. They ranged from Black students being verbally abused by White teachers to Blacks being discriminated against in the cheerleader selection process. They included such issues as wrongful death suits, violations of the minimum wage law, misuse of social security employee contributions, sewage problems, and poor county road maintenance. The investigation of this last issue started the political ball rolling.

The acting president of the NAACP received a call from a concerned White resident in one of the rural communities regarding what he deemed the obvious neglect of road maintenance in the Black community just past his own. The caller described the main road leading to the Black community enclave as being in good-to-excellent condition "just before the Black church." He said that he had placed several calls to the county supervisor for that district to voice his concern, but that nothing had been done. On a number of occasions, the road crews came out to fix potholes and other problems but always seemed to stop just before the church. He called the NAACP because he thought this might be an issue for them to look into. In addition, the caller advised that the incumbent district supervisor was not going to run for office in the coming election.

The membership was informed of the complaint early during the reestablishment of the organization; attendance was high and it was moved that this was an issue to be investigated. The investigation found the complaint valid, and the organization voted to send a letter to the supervisor addressing this issue. The initial response from the supervisor was a denial of discriminatory practices. However, after additional letters and a meeting of members of the executive board and the supervisor, a limited amount of work was done on the road.

The president of the NAACP seized the opportunity of the nonpublicized retirement of the district supervisor to find a willing African American candidate from the community of the church near the poorly maintained road to run for office. The decision was particularly reasonable since the incumbent was a Democrat and African Americans as well as a significant number of Whites vote Democratic tickets on local concerns.

At the same time, the police investigator had discretely begun to let it be known that he wanted to run for the office of sheriff. (It is important to remember that neither the police investigator nor the NAACP president were born and raised in the Oxford/Lafayette County community, although the police investigator's wife was. In Chapters 5 and 6 where identity is discussed, the significance of this point becomes clearer.) As one of his first steps after speaking with family and friends and forming an intimate culture support group, the police investigator asked to address the membership of the NAACP at a meeting a little more than two months before he had to declare his candidacy. Speaking unassumingly, he announced that he was interested in running and wanted to know if the members thought that this was something they might want to support. He advised the organization that he was ready to commit to the campaign fully but wanted to find out what the Black community thought before he made the commitment. The president and the body of the membership expressed enthusiasm for his candidacy.

Under the guidance of the president and vice president, the NAACP had decided to get involved in an effort to find a candidate for supervisor who could capture both the Black and White vote. However, after learning that national policy dictates that no branch can participate in the endorsement of a particular candidate, they decided that they could best serve the Black community by providing a forum in which members of the community could make decisions for themselves. The association could help establish a voter awareness program and a voter registration campaign could then be carried out. Meetings were set to be held in the churches of the district. Owing to low initial turnout, second and third meetings were scheduled to generate more community interest and involvement. After word reached a significant portion of the African American community of the district that the NAACP was supporting efforts to have a Black elected supervisor, at least three male residents expressed a desire to run for office. Although this was expected, there was no mechanism set up in advance to deal with competition within the African American community. The job of supervisor would bring prestige and a middle-class income to any individual elected to the position from the African American community. With the help of this nationally connected organization and the particular circumstances related to the incumbent, the possibilities looked promising; therefore, competition was generated. The competition became a great concern because the position of supervisor is not a part of primary elections. As a result, more than one candidate from the African American community would greatly jeopardize the chance of any African American being elected to the position. Discussions among the body of the association and at executive board meetings were often heated over this issue. Some members believed that this was the first real opportunity for an African American to be elected to a county office and that all the community's efforts should be directed toward one candidate. Others questioned whether the organization had the right to ask individuals interested in running for office to withdraw. Some members pointed out that if they did, the organization would be guilty of the same practices Blacks had accused the White community of carrying out. Still others argued that at least one of the entrants "didn't stand a snowball's chance in hell of getting elected [even] if he was the *only* one running."

During this same period, WW, one of two White members of the NAACP, noticed an announcement in the paper regarding an emergency meeting of Oxford's mayor and board of aldermen. Concerned about the reason for the meeting, WW attended. WW reported that the meeting was called for one purpose only, to make an addendum to city ordinances regarding the city employee practices and guidelines as they related to election candidacy. Without a discussion among the members or from the floor (which led WW to believe that the actual discussion had taken place in private), it was moved, seconded, and unanimously voted that any city employee running for office had to resign or take an unpaid leave with no guarantee of being able to return.

This particular addendum would only affect the police investigator who was considering running for sheriff. The executive committee members of the NAACP were disturbed by this move and questioned why this step was taken at this time. They questioned the sense of the move and asserted that it was simply a step to control the election outcome through the threat of a twisted form of economic reprisal. They based their questions and conclusions on the fact that only a year earlier, when city elections for the mayor's office and the alderman positions had been held, this new election protocol had not been of concern and no similar addendum had been offered. They also surmised that the addendum would be struck down before the next city elections because if the mayor or the aldermen were to seek new terms, there would be no one to run city government between the date for declaring candidacy and election day.

When the problem came before the association's membership, they decided three steps should be taken. First, an inquiry regarding the police investigator's knowledge of the newly instated policy should be made. Second, a letter should be drafted protesting the passing of such an obviously prejudicial addendum. And, third, someone from the association needed to attend every public meeting of the board. The body of the association also expressed disappointment with the one Black alderman who shared membership in several organizations because he was aware of the consequences of this addendum for the police investigator and should have objected, asked for a discussion or a tabling of the addendum, or, at the very least, abstained from voting. This alderman had been first appointed by the mayor, but as a result of being Black and representing a district that held the largest number of Blacks in the town (the district included the Freedman Town area), he was reelected in the following election. It should be noted here that this alderman, like the White mayor, was not born and raised in the community.

The NAACP learned that the morning after the addendum was passed, top White personnel advised the police investigator of the change in policy and told him that if he planned to run he had to decide which option he would take. He was also informed that a leave of absence with pay was not possible in spite of his considerable number of years on the force. This further complicated the decision to run.

Concerned members of the community advised the police investigator that perhaps he should unofficially declare his interest in order to test community support before he officially tossed his hat into the ring. Should he decide to run, he could wait until the very last date for submitting his entry into the primary. These suggestions were made out of economic concerns for his family, which included two young children and his wife. He decided to take these suggestions.

His testing of the waters led him to learn that fewer people knew of his interest in the office than he had anticipated. Members of his own church, where he was active, did not know or at least claimed they didn't know. He also learned that members of the community were committed to helping him attain his goal to the point of committing themselves to financial aid during the time he would be on leave. On numerous public occasions, presidents of clubs and organizations as well as individual residents told him that the Black community would not let his family down, that they admired his effort, and that if his family finances became strained during this process, the community would just have to tighten its belt to help support its own.

For a number of months, the police investigator attended meetings of different organizations and solicited their members' votes. Then he stopped. He did not even attend the meetings of any of the organizations in which he and I shared membership. After a couple of months of not seeing him and observing a lack of positive impact of his running for office among other grassroots intimate culture groups, I responded to his earlier request for my help by calling him to discuss campaign strategies. He admitted that it was a lot of work, but he thought he had a sufficient number of people helping to get the word out. We discussed getting the issues out and the campaign platform upon which he intended to run. Further, I suggested that he look at a documentary made about another Black Mississippian who ran for office in order to get a feel for and understanding of rural campaign strategies and problems.

The flurry around the bid for sheriff and the one supervisor's position sparked interest in other districts and other offices. African Americans had begun to declare their interest in other county supervisors' positions, the constable's position, justice court judge, county clerk, and others. Two weeks before the primary elections, twenty-two African Americans, an unprecedented number, had declared their candidacy for an office. The executive board of the NAACP was both elated and concerned about the exceptional number of Black candidates. The concern came as a result of anticipating some sort of backlash from the White community, particularly because of increased African American voter registration and poll turnout.

The NAACP decided to provide a community forum to which candidates of all races running for office would be invited to give their qualifications for office and explain why they should be elected. The association sent invitations and a list of questions related specifically to African American concerns to all the candidates. Unexpectedly, all the African American candidates responded as well as several White candidates.

At the same time that the police investigator was testing the waters, the issues of the use of block grant funds and annexation were the topic of a town council meeting. Several NAACP members were present. As mentioned in the previous chapter, block grant funds had been secured for road and sewage work in an unfinished development that included the county's third golf course and houses with prices ranging above $200,000. Also associated with the securing of these funds was the annexation of this new subdivision and a narrow strip of land surrounding it, which included another area under development that would house medical businesses. Members of the NAACP executive committee were irate. Realizing that construction (i.e., use of the funds) was to begin within a week, they looked for ways to block the construction and annexation until the courts could investigate the appropriateness of the allocation of funds. The executive board secured, on a volunteer basis, the local lawyer who headed the Ayers case to file an injunction preventing the city from proceeding.

In the meantime, through word of mouth, members of the association made efforts to inform the general community of this situation and asked residents of the communities surrounding the proposed annexed area, most of whom were African American, to come to a community meeting scheduled the day after the community election forum. An important point here is that the election forum was to be held in the district association church, while the community annexation/block grant meeting was to be held in a community church whose members are residents of county neighborhoods adjacent to the proposed area for annexation (see annexation map at *http://formypeopleprods.info* for affected areas). NAACP members went from door to door and called on the phone to inform residents living in those adjoining neighborhoods of the plans.

The effects of these two efforts were interesting. The election forum had a reasonably large turnout. With the exception of the two White candidates and a White reporter, the more than one hundred audience members were Black. Later it was discovered that many members of the audience were family and friends of some of the candidates. Attendance at the block grant/annexation meeting, which the mayor, the Black alderman, and city attorney were scheduled to attend, was sparse. Half of the residents attending the meeting were members of a single Hispanic family – a segment of the area's minority population that had never been considered in the mobilization efforts of the NAACP.

At the election forum, the speakers presented short speeches in response to the advance questions, and time was given for questions from the floor. The candidates less experienced in public speaking depended heavily on their families' residential history and church associations, while the more experienced speakers pitched their skills and goals and implied that their ethnic and racial identity gave them an edge in understanding the special needs of the African American community. Only one candidate directly stated that he/she would be unbiased in decision-making, and another stated that the particular circumstances of individuals would be taken into consideration, not in terms of final decisions but in terms of recommendations that perhaps could prevent recurrences of the same problems. Questions from the floor were mostly antagonistic and from nonmembers of a candidate's family, although it was possible to tell which candidates were the most favored. The younger candidates seemed less favored. To the disappointment of many who were in attendance, five African Americans were running for the same county supervisor's position, two for the position of constable, and three for the district supervisor's position discussed earlier in this chapter. The most startling announcement by any of the candidates came when a candidate running for justice court judge announced that she would be running on the Republican ticket.

After the forum ended, a few of the NAACP executive board members expressed their concern about the Republican candidate. A few mentioned that they had heard a rumor that she would run on the Republican ticket but did not believe that she would receive support from the conservative element of the White community. One executive board member commented that her speech and response to statements "made the most sense out of all the candidates," that her qualifications had been unknown before that night, and that they wondered if her campaign had been orchestrated by the Republican Party in order to hinder the election of Black officials running on the Democratic ticket.

The following night's meeting regarding the block grant funds and annexation proved to be a traumatic occasion for some of the local residents who had anticipated a more positive outcome or what Habermas (1994) describes as private persons meeting and resolving issues for the public good. Because of the perceived misuse of block grant funds some of the NAACP executive board members expected a compromise that would benefit the community in three ways. They expected the mayor's office would ensure annexation of the African American community that lay between the city and the proposed annexation location. They also expected a commitment of funds for development and repairs such as paved streets, lights, sewage, and city utilities. In addition, they sought a commitment to secure block grant funds to improve the quality of life for African American communities already located within the city limits. No one was prepared for what actually occurred.

The meeting started late because the mayor and his entourage were late. The president of the NAACP was even later and had, in fact, called me and asked me to stand in for him until he could arrive perhaps as much as thirty minutes late. Approximately ten minutes after the mayor arrived, the meeting began. One of the members of the church who was also a member of the association and a longtime associate of the mayor brought the house to order. A deacon from another church provided a prayer, which asked for a successful meeting. Then the mayor was introduced.

The essence of his speech was that he did not have a clear understanding of why the meeting was called but that he believed that he owed the community his attention to any problem they might have. That was the extent of his cooperation. Silence filled the air for what seemed like five minutes but in reality was only about a minute. I looked around the audience waiting for some of the people who had been outspoken in association meetings to clarify for the mayor exactly why we were here. There was silence.

Finally, the church member who opened the meeting stated that the African American community had concerns about the use of block grant funds to make improvements in the county as well as concerns about the effort to annex the area in question and not the predominantly African American community in between. Again, the mayor claimed he did not understand what the problem was. And again, there was silence. Waiting as long as I could, and armed with a copy of the block grant proposal, I addressed the mayor.

MTH: Your honor, we fail to see how your proposal benefits the community. Block grant funds are designated to help.

Mayor: My proposal? It isn't my proposal.

MTH: Didn't you and the city attorney sign and submit a proposal to the state for block grant funds to complete roads and a sewage system in the (XYZ) subdivision?

Mayor: Those block grant funds you are talking about are not for the subdivision. You know you people are acting like I'm the enemy here. You know I didn't have to come to this meeting. I came here because I wanted to set the record straight. You know, I'm on your side. I didn't just start doing things for your community. Way back before it was fashionable, I did things to help your people. Let me tell you this story.

At this point his honor proceeded to tell a story about a trip that he and his wife took to a conference in the Midwest. While sitting around the pool watching a group of young people (Blacks included) jump fearlessly into the pool, he got to thinking. He said to his wife, "Do you know why we don't see any of our young people [referring to Oxford Blacks] jumping in the pool?" She, of course, couldn't come up with an answer. "'Cause they don't have no pool, that's why," he said he responded. And that was when he decided he was going to build the "colored people, they were called 'colored' back then, a pool." He continued with another story, I attempted to interrupt, but he ignored me. I waited another minute or two and interrupted. "Your honor, the stories are nice but we are here to address the city's use of block grant funds for private gain." As the mayor again attempted to deny both his involvement with the funds and at the same time to defend the use of the funds by claiming that they were not being used inappropriately, the president of the NAACP walked in. After seating himself in the pew behind me, I filled him in on the progress of the meeting. The president interrupted another long story started by the mayor.

President: Excuse me your honor, did I hear you correctly, sir? Did you say that
             you didn't have anything to do with the proposal and that the funds
             were being used appropriately?

Mayor: What I said was that I was not aware of the funds being used inap-
             propriately.

President: Begging your honor's pardon, but how could you not? You signed
             the proposal, and the proposal clearly states what the funds are to
             be used for. It names streets that are clearly in the county and are a
             part of the [XYZ] subdivision.

Mayor: I don't read everything I sign. Besides, I don't need no Johnny-come-
             lately telling me what I know and don't know.

The meeting became "hotter than July." A few additional exchanges
took place between the NAACP president and the mayor. The church
member who opened the meeting tried to bring the discussion back to a
calmer tone. "Mr. Mayor, perhaps if you could explain to us how these
funds benefit the middle- and low-income families they are designed to
help we would better understand."

The mayor, appearing reluctant, proceeded to explain that the money
would be used for jobs that would benefit those communities. The association president interjected, "What jobs? Is there a Black contractor being
used to develop this area?" The mayor attempted to ignore the question
while at the same time addressing the larger issue by explaining that the
funds would develop the area. He also said there was a commitment by
a local business to open a pro shop at the golf course and the possibility
that the Marriott Corporation would build a hotel in the area near the
course and that these businesses would provide jobs for middle- and low-
income families. I interjected that the funds did not directly benefit the
segment of the community they were designated for, and that there was
no guarantee that whatever jobs those businesses might generate would
go to local middle- and low-income families.

To keep the flames low, an NAACP member switched the conversation
to the topic of annexation. The member wanted to know why that particular local community was being annexed to the city, especially when other
communities established long before had not been annexed. The mayor
responded by stating that the annexation process is handled through re-
quests. According to him, the residents of a community had to request
annexation and then it was up to the city to decide. The NAACP president interjected, "But nobody lives in that community. Who requested
it? The developer? He would be the only person who could stand to gain
from the annexation." The president continued by saying that the block

grant funds and the annexation were directly related. The developer, who probably had run out of funds, needed the $500,000 to complete development in the subdivision; however, he could not get the money unless the area was a part of the city.

Very angry, the mayor attempted to explain that the scenario created by the president revealed he had "no awareness as to how those funds operate." He explained that to get the funds, someone had to stand as a guarantor, and that, in the event the funds would not be used as designated, the guarantor would repay the funds. The president suggested that the funds then were just an interest-free loan for the developer so he could finish his project, sell the property he had finished developing with federal and state money, and then pay back the funds while making a huge profit.

Again trying to keep tension down, the church member asked if the city had any plans for securing block grant funds for any African American communities. The mayor responded, "You got somebody in your community who can guarantee a $500,000 loan?" The president and I both jumped on the answer at the same time.

MTH: Are you saying that only people who have money can get these funds?
President: Isn't that why you are elected, to find those kinds of funds?

Totally frustrated by what must have appeared from his perspective as an inquisition, the mayor used profane language as he struck out at both the president and myself. The church member officiating over the meeting quickly got up from his seat, declared the meeting over, and advised the mayor that he owed the members of the church an apology for committing blasphemy in their house of worship. The mayor, still highly upset, walked out followed by his entourage and mumbled something about when the Black community could get enough people to show up at the polls to determine whether he wins or loses, then they could start telling him how to do his job.

Still in a state of shock from the mayor's use of profanity in the church, residents of the community agreed that they should draft a letter to the local newspaper asking for a public apology from the mayor. This resolution for action, like numerous others, fell by the wayside of day-to-day survival as matters of more immediate concern took its place. The coming election was one of them. Focus is often drawn from one important issue and shifted to another. On the surface, this behavior can give the appearance of inaction or acquiescence. However, this is often a result of the complexity of hegemonic structures and how well they are integrated into every aspect of the operation of the community.[1]

At a general meeting of the NAACP, concern was voiced about a possible split in the Black vote owing to the prominence and roots in the community of the Black candidate running on the Republican ticket. The issue was temporarily tabled. On the agenda was a knowledgeable member of the Democratic Party who explained that the design of the primary ballots had changed, announced switches in poll locations, and discussed the qualifications of all candidates on the Democratic ticket running for offices on the state and local levels.[2] At the end of the evening, the issue of the Black vote being split was brought before the body again. A decision was made to adjourn the meeting and have a public discussion of the issue since the association could not in any way appear to be endorsing any candidate. The president of the association then relinquished the floor to any member who wanted to bring up the issue.

One resident who had run for public office in the past opened the discussion by stating the problem. The primary voters had one choice before they entered the voting booth; they had to choose a Democratic ticket or a Republican one. It was at this point that they could make or break the chances of the Black bid for the supervisor's position, which they believed stood the best chance of success. In their support for the bid for sheriff, they were counting on the White community to be ready for new blood and dissatisfied with the incumbent who had held the office for more than twenty years. The assembled group reasoned that if they split their votes between the two parties (in order to get a Black judge), they stood a good chance of losing all around because they believed that White Republicans would not vote for the Black candidate. A decision was made. It was important to impress upon the members of the larger African American voting public that voting the Democratic ticket in the primary was important to the goal of getting an African American elected to office, and if, by some luck of the draw, the African American Republican candidate made it through the primary election, then the November election would be the time to decide upon merit.

The following information regarding the move to elect a Black official was gained through newspaper articles and telephone interviews. I used this method because my research period ended in May of 1995; the

---

[1] Another example of this phenomenon is the distraction of parking requirements in the building fund drive of ODA.

[2] Only one candidate running for state office on the Republican ticket asked to speak before the association's membership, a bold move on his part.

primary was held in August, and the regular election, in November when I was no longer a resident of Oxford.

Two of the three African American candidates for the NAACP-targeted county supervisor position dropped out of the race leaving that position unchallenged by any Democrat. Voter registration activity increased. Some candidates actually picked up people from their communities and took them to be registered. The Motor Voter Drive, established by the state, is also credited with helping increase the number of voters, although these newly registered voters were not eligible to vote in the primary. Finally, with the large number of African Americans running for office, an increase in voter registration occurred because practically every family member of voting age registered so they could get their family member elected.

The primary resulted in two Black females running for the position of justice court judge, while the Democratic Party's seat for sheriff remained in the hands of the incumbent. The Black candidate for sheriff considered the race close. He stated that his percentage of the votes was around 37 percent, while his opponent's was approximately 53 percent, with the difference in actual votes being around 1,800. The November election results also proved to be informative. There were seventy-two candidates running for various positions. Fifty-one of those were Democrats. Of the twenty-one African American candidates, three were elected to office: one county supervisor, the constable, and the Republican justice court judge. Democratic Party officials and community leaders strongly believe that additional county supervisor's positions could have been won if five African Americans along with one White candidate were not running against each other.

SOCIAL CHANGE: WHO WANTS WHAT AND WHY?

When I asked people why 1995 brought a significant difference in the political participation and interests of Oxford/Lafayette County African American residents, a variety of reasons were given. Most residents, however, expressed the idea that the community was "waking up." They made comments such as: "People are beginning to realize that if they want change, then they have to *make* a change"; "They have stopped being afraid and stepped up to make their wants heard"; "If Black people are going to get anywhere, they are going to have to take advantage of what they already have"; and "They have to stick together and fight for what they want."

These responses spoken to me on a return visit a little more than a year after the election, however, came from members of the community who vote. They are community members who expressed their reason for voting as exercising their rights – as a part of being a citizen. There is, however, another segment of the African American population who does not exercise its rights. This segment can be divided into two groups. One is composed of grassroots people born and reared in the Oxford community or one similar to Oxford who see no advantage in voting or who simply do not desire to put forth the effort. The other group consists of African American faculty, administrators, and students. This group does not see itself as a part of the community. They arrive as strangers and remain strangers to the community throughout their stay. There are a few exceptions, but, for the most part, this population does not concern itself with the day-to-day operation of the community. Neither group, however, is short on opinions about what's wrong with the community, particularly what's wrong with the African American population.

The year 1995 constituted a significant upward change in voter registration and voter turnout in Oxford/Lafayette County. The description in this chapter of the various efforts spearheaded by the newly reinstated local NAACP branch provides a base from which to understand why 1995 was different not only from past election years but also from the voter turnout of the 1996 presidential election year.

An historical look at leadership helps to give a profile of how and why the movement began when it did. Most of the traditional African American leadership in Oxford/Lafayette County came from a segment of the community culturally and socially in a position to lead – ministers. A secondary source of leadership came from the educational system. Since community leaders, for the most part, are passed down from the church, the profile of Black leadership reveals that they are traditionally religious and male. This does not imply that women did not have outlets for their voices, but even in those positions, as we will see later in this chapter, they conduct a kind of "public women's work."

Throughout most of the community's history, religious leaders were residents born and reared in the community, with social roots that tied them both to the area's African American society and the dominant White society. This early leadership could be viewed as having two forms, radical intraethnic leadership and moderate or conservative interethnic leadership. In other words, the self-help activities they became involved in could be as radical as their constituents would allow as long as the activities did not interfere with the smooth functioning of the larger White society.

A couple of stories, one post–emancipation/reconstruction and the other post–World War I, are the only examples I know of indigenous radical interethnic behavior in the area of social movements.[3] The decision by Black members of the White Baptist church to break away and establish their own church in the 1860s was the first. The move was radical at the time, although the steps taken to accomplish the break would not be considered radical by today's standards. Five women petitioned the church for the land and resources to build their own sanctuary, and that petition was granted. This move by women and the matter of worship might well have set a precedent for the next one hundred years, particularly given the next attempt prominent in the minds of members sixty and over who either heard the story or witnessed this next event.

In this second story, a fairly young spunky minister who had served in World War I returned to his hometown. Disappointed about the state of race relations and the condition of his people, he proceeded to try to organize them. His outspokenness caught the attention of what was reported to be the local chapter of the Ku Klux Klan. Determined to still have an impact on his community, he tried to organize groups of workers who were interested in migrating to Chicago. His family, having gotten word from some of the local White liberals that he was going to be lynched if he didn't stop, concocted an elaborate scheme to get him out of town and to safety. The plan worked, and the young minister never returned.

Here we have two stories about early radicalism in the community, one that succeeded in its aims and one that did not. During one of my interviews when the latter story was related, my collaborator, an elderly Black male, added, "It goes to show you, the Black man don't stand a chance. Every time you try to do something positive, the White man'll try to knock you down." Both males and females often told these kinds of stories. The collective memory of these two prominent stories and other similar stories about interethnic interaction has helped construct the particular profile of Black leadership and social action in the community up to the 1970s. Direct action initiated by Black males that affected the status quo for the White dominant society was dangerous in Lafayette County. The fear was grounded in both local lore and the awareness of White terrorism in other areas of the state and nation.[4] The success of

---

[3] The two CRM activities related to the integration of a lunch counter and the integration of the schools are the only stories told to me about radical steps taken by individuals from the community. Black females initiated both.

[4] Walker states: "Between 1889 and 1946 almost four thousand Black people were lynched" (1991:30).

the women perhaps became symbolic of how the culture of race relations should be approached and who should handle the matter. In response to my inquiry as to why more males, particularly ministers, are not more active in the community, one gentleman in his seventies quickly responded, "They're scared." He was one of the first people to tell me the story about the young minister.

Between the 1930s and 1960s, the Black community insolated itself as much as possible under Jim Crow and the paternalistic system in place. During the 1970s, slight changes in the leadership profile began to occur. RWJ, an enlightened young minister, returned home and established North Mississippi Rural Legal Services. RWJ instituted a number of self-help programs such as a childcare facility, a cooperative store, the local Black newspaper, and ODA. THW, also a minister, who had remained in the community from birth, instituted other self-help projects such as a Black community bus service that picked up children for Head Start and carried the elderly and those in need of transportation to church and shopping. These roles were totally different than the roles assigned by the dominant society. In addition to being spiritual leaders, Black ministers were generally called on by Whites to stand for bail; relay concerns, ideas, and policies of the dominant society to the Black community; and help "keep the peace." However, it was the women who demonstrated the Black community's disapproval of the social disparities. Consider MQ, a Black woman, who was the only local-born adult resident to take part in a march for better housing, and WOH, another young Black female hometown resident, who single-handedly marched to and sat down at the segregated lunch counter owned by the same mayor mentioned earlier. There also was the young mother who fought to integrate the public school system. A new more socially active pattern began to form; nevertheless, the women were on the more visible radical side, and the men were on the publicly moderate or conservative side.

The 1980s brought about a period when both males and females sat back and enjoyed the fruits of their labor, but time was marching on and the concessions made by southern society – influenced by the movement – paled in the light of the needs and problems that continued to grow. During the two-decade period of the 1970s and 1980s, however, the young African American lawyer from out of town who was employed by NMRLS had been offending Whites on campus, in city hall, and in the capital left and right. He was so outspoken that both Blacks and Whites often described him as "rude," "loud," or "crazy." Although while in private both male and female Blacks marveled at his fearlessness, none followed.

During a period between approximately 1970 and 1990, moderates periodically got into battles over the location of facilities, the names of buildings for Blacks, and similar matters; these concerns, however, rarely involved a move that could be considered radical. Variation from this structure did not occur until the young out-of-towner who attended the University of Mississippi and refused to carry the Rebel flag in his capacity as Colonel Reb, came to the community. Taking up the ministry and making his home in Oxford in 1993, he began to influence the Black community as a whole, and members of that community began to challenge the status quo aggressively. When a few of the moderate hometown males and females and a number of the radical females joined him, some of the old fears of reprisal that kept many of the residents in their places began to subside.

Some moderate and conservative elements of the community, which included men and women and cut across class and educational boundaries, tried to quell the fires that had begun to burn. At times they were successful. Some of this conservative element joined the local branch of the NAACP to keep an eye on what was going on and report that knowledge to those they deemed should be aware or prepared. This at times caused confusion, suspicion, and intragroup sanctions. Some plans became more secretive, but, on the whole, a number of young hometown males and females were beginning to see that the 1990s was a new era in Oxford/Lafayette County. If they wanted something, they had to go after it, and that they did.

Does African American participation in the political process constitute acculturation or assimilation or some other cultural change from an analytical view? Does it constitute a change from an internal perspective of practice? If so, then what does it mean in practice for African Americans of Lafayette County? Do they look at it as a step away from Black culture and one closer to White? What is the perceived loss? Power? What kind of power? These questions are difficult to answer because of the complexity of the community and the lack of a coherent social agenda. Because efforts to elect Black officials became the only form of social action that attracted a significant number of Black residents during the research period of this work, I have chosen to focus on that aspect of political participation in order to address these questions. Descriptions of voting practices and the possible meanings that can be attached to them follow.

In practice, there are three distinct points of view related to participation in the political process in this seemingly homogeneous population. Some African Americans view voting as a step toward integration into the larger society with full realization that it is identified as a domain of the "White dominant" society. Others view participation as an act of self-defense that concentrates on the goal of equal treatment and a promise of change, which in their view is not equivalent to integrationist ideals. The third point of view sees the whole process as a culturally and racially alien operation designed to benefit those Whites who initiated it. Many who see the process as alien choose not to participate in the voting process, always evoking as their justification the epithet: "White folks are going to do what they want to do anyway."[5] Some of those who have this latter perspective vote because it's their right, but they never expect anything to come from it. The self-defense group becomes divided in terms of participation by the nature of the cause. Generally the cause must be overt, and a direct link must be evident between cause and effect as it relates to equality or benefit. An immediate and direct benefit must be perceived. Consequently, only two situations bring about social action with this group – overt racist or discriminatory acts and the direct advancement of a cause they support. The first group represents perhaps the only segment of the African American community that can be viewed as "assimilators." Among this group, having a piece of the pie includes accepting participation in all the processes that are incorporated within that pie. Partaking of only the crust or the filling does not constitute full participation. Their understanding of how society operates gives many members of this group the impetus to participate in voting, while other assimilators no longer participate because they now have it as a right, which is often viewed as having achieved equal rights. The structure of these three groups is mostly ideological, and their boundaries cut across class, gender, kinship, age, neighborhood, and educational lines.

Does the increased political activity of the 1990s constitute a change from an internal perspective of practice? Historically speaking, the various intimate culture groups of the community have nurtured their specific worldviews and ideologies as long as the groups have existed, and surface analyses of political participation would conclude that a considerable change has occurred, but from the level of some of the intimate culture groups, the change is strictly cosmetic. It is not cosmetic in the sense of being superficial; instead, their outward appearances are now being matched to their inward desires, and they believe that they no longer need

[5] This group does not include the religious sect of Jehovah Witnesses who do not vote because it is seen as a form of idolatry. The issue of social action is less fixed among Witnesses. As such, they may join other African Americans on such matters as demonstrations and protests.

to wear a mask. In practice, it means that most African Americans in Lafayette County are beginning to do and say what they have wanted to all along. Practice, therefore, is not just an outward manifestation of their internalized beliefs but rather is shaped by the political and economic realities of the moment.

Instead of "quiet resistance," it was "patience," a patience that allowed both the intraethnic and the interethnic cultures of social relations to mature to a point where change in the political arena could be made. It is evident from the 1995 elections that both Blacks and Whites in the community have matured in the levels of acceptable social interaction and relations. For some African American Oxonians, there is a bit more trust, less fear, and an increasingly positive culture of social relations between themselves and Whites. This new understanding developed in its own time and space and as such validates the religiously influenced concept of "patience" so often referred to by older and/or religious community leaders. This patience constitutes the difference between *waiting for an opportunity* for action and *making an opportunity*.

In Part Three, however, this work discusses intraethnic problems connected to the crises of identity within the African American population that possibly were responsible for only three Blacks, out of the twenty-one who ran, being elected to office. The many views regarding what it means to be Black in Oxford/Lafayette County fracture the coherence needed for social action, particularly efforts to get members of the community to rally around a political candidate. One official connected with the Democratic Party tried to sum up the significance of the Black vote in the 1995 election and make sense of problems within the Oxford African American community that limited the power of that event. Grappling with the intraethnic and intraracial culture of social relations, he focused on individualism and its influence on African American's sense of community and concluded that African American Oxonians as a whole need to:

Support our own. Talk to our own folks. They're the ones that are going to come to your funeral. They're the ones that are going to come down to the hospital to see you. They are going to be part of the ones, if they don't talk about you too bad, gon' come by and see you when you burnout, or when you sick. Regardless of how high we get up the pole, we got to remember who we are. . . . I'm making apologies now. I hope I don't sound too harsh or too hard, but as far as I'm concerned about the African American race, we are a self-sufficient race of people. We've been here, we exist here. We're dealing with a holiday season right now, in regards to why Christ went to Egypt, better place to hide among them than among your own folk.

PART THREE

CONSTRUCTION OF AN INTRARACIAL IDENTITY

5

"What's Race Got To Do With It?"

In cultural, community, and regional studies, the anthropological tendency to describe and construct the whole can often lead to glossing and misunderstanding the parts. This has been particularly the case in studies that focus on African Americans. Although anthropologists note the diversity of the population, little attention is paid to the significance of that diversity from an internal perspective. The descriptions in Chapter 3 of a number of Lafayette County's intimate culture groups identified various heterogeneous group identities existing within the Black community. The underlying reasons for the construction of such groups give insight into the importance of identifying and understanding such "heterogeneous identities." This is more than ever the case when analyzing the cohesiveness of any regional culture, particularly one with group identities that cut across kinship, economic, spatial, educational, and political lines.[1] These intraethnic/intraracial identities, for the most part, become key determiners of social behavior and perceptions.

The manner in which intraracial identities are constructed is important to understanding the meaning of "Blackness." Cohen points out "that the simplified identity that a collectivity presents to the outside world . . . is informed by its internal intricacies" (1982:12). To understand African Americans in Oxford/Lafayette County or any other community, we cannot gloss over the complexity of "belonging" by simply conceptualizing them as a homogeneous group divisible only by such social phenomena as region, kin, and economy. To be assigned membership

---

[1] See Gregory for a discussion of how multiple constructions of difference and complex relations of power are connected to the formation of racial identity (1996:27–32).

in the African American cultural, ethnic, or "racial" group contributes to the perpetuation of myths and stereotypes that do not consider local and particular individual experience. Cohen suggests that "the discreteness of local experience is all the more important in societies whose communities see themselves as peripheral or marginal and in which the reality of difference is continually being glossed by the appearance of similarity" (1982:13). To gloss over the differences in identity constituted by local tradition and experience further marginalizes the diverse groups that form the larger African American community.

"Local experience mediates national identity" according to Cohen (1982:13). I suggest that local experience mediates ethnic, racial, and regional identity as well, and an understanding of these broader identities cannot proceed without knowledge of local experience. Therefore, it is important to look at the relationship between the African American community of Oxford/Lafayette County as a regional, ethnic, and racial collectivity and the various intimate culture groups that are its components. The culture of the social relations of these intimate culture groups sheds light on the meaning of belonging to members of the larger African American community.[2]

THE INTERCONNECTION OF PLACE, SPACE, AND BELONGING

Belonging is an important aspect of everyday existence for Lafayette County's African American population. Cohen (1982) suggests that in conditions of frequent contact with other cultures, the valuing of distinctions of one cultural group from another is a condition of a culture's survival. He further suggests that "the awareness of commitment and of belonging to *a* culture...is a ubiquitous feature of peripheral communities" (1982:6). As a result of the value placed on belonging, attachment to signs of local social and cultural identification is an important process for both those born and raised in and those who migrate to an area. The peripherality of which Cohen speaks is not tied to geography alone but includes the social marginality of the individuals being placed. He suggests that peripherality can be a state of mind as well as a collective self-image. This collective self-image influences and is influenced by perceptions of powerlessness. Cohen suggests that it is often expressed as a dependence upon very limited exploitable resources and competitive

---

[2] Geertz (1983) also emphasizes the importance of weaving pieces of knowledge for understanding culture.

disadvantage. The two building projects mentioned earlier and the recy-
cled fifty dollars are primary examples of this phenomenon in Oxford.
He also suggests that this perception of powerlessness is "often expressed
politically in dependence upon centralised patronage and in a consequent
resentment" (1982:6–7). The process of sanctioning Black leadership by
the dominant society contributes to individual as well as collective self-
images and underscores the Black community's view of itself as misun-
derstood, powerless, misrepresented, exploited, ignored, or patronized
(Cohen 1982:6–7). The lack of respect by the mayor for the issues brought
before him by Black leaders of the community and his additional abuse
of the one symbol of Black power – the Black church – without a doubt
influenced the state of mind not only of the leadership but also of the
community as a whole.

While I agree with Cohen's conclusions about the impact of peripherality, my analysis of processes and structures within the Black community
of Oxford reveals a more complex web of intragroup interaction based
on ideas of place, belonging, and Blackness that shape the collective and
individual self-images of that community. The creation of various clubs,
societies, associations, and councils that form a range of intimate culture
groups within African American communities constitute efforts to change
the balance of power. Each group helps to establish "place" and satisfy
for its membership a sense of "belonging."

Belonging, in Oxford/Lafayette County, is not always related just to
family ties but more often involves lifestyle and ideological identifiers.
Although, at times, family plays an important role, the church, organization and association membership, and fraternal and social clubs are the
most significant identifiers of an individual's belonging and that person's
relationship to the community. Members of the community use these identifiers in terms of their positive or negative qualities to evaluate residents
and newcomers. At times, the same characteristics may be considered as
having both qualities. This view depends upon which groups are inter-
acting with each other as well as the "place" the member holds within
the larger community that is classifying an individual's belonging. For
example, most, if not all, of the churches compete for employees of the
university community to attend worship services and become members.
Many members wear the attendance of students or faculty members from
the university as a badge of honor. Non-university members of the church
often find reasons to bring up the fact that a university member attends
their church. Yet, sermons often criticize those individuals who dedicate
themselves to the pursuit of higher learning. Comparisons are regularly

made between students and professors who miss church because of institutional obligations and people who go fishing on Sundays. Ministers also make comments in the pulpit. One prominent pastor commented, looking at me, "Book learning ain't everything. This [referring to the Bible] is the only book I know that can get you into heaven." Although churches clamor for an educated membership, there exists a certain disdain for the changes education often bring as is exemplified by the following comments. "I wish I had a praying church sometime. Everybody's just too proper now-a-days." The minister goes on to conclude that education has made the congregation "too proper" to respond with "amens," "too proper" to respond to the spirit.[3] The latter example reflects the minister's belief that either he or his educated membership does not "belong" to this particular church community. Education possesses both positive and negative qualities. The minister is able to make such statements because his position is that of the authority figure in this particular setting. I have heard the same kinds of remarks made by Sunday School teachers, but the comments elicited little or no response.

The number of positive intimate culture groups an individual is associated with has significance for the total value placed on one's belonging to the larger African American community. Some individuals belong to no specific group other than the larger African American community, and, as such, their importance within the community is marginalized. This peripheralization cuts across neighborhood, economic, and educational boundaries. Members of the community who are peripheralized are still expected, however, to interact with and give support to members of the larger community when issues are defined as racial matters. The voter registration drive and the block grant funds issue are primary examples of those expectations.

What's race got to do with it? Belonging is *the* major ingredient of a public persona among African Americans, and it determines the culture of social relations both inside and outside the African American community. Race is the key influence in the peripheralization of African Americans. I suggest that the peripherality of Oxford/Lafayette County's African American population contributes to the importance given to belonging to local intimate culture groups and the formation of a cohesive larger group identity. Perceptions of powerlessness that accompany their peripherality are also significantly related to the number of intimate culture groups

---

[3] Admittedly, there appears to be an inverse relationship between educational levels and the quality of the worship service interaction.

(churches, church organizations, fraternal and social clubs, civic and political organizations) formed within the community. The plethora of organizations exists because belonging provides a sense of power and self-determination for intimate culture group members and multiple senses of belonging seem to be more satisfying than only one.

This also explains why members of the community who do not "belong" or have associational ties are peripheralized within the community. The advantage of belonging is in its potential. The show of minimal amounts of effort within intimate culture groups is cause for leadership placement. Consequently, there are as many committees or leadership responsibilities within the intimate culture groups as there are energetic members. Introducing an idea typically leads to being assigned to lead that project. One's ability to accomplish the task is seldom a consideration. At most of the meetings of the various organizations, the importance of that placement could be seen in the way committee chairs or project leaders were called upon to report, stood up, and reported there was nothing to report. Or the way in which one heavyset woman struggled to her feet, slowly walked from the middle of the room to the front, paper in hand, looked down at the paper, and said, "the ... committee was supposed to meet last week. We didn't, so the ... committee has nothing to report." Then, just as slowly and with dignity, she returned to her seat. This is perhaps her monthly opportunity to contribute and feel valued.

Taken together, each group has a number of social functions and varying internal levels of power. They can be religious, they can be secular, or, as is the case in Oxford/Lafayette County, the boundaries between the two can often be blurred. Groups can also be as small as age-mates and social buddies or as large as churches, neighborhoods, or the Oxford/Lafayette County community. Belonging is important to intragroup allegiances or responsibilities and thus carries significance in shaping roles in larger community interaction and the expected behavior that distinguishes the culture of social relations.

Belonging constitutes the degree to which one's association to the community is valued and made valuable.[4] It determines how much allegiance is expected not just to one's intimate culture group but also to the community at large. The ideology of this association has primary significance for understanding the criteria that constitute the relative

---

[4] Evidence of this value is observable even in burial practices. See Krüger-Kahloula (1994) for a discussion of the way "spatial structur[ing] of Black cemeteries in the United States reflects ordering principles such as biological descent, cultural community, and social hierarchy" (1994).

nature of "Blackness" for each member. Belonging is determined not only by intragroup association but also by distance from those aspects of society associated with Whiteness.

I argue, therefore, that owing to the interconnectedness of the concept of belonging (which includes the value placed on one's group/intimate culture associations) and the local historically defined meanings of Blackness and Whiteness, the various structures of social organization formed by the process of belonging take on greater meaning for the community than simply frames for social organization and action. These structures have become symbols for legitimizing associations and maintaining cultural continuity. I further suggest that the history of the culture of interethnic and interracial social relations contributed to a devaluing of the various social and political structures of the dominant society as frames for social action. Instead, more emphasis is placed on their meaning as frames for maintaining racial separation. As such, this emphasis provides parameters for racial and ethnic group identity and a sense of stability in the Black community. In addition, these frames that divide racial and ethnic group identity are infused with the human desire for self-determination. Therefore, these local organizations or groups embody in their structure and function the rarely discussed understandings of what it means to be Black in Oxford/Lafayette County. These understandings are then played out in public arenas.

The ways in which individuals manage their participation in the social changes that have occurred within the community is related to the maintenance of their social identity and, as such, strongly affects their ability to belong. For example, the increase and survival of Black-owned businesses are partially due to the Civil Rights Movement's goal of desegregation. One of the few African Americans (referred to here as NQS) who owns a small, reasonably successful business in the community and has few associational ties is not perceived as holding a place of value in the Black community. In spite of being located on the border between two African American neighborhoods, patronage by members of those neighborhoods and the larger Black community is poor.[5] NQS's business practices, which are equated with practices of White businesses, are the primary reasons for her/his being considered peripheral to the operation of the neighborhood and larger African American community in spite of the business being located within and serving that community for over twenty years.

---

[5] NQS's business is located in a high-traffic area and is convenient for traffic traveling to two White subdivisions. As a result, it is patronized by a significant number of Whites, who offset the small number of Black customers.

Another example of the relationship of degree of belonging to perceived value to the community is that of HJ who also owns one of the few Black-owned businesses in the community. Also located on the edge of a Black neighborhood, HJ's business is the only one that provides a particular service for the Black clientele. HJ is active in church and church organizations; however, HJ belongs to a church that occupies a borderline position of value in the larger African American community.[6] Although a member of most of the prominent civic, political, and social organizations, HJ rarely attends meetings. Within HJ's history, there is a myth (discussed by others) that emphasizes paternalistic relationships with members of the dominant society. HJ's access to institutional financing is seen as evidence of the continuation of such a relationship, a privilege that is not enjoyed by other Black owners of businesses that service only African Americans and that is available to less than a handful who serve an integrated clientele.

The mythological culture of social relations with the dominant society casts an element of suspicion on HJ's place in and commitment to the Black community. A considerable number of community residents see economic indebtedness to members of the dominant society as carrying coexisting social obligations. The community perceives the gift of cosigning or granting a loan as having an additional obligation other than repayment. They assume that the second – socially oriented obligation – most often is repaid with information or cooperation that negatively affects the Black community. Other members of the community who share HJ's position within the community are often spoken of by people of various economic, educational, and religious standing in this manner: "You better watch her" or "I don't trust him." When efforts are made to pin down the particular infraction HJ has committed, the response is usually a reiteration of the same warning with no further insight.

Although it is possible for a number of people from one family to be attached to the same social or cultural identifiers, such as poor/well-off or church-going/non-church-going or selfish/good-hearted, their value to the community may vary considerably. Members of the community do not always agree upon the particular social or cultural identifiers, but generally any member of the community who disagrees rarely contests the public assertions. The disagreement is saved for comments in private arenas. Assessments of the individual personalities of each family member

---

[6] On the whole, churches are considered borderline if the reputations of their ministers are questionable, if other members of the community consider the members elitist or snobbish, or if their ideologies vary from mainstream Protestantism. In the interest of anonymity, the aspect that labels this particular church borderline is not defined.

appear to be the base for the resulting variation in perceived community value. Although family ties influence expected value, perceived value is individual. For example, ministers' wives may be treated with respect because of their relationships to their husbands, but their worth to the congregation or larger community and the accompanying level of prestige depends strictly on their own contributions and the intimate culture groups to which they do or do not belong. The interesting phenomenon about family was the rarity of cohesion in terms of intimate culture groups. Husbands and wives may "belong" to the same organizations, but they rarely were active in the same organizations or attended organizational activities together.

Belonging on its own merit brings with it little or no power. "Place" is an important aspect of belonging. Belonging, however, becomes powerful when it is combined with specific places within organizational structures because it establishes power relations. Belong is a group identifier, while place is a level-of-power identifier. Place, from the community perspective, is an association with and ranking of traits, ideals, economic and educational positions, and background. It is directly connected to the perceived social history of the individual or group. The ranking system itself is also very complicated. For example, an individual placed as an educated, rich outsider can be ranked lower than an individual placed as a not-having-book-sense, struggling insider. In this case, the primary qualifier for rank is known history versus unknown history. Knowing one's history is important because an individual's past behavior and group associations are used to determine place.

Power from the perspective of the African American community in Oxford/Lafayette County is the legitimate right to tell others what to do, to suggest and make changes that affect others, and to represent others. Each of these aspects of power can be seen individually and in varied combinations. And, individual's or a group's ability to use each aspect of power is determined by that individual's or group's place. Therefore, power exists within the community only through authority because place exists only through mutual consent. In other words, one can aspire to have power within the community/organization or see her/himself as occupying a particular place within the community/organization, but neither place nor power is legitimate without mutual consent. The interconnection of place, belonging, and power is complex within the Oxford/Lafayette County African American community because to have an untarnished reputation, each person must understand what aspects of power are associated with specific levels of place.

Both groups and individuals have their place. Groups that are deemed as having low value for the community are marginalized and, as such, are perceived as having very little power. Value is dependant upon one's contribution to Black society. Visiting the sick and shut-in, carrying suppers to the incarcerated, and donating money or clothes to the needy or deserving are some of the characteristics by which ranking/value are determined. Equally important is the fact that one can belong to a low-ranked group but have a tremendous amount of power, though it is mostly within the group. For example, those members of The Yard intimate culture group that have automobiles, regardless of their condition, have a tremendous amount of power among the members. They are often asked to run errands that keep the products of the underground economy readily available.

It is possible to belong to a group but at the same time "not know your place" both within the group and in the larger society. An important part of knowing one's place is giving proper respect to others. When individuals operated above their place, others often commented, "I don't know who she/he thinks she/he is." Individuals who belong to the same group and often share membership in several intimate culture groups frequently make this type of comment. "That child know he's something else" is also a phrase used to indicate that an individual is acting above the level of his/her placement by others, either in words or deeds. For example, one of the local civic organizations has an annual membership drive designed more for renewing memberships than for securing new members. A membership committee organizes the drive. Each membership-committee member is expected to contact less active or out-of-state members and collect membership fees. A list of all active and nonactive members was divided among the members of that committee. TN, a very aggressive committee member, contacted and secured fees from members who, in previous years were contacted by IG, another committee member who is also a lifelong friend of TN. IG expressed the opinion that TN was out of place to contact those members whose fees had been previously collected by IG in spite of the fact that the names occurred on TN's list. Although this issue was not brought before the organization or the committee, I learned at the next meeting that other members of the committee either collected fees and attributed them to those members who had secured those fees in the past or asked the committee member if it was okay to contact the inactive member. TN was out of place because proper respect was not given to IG, who was due a certain amount of consideration regarding solicitation of membership renewal from IG's longtime contacts.

TN was expected to know the details of prior lists.[7] One can see how a stranger to the organization could generate a tarnished reputation. That is why the phrase, "If you don't know, ask," is vitally important.

If people are always in their place, they never step on anyone's toes. In spite of how well meaning the act may be, stepping on someone's toes disrupts the smooth operation of the organization or group. Therefore, a disruptive action is to be avoided if a person wishes to have cooperation and goodwill on any project that he or she heads. Perceptions of being out of place diminish one's power.

Place and belonging often are connected to physical markers that determine spatial rights and the use of particular locations. These markers often cut across the spatial boundaries of other social identifiers such as economic, religious, private, and public borders. There is, however, established protocol in practically every situation. It is important to mention that protocol in Oxford is in the process of changing owing to the recent introduction of new intimate culture groups that do not have deep attachments to the larger Black community. For example, over the past three years, Lafayette County has experienced intimate culture groups with "street gang" connections. The members are the sons and daughters of children and grandchildren who migrated but still maintain interpersonal relations with those who stayed. They live with grandparents, great-grandparents, aunts, uncles, and cousins. They are children of parents who sent them south as a method of preventing or curbing their chances of getting into trouble. Again, the formation of these gangs responds to the need to belong. The culture of social relations between the newer intimate culture groups and the more traditional ones is exemplified by a lack of respect. The practice of exhibiting respect for spatial boundaries and the power of place practiced by the traditional intimate culture groups has deteriorated with the introduction of newer ones that violate community norms. A clearer sense of this can be provided best through the following examples.

One enclave in the county has spaces that could be labeled "sacred" and "profane." As a meeting space for intimate culture groups, the enclave is shared by a religious intimate culture group and a worldly intimate culture group. The two homeowners in this small space are the leaders of these intimate culture groups and as such have considerable power. My labels for these spaces have been guided by the main activities the

---

[7] This interaction is an example of what Geertz (1983) refers to in his work on "local knowledge."

intimate cultural groups perform. At the mouth of the enclave is a church and at the enclave's greatest depth is the house of a man who operates on the level of a "Big Man" for the profane element of the enclave. Although the religious intimate culture group ranks higher in value in the larger African American community, a ritualized form of respect is practiced by both the religious and the profane groups in terms of the use of space. For example, a female who heads the religious group holds regular meetings during the week and on Sundays at her home – sometimes on the porch, weather permitting. During these periods, the Big Man of the profane group refrains from conducting his activities, which consist of the selling of beer and alcohol. He also exercises control over lightweight gambling on the porches of his premises.[8] Correspondingly, the owner of the home that serves as a space for religious activities limits the days and times the activities take place, particularly on her porch, in order to allow the profane element to operate. While the religious use of space is a prearranged event that determines the gathering of this intimate culture group, the profane use of space is strictly determined by the Big Man and is signaled by a ritualized performance. The Big Man comes out onto his porch, walks to the edge, lights a cigarette and then sits on his porch. Soon after, crowds begin to gather, and it is business as usual. If the Big Man simply comes out and sits on his porch without the other aspects of the ritual, crowds do not gather. This considerate sharing of space by two extremely different intimate culture groups constitutes the development of protocol that acknowledges the legitimacy of both groups and their place in the society in spite of the different values attached to them.

While standing in the yard of TIM, one of my collaborators, I observed the following incident, which is a good example of the deterioration of respect brought about by the formation of new intimate culture groups. A working-class family consisting of a husband, wife, and their two sons lives at the mouth of the The Hole. Various members and friends who periodically reside with them extend the family from time to time. The house, owned by TIM, sits a considerable distance from the road, but TIM converted a piece of his property that is close to the road into what he calls a playground for his kids. The grassless section of the hard clay plot has a makeshift basketball court and an area big enough for small-scale bike riding.

---

[8] The Big Man owns several of the shotgun-style buildings in the enclave. One building appears to be a converted chicken coop.

While discussing changes that had occurred since I left four years earlier, a group of young African American males passed his property headed to The Hole.

"Look at 'em. These young people just don't have any respect nowadays."

"How do you mean?"

"Just look at 'em. They don't care who see what they are doing. But I got something for them."

At that moment TIM yells across the street at the young men.

"Get on out of here. Don't you stop in front of my house. I mean what I'm saying now. Get on out of here with that crap. Don't you see these children playing here in this yard? I ain't gon' tell you no more, get on from in front of my house."

TIM headed for his house and I followed, thinking that perhaps he might be going to get a gun. By the time we entered the house, the young men had moved on.

"They know I mean business. They ain't gon' disrespect my family like that." Sitting down, he continued, "Now you know I smoke a little pot every now and then. Well, maybe more than now and then. And so you know I don't have anything against folks selling it. But the point is I don't do it in front of my kids. There used to be a time when I didn't have to say a thing, but now these young people just don't care. So I don't care either. I'll call the police on their ass in a minute. I don't care what they do any other time, but they ain't gon' do it in front of my kids."

An understanding had developed between earlier drug dealers and TIM in the use of intimate culture group space. Formerly, the use of that space was controlled by TIM's family as one of the intimate culture groups that made use of the general community space. Out of respect for their use of space, the drug activities were conducted out of the sight of his children. TIM correspondingly adopted the attitude of "live and let live" in regard to the culture of The Hole. Recently a group of young drug dealers and users have begun frequenting The Hole and often show no regard for the presence of TIM's family's use of the space. This change in respect has produced a reciprocal change in TIM's attitude and behavior. In the late evenings when the children are in bed, and dealing and gambling escalates to an almost frantic level, TIM does not concern himself with the moral aspects of the activity. In fact, he often sits on his porch or in the yard in the dark and observes the activity of The Hole commenting on the craziness and destruction of human potential. Occasionally, he visits The Hole himself.

The culture of social relations between the traditional intimate culture groups sustains the ideology captured in the saying "There is a time and a place for everything." However, the newly formed groups have not adopted this ideology, which provides social order for the multiple cultures of African American neighborhoods. As such, they are beginning to constitute a group of low value for the community and are perceived as extremely peripheral. The significance of the respect that exists among the traditional intimate culture groups is that the members of each group perceive themselves and the members of the other intimate culture groups as belonging to a larger racial, ethnic, or regionalized group.

PLACE: A COMPLEX CONSTRUCTION OF HISTORY AND TRADITION

What's race got to do with it? And why does place play such an important role in the lives of African Americans? The diversity of Lafayette County's African American community, as reflected in the numerous churches, religious organizations, and other intimate culture groups has its base in history. It is not a recent phenomenon developing out of contemporary educational, economic, or social disparities, nor is it simply the history of the specific place that forms the foundation for that diversity. Rather, it is a complex mixture of the history of stratification in the early settling of the United States as manifested in national, regional, and local practices. The manner in which this country, the southern United States, and Oxford/Lafayette County treated the indigenous population, various groups of immigrants, and the forced immigrants has contributed to the various levels of segmentation within Lafayette County.

Because of the structure of the institution of slavery, race became the primary means through which the various ethnically and culturally diverse Africans who were forced to immigrate to the Americas were identified. This racialization of the immigrants constituted the construction of an identity that both grouped individuals from varying African nations and ranked their place in that society.

The formation of America's forced immigrants' identity is similar in structure and process to that of the formation of "British-ness" as described by Williams (1989) in "A Class Act: Anthropology and the Race to Nation Across Ethnic Terrain." She describes the formation of one identifiable group, the British, from several cultural groups rather than two. This multicultural heritage is responsible for the "resurgences of subordinated ethnic groups in the United Kingdom" (Williams 1989:422).

I suggest that, like the British process of becoming, the process by which Blacks in the United States became Americans (albeit second class) also serves as a base for a resurgence of differentiation.

Although the processes in the formation of British and African American identities are similar because they both consist of an artificial collapsing of borders in order to create a larger body, the similarities are only processual and structural. They differ, however, in both intent and purpose, and *that*, I propose, is what distinguishes the particular forms that resurgence of differentiation takes.

Williams (1989) explains that long-term development of identity formation differs in First and Third World nations. In the case of African American identity formation, I suggest that the violent revolutionary form of change and the abrupt removal from the familiar to the unfamiliar engendered an immediate need for cultural adjustment. This included the immediate establishment of a new historically based foundation for an adapted identity.

There are other ways in which the formation of British-ness differs from the formation of Blackness – which is the first African American identity. With the British, political borders were collapsed while the spatial divisions remained; in different periods of British history, however, physical boundaries changed as well, but this also was a slow process. On the other hand, the many cultural groups that constituted the category of "Blacks" in America were first physically removed from the ties of geographical boundaries and then scattered over a large area. This early creation of the African Diaspora broke the ties of historically geographic cultural boundaries. In addition, the area they occupied as forced immigrants was divided not only in terms of geography but also in terms of ecology, ideology, politics, and economics. The Americas, and more specifically that region that came to be known as the United States, constructed *for* the forced immigrants a previously insignificant boundary of group identity formation – a phenotype that became commonly referred to as race.[9] This generalization constituted a collapsing of sometimes-significant cultural borders among the forced immigrants. Cultural practices and regional ties rather than color and facial features had been the criteria for group

---

[9] It should be noted that this was especially true of race during the beginning of White–Black contact and that the concept of race evolved to symbolize more than physical markers – like culturally defined principles of descent (hypo-descent for African Americans) for reckoning socially significant ancestry. See Harrison (1995a), Gregory (1996), and Shanklin (1994) for insights into the social significance of racial categorization.

identification. Upon their capture and arrival, the forced immigrants had to begin thinking of themselves in different ways based on the practices of the nation (the institution of slavery), the various regions (the North and South and the variation on structure of the institution and use of the forced labor), and in Oxford/Lafayette County the specific meanings attached to slave ownership and the ways in which those meanings get translated into the individualized treatment of each slave.

As time progressed, Euro-Americans divided the country's forced immigrant population into Blacks and mulattos, freedmen and slaves, field and house servants and then proceeded to stratify those categories as well. (There were even more/different categories depending on locale.) These various categories represented different life chances and lifestyles for Blacks. In addition, these differences carried with them varying levels of power, prestige, and opportunities as all life chances in stratified societies do. We know, for example, from slave narratives [classical and Works Progress Administration (WPA)], diaries and papers of prominent and not-so-prominent White citizens (in both the North and South), and from the creation of Black codes and state laws, that the treatment of the forced immigrants varied by region, crop, and individual master. Differentiation of treatment was also a part of the freedmen experience in both the North and the South. These new divisions created different ways of being that influenced interaction between the different groups of Blacks in terms of the place one's group held in the larger society and the specific individual's place within that group.

Recognizing the newly constructed group identity, the forced immigrants created institutions to accommodate it. These new forced-bondage identities were created originally along racial and class lines, but they also worked to sustain aspects of a heritage that continued to hold meaning and give direction. For the most part, however, during the early years of the slave period, race – which served as a metonym for the shared history of suffering of the diverse group of people – became the most prominent boundary and visible reminder of group identification. Although stratification of that group created varying degrees of enslavement, total freedom became an issue around which the larger group identity would at times be able to organize social action.

After freedom, a new process of group identity formation was put into place – this time with stronger impetus from within the group to reestablish identification. The formation of a national identity would accord all the rights and privileges of that identity, or, in essence, what it means to be an American. (Race takes on new shades of meaning, deepening the chasm in some respects.) The ideology of race, however, continued to subordinate the sons and daughters of forced immigrants, placing their national status as second-class citizens of America. This status has often been referred to in academic circles as "the caste system" of the United States. I suggest that the differing spatial and ideological practices that developed during slavery as well as the different ways of being and social practices that solidified for African Americans in various regions and communities after freedom became the basis for the formation of varying worldviews. These diverse views found venues for expression in the various institutions and organizations the African American community created; those institutions had a place both in the African American community and the larger American society.[10] I further suggest that the increased interaction of an organization with the dominant society and the increased association of its members with the ideology of the dominant society by groups with little or no previous interaction between the two is directly related to understandings of how such relationships historically had contributed to differentiation among the larger African American community. This occurrence resembles Lomnitz-Adler's (1991) understanding of the ways in which the culture of social relations strongly defines boundaries of identity and constructs intimate cultures. Years of enacting those social roles that required constant or frequent contact between Whites and Blacks as well as performing those that required very little interplay, reified the worldviews and manifested themselves in the different forms of inter- and intraethnic interaction evident in Oxford/Lafayette County.

Pre–Civil War census reports indicate that the majority of Oxford/ Lafayette County's slave population was spread among the various White families of the community. Contemporary interpretations stress the importance of the size of antebellum slave holdings to the culture of social relations between enslaved populations and their masters. These interpretations support Sobatka's (1976) inferences that the culture of social relations between slave and slaveholder, Blacks and Whites, was more intimate in Oxford/Lafayette County than in other areas that managed larger or more plantations and where the majority of the population was Black. The fact that many Black families after freedom made their homes on or near the very tracts of land to which they previously had been

---

[10] Such ventures as the "Back to Africa Movement" attempt to establish a separate Black state; the creation of the NAACP, the establishment of formal Black churches, and the development of other organizations reveal the varying degrees of connected Blackness and varying ideological perspectives of what it means to be both Black and American.

bonded also indicates that the level of the culture of social relations prior to freedom was not totally alienating. In spite of this spatial fact, questions remain. Does the amicable social climate serve as an indication of ideological cohesion? Does it correspond with the intimacy of interaction such that the enslaved Blacks agreed with White perceptions of the "nature of Blacks" and accepted their low-ranked position in society? (See Appendix E for testimony in Susie Marshall's unpublished Freedmen Town marker dedication speech that could imply such an acceptance.) Or should the behavior, often referred to as subservient, be viewed as a forced and enforced manifestation of respect?

Such simplistic assumptions about the culture of social relations do not take into consideration "masking," a part of social life that is almost as prevalent among Southern Whites as among Southern Blacks, or "fronting out," defined by Willis as the expression of resistance in a "style concocted out of discards and the affirmation of everything the bourgeoisie sees as loathsome" (1994:181) in the behavior. In addition, they do not take into consideration the lack of opportunity for social action of those enslaved. Here I suggest that because enslaved Blacks in Oxford/Lafayette County had few opportunities to interact with each other owing to the tremendous number of small holdings in that community, they saw an advantage in putting into practice protocol for maintaining an amicable level of interaction with Whites, or one reasonably close to it. This suggestion is not intended to imply that all the enslaved instituted the practice of masking as a means of balancing power relations, but I submit that contemporary maintenance of a separate Black society carries weight for evaluating the independence (in terms of free will) of those actions, often labeled subservient, which have in past analyses of such behavior been based on understandings of the required "caste-like" deference of the South.

The culture of interracial social relations prior to freedom is important for our understanding of the culture of social relations afterward, particularly the manner in which it influenced the culture of intraethnic social relations. Given the wide range of human attitudes and emotions, it is perhaps safe to say that enslaved Blacks – who enjoyed privileges that other enslaved Blacks did not – experienced a range of attitudinal and emotional reactions in the intraethnic culture of social relations. For example, the disassociation by members of the same family through the variation in spelling of last names reveals a division by complexion and property ownership. Darker-skinned family members' property ownership does not stem from pre- or even postemancipation relationships with Whites, as does much of the property ownership by fairer-skinned members. The original difference in spelling, although unverifiable as to cause, reasonably can be considered a result of the race mixing that occurred on one side of the family, and that one side of the family wanted to distinguish itself from the other side based however loosely on the history of White/Black interaction and the privileges that interaction afforded.

A more contemporary example is the labeling of offspring of housekeepers as rich because they often wear clothes that have been passed along from White employers to their Black workers. The term "rich" is used to separate this particular privilege from that of the majority. It is often used to alienate those youth who in turn struggle to overcome that stigma, adopting behaviors that work to their own disadvantage, as they try to prove they belong.

A final example of the ways in which the interethnic culture of social relations influences the intraethnic culture of social relations is the attitude of many of the members of the African American community toward the first African American appointed to the board of aldermen. I have never heard any complimentary descriptions of him or his performance in office. Further, it is strongly suggested that his relationship to the White members of the board and the maintenance of the position are far more important than caring for the needs of his Black constituents. Many view his disassociation from the Black community on the whole as the reason he was chosen for the privilege. It is also safe to say that these kinds of attitudinal and emotional responses exist and existed regardless of the reason for such privilege. Whether it was given because of sincere dedication or masked contestation, it can be assumed that the enslaved individual or any descendant who had or has the privilege of forming an intimate culture relationship with the master or other members of the dominant society was and is often looked upon with mistrust, suspicion, jealousy, disdain, and envy, as well as admired and depended upon for knowledge and information not accessible to those who did not share such privilege.

These reactions can be viewed as the base for the local African American community concepts of "Uncle Tom" and "Aunt Thomasina," and "acting White" or "trying to be White." Reification of these concepts then forms the boundaries of group identities divided along racial lines and establishes what is to be expected of group members.[11] This

---

[11] The association of privilege to negative behavior, particularly the label "Tom," and increased interaction with the dominant society has been legitimized for African Americans through mass culture appropriation of Black culture. From the minstrel era through the

understanding is important to the analysis of the culture of both inter- and intraethnic social relations throughout the history of any community. It also provides a base for understanding the diverse reactions to both the Civil Rights Movement and its gains, which redefined interethnic interaction and in many social arenas reconstructed the interracial culture of social relations.

HISTORY AND MEMORY AS DEFINERS OF IDENTITY

Remembered history also plays both an essential and a complex role in the formation of an intraethnic identity. Family histories of Blacks in Oxford/Lafayette County tell of Whites and Blacks working on each other's land and selling land and livestock back and forth after freedom. Because such activity was out of the ordinary in terms of interracial interaction and economic standing those who tell the stories consider this level of interaction prestigious. Whether these relations occurred under some unknown duress, or even at all, is not as important to the analysis as the perception of the event or the story that has found its way through the family history for over a hundred years. Having the funds to purchase land and livestock after emancipation implies also a preemancipation position of privilege. No doubt the telling of such stories provides a means by which nonscholars can challenge the generalizations of American history that at times either excludes Blacks or is selective at best.

Many members of the families that have similar stories as part of active memory constitute a particular profile in Oxford/Lafayette County. Regardless of their economic standing, family members who relate such stories of "prestige" have considerably more interethnic interaction than those who do not have such data as a part of their active memory.[12] For example, those members of the Oxford/Lafayette County community who attend weddings, funerals, university events, and special church functions held by the White community are usually those members of families with stories of early nonoppressive or nonconfrontational interracial

blaxploitation films of the early 1970s, the image of African Americans who shared intimate associations with Whites has been negative. Therefore, contemporary association with that relationship by Lafayette County Blacks as being negative can be seen as an extension of that image.

[12] This is not to imply that such a story does not exist in the history of individuals who do not relate them; rather, it simply suggests that memory of stories of the distant past are overshadowed by more recent memories that also influence certain levels of interethnic interaction.

interaction as active parts of their cultural tradition and who currently maintain interaction through employee/employer or religious association relationships. One very active couple in the community, SG and his wife VG, exemplifies the influence of this kind of tradition in the culture of social relations. Social activities within the Black community are most often extended to both the husband and wife who usually attend. But invitations to activities within Oxford/Lafayette County's White society are often only attended by the wife and rarely by the husband. This tradition exists in spite of the fact that much of the prestige accorded this couple by White community members stems from the husband's position as a minister in the community. For many years, SG also occupied the position of leader of the Black community appointed by White society and was often called on to address potential problems, stand bond for Blacks who were arrested, and endorse White political figures. However, VG, his wife, has active memories of a number of stories regarding her father's, her sibling's, her husband's, and her own childhood interactions with the White community. It is important to note that even when asked, SG simply shrugged off the stories that reveal his own family's culture of interracial social relations. The fact that SG places little value on past or present relationships but does not deny VG the right to capitalize on the opportunities is evidenced in his response when asked why he does not attend. "That's VG's thing. She enjoys that kind of thing. It's important to her to be there."

Community liaisons, chosen by members of the dominant society, are usually selected from this group with histories of cross-race connections. Additionally, this selection is not based on socioeconomic standing. Although this level of interaction can be translated into economic rewards, such as medical treatment or loans for automobiles and homes, the dominant society must sanction these rewards as being suitable for that individual's place within the community. For example, through the middle 1970s, Whites perceived brick houses as being inappropriate housing for Blacks. As late as the mid 1980s, a new car was also viewed as being inappropriate. According to CTL, who remembers the response of his family's White patrons (revealed in the story told in Chapter 2) when he built the first brick home to be owned by African Americans in the community, these perceptions were based on the number of times African Americans were refused bank loans for the purchase of such items and the efforts of White potential cosigners to discourage the building of such homes or the purchase of such automobiles. These types of restrictions on Blacks prevailed in spite of privileges. As a result, many of those who attained prestige in the dominant society also sustained prestige in the African American society because of perceptions of a history of shared discrimination and suffering albeit relative. That understanding of shared discrimination and relative suffering is often intensified because members of the Black community see those restrictions, many of which are public knowledge, as "White folks making examples out of you when you get out of place." Members of the Black community feel a connectedness to those members who have been "put back in their place" through negative sanctions. If, however, those members of the community with positive interracial interaction memories sustained no visible evidence of negative sanctions, their actions would be closely scrutinized and held suspect. They must clarify the culture of their social relations with Whites or be viewed suspiciously and at times labeled as "acting White" or "trying to be White," particularly when their activities appear to go unrestricted. For example, interaction between local Black males and students on campus is usually discouraged by campus police harassment. Therefore, local Blacks are looked upon with suspicion if they have a considerable amount of activity on campus and more so if that activity is with Whites. They are likely to be thought of by members of the Black community as "trying to be what they ain't" or "up to no good."

A final aspect of the profile of those whose memories include stories of prestige is that each individual works toward achieving some aspect of the American dream. It should be made clear that this group has sustained for more than a hundred years a tolerance at least and intimacy at most in a culture of social relations with members of the dominant society. They had, as a part of their memory, stories about distant family members or other community members who incurred conflict and deceit as the culture of their social relations with the dominant society as well. And although they may be saddened by the particular incident, it has not killed the quest for the privileges of being a "first-class" citizen as it has in members of the Black community who have adversarial memories as their primary interracial relationship experience. These adversarial memories, however, at times have an impact on behavior in terms of perceived wrongs, which often results in a withdrawal from active contact with White society. Civility, patience, dedication, and hard work are expected to produce rewards from the larger society. This is perhaps a result of the combination of the paternalistic culture of social relations that has existed through time and a folk understanding of the operation of "the gift," exemplified, for example, by "the gift of cosigning" mentioned earlier in this chapter.

Let me take a moment to discuss members of those same families who do not have that history of positive interaction as an active part of memory. A gentleman who served as liaison and whose nuclear family enjoys prestige and power among Whites and Blacks even in his later years (when he is no longer active in the community) is a member of a family who has stories of positive interaction with the White community as far back as slavery. (The wife of the master taught his great-grandmother to read, and his grandfather like the brother of the master was a minister and carpenter.) The male side of the family carries to this day the surnames and the initials of the given names of members of the slaveholder's family. All the immediate descendants of the progenitor who lived in the community enjoy varying levels of preferential treatment. However, those family members who did not tell the story, even when prodded, do not interact with the dominant society on the varied levels of those who did. The relating of the story also appears not to be a generational phenomenon because the half-brother of the previously mentioned liaison did not relate the story but did tell several adversarial tales of what life was like. The granddaughters, however, related stories that showed they had an active memory of positive race relations for their great-great-grandfather and his family. The half-brother avoids situations that could potentially appear adversarial and usually avoids conversations related to contemporary interethnic/interracial problems by making jokes. This behavior is very different from the behavior of the other members of the family who do not make excessive efforts to avoid confrontation and who actively speak out about perceived racial injustices. Although these brothers occupy the same land, they belong to different intimate culture groups, and the interaction among these other groups within the African American community is vastly different.

Friedman suggests that identity is a question of empowerment when the construction of a past creates an appropriated representation of a life leading up to the present for individual subjects as well as any collectivity (1992b: 837). Thus the selective memory phenomenon of positive interracial interaction exhibited by various family members and members of the larger Oxford/Lafayette County community constitutes a transfer of power associated with the remembered act to the identity of the individual(s) who are reconstructing the past through the stories they tell. For example, those residents who include within their life histories stories about interracial/interethnic interaction that imply shared understandings of equality or a sense of unity, no matter how brief the moment, transfer that meaning into an identification of place within today's society and use it as a claim to place and prestige and power that accompanies that place.

What does race have to do with it? Race enters the picture again, this time from an internal perspective. The individual constructing the life history in essence is stating that I, as a person different from "the other" or "them," have this particular relationship of interaction or culture of social relations as a part of my history. The acknowledgment of difference constructs an I/other or we/them dichotomy, which relates to several historical issues that, when summarized, points to the problems of identity created by the larger social construction referred to as race.[13] The positive interethnic/interracial life history construction constitutes an attempt to attain empowerment through identity construction in two arenas – that of intraethnic interaction as well as that of interethnic interaction.[14] Other efforts to establish identity can be seen in the efforts put forth by family members to get articles about family histories published in *Soul Force*, the local African American (for the most part monthly) publication, and the desire of individuals to be recognized for contributions made to the community.[15]

AUTHENTICATION OF BELONGING

Among Oxford/Lafayette County's African American community, a positive assertion of Blackness is important for day-to-day living. Maintaining this distinctive identity is a practical problem for those members who are agent (e.g., politicians, civil service workers, police, professors at the university, and foremen). The most visible sites of struggle for this maintenance are the interaction of these authority figures with members of the larger African American community in the workplace. Although these authority figures may belong to a number of African American intimate culture groups deemed positive and ranked high in value to the community, the figures occupy a particularly ambivalent place in that community.

---

[13] The historical issues referred to here are privileged/underprivileged, exploiter/exploited, economically advantaged/disadvantaged, and colonizer/colonized in America.

[14] See Ginsburg (1989) for a comparison of the way life histories shape identity and provide an understanding of worldview.

[15] Family-submitted articles carry such titles as "Generation-To-Generation With Love" (March 1995), "In Loving Memory of the Mrs. Vivian D. Mitchell Jenkins: *A True Pioneer an Dedicated O. D. A. Historian and Member*" (March 1995), "Friends of Yates Honors 24 For Black History Month" (April 1995), and "Salute to Mrs. Annie Lee Burt: Our Rosa Parks" (January 1993).

The arbitrariness of what is defined as Blackness and the importance of belonging complicates their place in society and community perceptions of their allegiance to the Black community.

For African American authority figures, authentication of their identity must be constituted in perceptions of their belonging and place. First, belonging to the community is a primary prerequisite. For some purposes, belonging to the community means being born there; for others, it means being born and brought up there or having strong relational ties (e.g., marrying someone born and reared there); and for others, it requires living there for varying lengths of time, developing positive organizational connections, and occupying a prestigious place within those organizations. The length of time and distance away from the community also play key roles for those born and reared in the community. For example, suggestions offered as possible solutions to particular social problems can be labeled "New York" ideas or some other "foreign" area if the person who puts the idea forward is perceived as being influenced more by their stay in that other region or community. Or, recall the case of JD (mentioned in Chapter 2), who came from central Mississippi and was told that "We do it differently up here" in response to his suggestions for ways to improve housing conditions within the Black community. Making a home in Oxford/Lafayette County does not necessarily constitute belonging to the community. The community determines whether you belong, and the grounds apparently shift according to issues/context. Although, there may be disagreement among community members as to the status of an individual, those members who hold high ranking within the various groups that constitute the community greatly influence group perceptions of an individual's position and relationship to the community.

Second, belonging to the ethnic group, as distinguished from the racial group, must be affirmed in a number of ways. The culture of interracial and interethnic social relations and intraracial and intraethnic behavior patterns, which change over time, are the primary methods for authenticating Blackness. Language is included in that authentication for both community and ethnic group identity. For example, pronouncing the county *Le-'FAY-ette* is a local community identifier (for both Blacks and Whites), whereas pronouncing "usher" as *er-sher* is ethnic.

For ordinary community members, the struggle for authentication of belonging to the community and the ethnic group is not as much a primary experience as it is for authority figures. The performance of authority figures in the workplace presents a constant challenge to their authentic community/ethnic identity. For them, the community-desired behavior is

not the behavior expected of their position. Authority figures are expected
to support the dominant society's role in the community, although it is desired that they champion the causes of the African American community,
and they must continually prove their belonging. Members of the community hope that Black probation and parole officers, college professors,
supervisors, and police officers will be more lenient with those with whom
they share a community and ethnic identity. It is believed that one should
be able to rely upon one's politicians and civil service workers to provide
information to which they alone are privileged and which they know the
larger African American community needs but cannot otherwise acquire.
If they do not perform these services they are not deemed useful to the community and are consequently perceived as choosing to belong to "them."
This often means that African Americans who occupy positions of authority must choose between being agents of the dominant oppressive society
or of being deceptive to the dominant society – wearing the mask[16] – or
ambiguous in their functioning, which often appears as inefficiency. For
those born and reared in the community who stayed there, the options
boil down to an inescapable choice between belonging to them or to us.[17]

The process by which African Americans became Americans serves as a
base for a resurgence of differentiation among Blacks in Oxford/Lafayette
County. The artificial collapsing of ethnic-identity borders masks the diversity that existed within the larger group. Because of this national collapsing of identity, Blacks began to think of themselves in these larger
terms of race, the associated position of servitude, and the expected con-
comitant behavior. When that behavior begins regularly to vary from
what is expected, the larger group becomes segmented around those lines.
However, the dominant society historically continues to ignore internal
differentiation within the African American community in favor of a racial
identity that rarely considers the now firmly set differences existing as a
result of the varied regionalized histories. For African Americans, this
process has produced false understandings and misinterpretations of the
meanings of behavior in the culture of social relations and intimate culture ideology. The unsatisfied expectation of coherence within the larger
African American community produces negative perceptions of self as a

---

[16] In a position of authority or privilege, wearing the mask is often mistaken as allegiance
to the dominant society, just as the category Uncle Tom was a misinterpreted relationship
of the oppressed to the oppressor.

[17] See Emmett (1982: 171–3) for a comparison of the struggles in the workplace for agents
who struggle to maintain a Welsh identity.

racial or ethnic group and the mistrust and suspicion that occur on the individual level.

What is often missed when the varying borders of "Blackness" are collapsed into a homogeneous group identity constructed by the historical fact of enslavement – whether by scholars, grassroots groups, Whites, or Blacks when trying to make sense of the lack of coherence within the African American community – is the role African Americans themselves played in the identity formation process. Across the Americas, they constructed various group identities and created institutions to accommodate their new identities formed in response to the dominant society's treatment along racial and class lines. Blacks, mulattos, Free Blacks, slaves, and field and house servants were new groups that created different ways of being. These ways of being, in turn, influenced the level of interaction, which was determined by the place of an individual's group within the larger society and by the individual's place within that group. Oxford/Lafayette County's African American community presents an excellent example of the relationship between ascribed status, history, individual sense of belonging, place, power, perceptions of the significance of these, and problems faced in the construction of a coherent ethnic identity. The simplified identity, which Blacks as a racial or ethnic collective present to the outside world, masks the Lafayette County structure as a complex group. One can only understand many of its interethnic and interracial problems by examining these internal intricacies and the problems they present for collective social action.

6

It's a White "Thang"

Ethnic Identifiers and the Loss of Cultural Codes

I, Too, Sing America!
by Langston Hughes

I, too sing America.
I am the darker brother.
They send me to eat in the kitchen
when company comes.
But I laugh, eat well and grow strong.
Tomorrow I'll be at the table
when company comes.
And no one will dare say to me
eat in the kitchen then.
Besides they'll see how beautiful I am
and be ashamed.
I, too, am America.
                        (Chapman 1968)

"Black enuf fuh ya," "Negritude," and "Brothers and Sisters" along with such contemporary terms as "homey," "from the hood," and "peeps" are some of the linguistic signs that denote the grassroots identity of the descendants of North America's forced immigrants.[1] They signify history, heritage, hopes, and ways of being of a people. These phrases, unlike the color of one's skin, are signifiers of a particular group's ethnic identity, cultural heritage, and shared historical experiences. I am reminded here

---

[1] The term "grassroots" from an insider perspective is a socioeconomic term that refers to an identity drawn around "poor, hardworking, Christian" people. Their lives are viewed as the foundation (mainstay) of African Americans as a people.

of the monologue in Charles Gordone's award-winning play, *No Place to Be Somebody*, that heralds: "There is more to being Black than meets the eye." As the monologue goes on to say, it is a way of walking and talking, dressing, and loving. All these social behaviors have developed in the same way Black English has emerged; they are a recreolization of Black culture,[2] and as Harrison points out, in the United States, "particularly in nationalist and Afrocentric discourses, Blackness has come to marginalize mixedness and cast it as a mark of oppression and a threat to racial survival" (1995a:61). The concept of Blackness has also come to marginalize mixedness of cultural practices, particularly in forms of acculturation that include integrationist ideologies.

It is in this cultural mixedness that mobilization around racial and ethnic solidarity often is ineffective. Many members of the Black community attach ideological significance to the material culture and lifestyle choices of the integrationist. Integrationists are viewed as "sellouts," "crossovers," or "Oreos," which leads to alienation of particular groups within the larger Black community. In these instances, Blackness is constructed against what is perceived as the integrationist's relationship to the oppressor. Although analytically this distinction is heavily class based, in the area of grassroots understanding/interpretation, the differences are categorized on the level of practice as acting White.

A part of the identification of what Blackness is, however, also constructed against perceptions of Whiteness. For example, in general conversations among African Americans, members of White communities are heralded as cooperating with each other, while members of African American communities are deemed unable to organize. Some sociological discourse has contributed to Black grassroots beliefs that view the construction and operation of the Black family as dysfunctional, while White families represent strong family values. Furthermore, older generations of Blacks make comments such as "White folks got all the money," while "Black folks ain't got a pot to piss in." Most of these African American perceptions of Whiteness are based on dominant society myths (and some first-hand experiences of "unified" White action) that imply homogeneity among America's White Euro-American population. Good, proper, and right are the positive images these stereotypes signify about Whiteness.

Perceptions of Blackness against Whiteness, however, are not always negative views of African Americans. For example, Black folks are "hip," whereas White folks are "corny." Blacks see themselves as expressive,

---

[2] See Smitherman (1986) for a discussion of the decreolization and recreolization of Black English.

while they see Whites as stiff. Blacks also see themselves as athletically and musically inclined or gifted, while "White folks can't jump" or "got no rhythm." These characteristics, while admirable, are not designated as required standards of achievement by the dominant society. Thus, in spite of their positive image, the functions are peripheralized in terms of importance as social skills or abilities. The positive and negative constructions of Blackness against Whiteness place African Americans, on the level of the individual, in a perpetual state of identity construction as meanings assigned to different phenomena change. These constructions of Blackness against perceptions of Whiteness can be problematic when the construction of that identity is a major aspect of collective social action.

What comes into play here is, again, DuBois's concept of "double consciousness." It is difficult to be both Black and American, not just in negotiating day-to-day interaction in the dominant society but also in establishing the culture of social relations within Black communities, particularly when "America" is metonymic for White and middle class. This problem for intraethnic interaction has an historical base. Whiteness has operated as the key site of racial domination. "Page and Thomas[3] characterize this hidden site as 'White public space,' which in many material and symbolic forms 'routinely, discursively, and sometimes coercively privilege Euro-Americans over non-Whites'" (Harrison 1995a:63). I suggest that in Oxford/Lafayette County recognition of this privileged position and the association of it with material and symbolic forms, such as segregated public facilities, housing, neighborhoods, and lifestyles, greatly influences perceptions of racial and ethnic allegiances when those segregated and distinctive boundaries are crossed. When these boundaries that define areas traditionally privileged by Whiteness are crossed by Blacks, many African Americans believe that "you have to give up something" to operate in those arenas. Crossing the boundaries jeopardizes one's standing in the Black community because of the community's uncertainty as to what aspect of Blackness is given up for the privilege. This uncertainty often generates suspicion and distrust, which at times is also complicated by envy. In Oxford/Lafayette County, those boundaries can be as ordinary as the way you talk, the kind of car you own, or what you do for entertainment, or those boundaries can be as uncommon as having interracial friendships, owning a successful business, or being in positions

---

[3] Helan Page and R. Brooke Thomas discuss White public space in their article, "White Public Space in U.S. Health Care: Fresh Concepts and a New Model of Analysis," published in the 1994 *Medical Anthropology Quarterly,* new Series vol. 8, no. 1.

of power such as that of a public official. An important aspect of crossing these boundaries traditionally seen by Blacks as White public space is
that the perception of what the crossing means is situational. Before pre-
senting ethnographic examples of this phenomenon, I reiterate that from
an external anthropological analytical perspective, the issues appear class
oriented.

Because of the satellite-type enclaves, the lack of public transportation,
and the distances residents had to travel to get from one side of the county
to the other, access to automobiles was important for handling business
in town. One collaborator with whom I lived, PWC, has a small two-door
car and often chauffeurs other family members and friends who need to
take care of personal or family business matters despite the fact that her
car does not have air conditioning or working heat. One hot Mississippi
summer day when PWC was on mandatory vacation from her factory
job,[4] she promised to drive around a family member who had to take care
of necessary business. I offered the use of my car because it had a working
air conditioner and was large enough to accommodate PWC, her two sons,
her unmarried sister-in-law, SIL, and myself. On this particular occasion,
I observed the extent to which perceptions of what it means to be Black
were manifested in both inter-and intraracial cultures of social relations.

SIL lives in the northern end of the county in a small four-trailer cove.
After picking her up, we traveled to the home of another one of PWC's
sisters-in-law who lived on the southern end of town in an African American enclave that consists of modestly built working-class homes. The trip
was made to pick up a disability check that family members continued
to collect in spite of the passing away of the designated recipient. This
money was used as a fund available to all members of the family. Often, nonworking members of the family borrowed advances against their
share from working members of the family.

We exited the neighborhood by another route after picking up the
check:

PWC: Isn't that MC's house?
SIL: Yeah. Boy, you can't tell her nothing now.
         [The now refers to the fact that MC formerly lived in the projects and
         has managed to buy a home.]
PWC: Have you been inside? They sure did fix it up nice outside.

---

[4] "Vacations" are factorywide closings that actually accommodate slow seasons. These
vacations are paid holidays only for the few classified as full-time and permanent. PWC
is one of the fortunate few.

SIL: No chile. I ain't going in there. You know she think she White now. Look at how she got them lights out there in her yard.
[This reference is to lights that illuminate the driveway and walkway path.]

SIL: Ain't nobody care 'bout seeing her house.

The conversation ended on that note. On the surface, it may appear that SIL is putting her down for getting up in the world. However, the root of her put-down is related to her own perception of what constitutes the conspicuous display of consumption.

The next stop was to get the check cashed. A discussion ensued as to where the check should be cashed. PWC suggested cashing the check at a Black-owned business but SIL insisted that the check be cashed at a White-owned business where the clientele are predominantly Black. (It is important to mention here that this business is not located in or on the borders of any Black neighborhood.) SIL's explanation for wanting to do this was "I don't want them Black folks all up in my business." This statement was made in spite of the fact that the clerk at the business where she cashed the check was Black.

After SIL deducted her share of the money, paid PWC on her loan from PWC's husband, we took her home. On the ride back to PWC's house, the oldest of her sons (12-year-old P'sS) asked for five dollars.

PWC: What you want five dollars for, boy?
P'sS: I want to buy something.
PWC: I didn't think you wanted to eat it.
P'sS: I want to get me a gold necklace.
PWC: For what?
P'sS: To wear to school.
PWC: What you want to wear a gold necklace to school for? For somebody to take it?
P'sS: No! So everybody'll think that I'm rich.
PWC: Rich? Boy, we ain't rich. We're poor.
P'sS: They won't know that.
PWC: Where you gon' get the rest of the money for this necklace? How much money you got saved?
P'sS: Five dollars.
PWC: Boy, you can't buy no gold necklace for ten dollars.
P'sS: Un huh. They got 'em at Wal-Mart.
PWC: Boy, I don' told you you can't buy no gold necklace for no ten dollars.

P'sS continued briefly to argue the point with his mother, and I asked why he wanted his friends at school to think he was rich. He answered, "So they won't think I'm poor, like them."

PWC: If you want somebody to think you're rich, you need diamonds.

Each of these conversations reveals how lifestyles influence interpretations of Blackness and degrees of Blackness. The acquisition of material culture such as lights to illuminate the outside of a house by members of a cultural group that struggles to maintain services for lights on the inside of the house is viewed as buying into the practices (wastefulness/ extravagance and conspicuous consumption) of the dominant/White society, or acting White. This view regarding wastefulness is not the view of a particular economic level. SIL's perception of Blackness makes owning walkway lights "matter out of place" and as such the individual's allegiance to the Black community is questionable and the act becomes a stigma.[5] This perception is exacerbated if the owner lives in a Black neighborhood. In addition, the stigmatization of this act has an impact on other kinds of interaction such as SIL's refusal to go inside the house. Alienation occurs when people or things are considered to be out of place. The purchasing of goods considered to be representative of White culture by Blacks is considered being out of place by both Blacks and Whites – as per the story of the first brick house owned by a Black in Oxford.

The culture of social relations in business practices in Oxford and SIL's understanding of place influenced the choice of check-cashing location. Banking is looked upon as something White folks do. Therefore, it stands to reason for SIL that Whites should carry out all business related to banking. My explanation was formed after careful evaluation of both places of business and the identities of both the individual who actually handled the cashing of the check and the individual who potentially would have handled the check at the Black-owned business.

The Black-owned business, which is located on the border of two Black neighborhoods, employs two workers – the owner, born and reared in the community, and a cashier-manager who was born, reared, and continues to live in another county.[6] The cashier-manager is not an active member of

---

[5] See Mary Douglas (1991) for a greater understanding of the concept "matter out of place."

[6] The clientele of this business in the past has been balanced between Whites and Blacks because of the nature of the business and because it is located on a main street. Near the end of my research, a new road was being built that would provide access for Whites to their community without their passing this business. I anticipate that this will bring about a difference in the number of Whites who patronize this business and, therefore, subsequent changes in policies. A 2004 trip to Oxford revealed this long-standing Black business has gone out of business. Some interesting questions are: Why was the road

the community. African American members of the community continually criticize the Black owner for his business practices. For example, he refuses to extend credit, which is a necessity for low- and no-income people. He also has instituted a no-check policy that has been interpreted by some members of the African American segment of the community as "my check ain't good enough for him." These are policies practiced in many of the locally owned White businesses. Yet he is highly criticized for both practices because of the financial strains and ill will the practices have caused in the past. (His business has sustained a number of returned checks from Blacks in the community and collection of the debts has been difficult. He has often had to appeal to family members to handle the debts.) In spite of these problems being common knowledge in the community, his business practices are perceived as unfair and prejudicial to Blacks, which in turn translates into the owner trying to be something he is not – "just 'cause he owns a business." Some customers rationalize that his no-credit policy was what caused community people to write checks without sufficient funds.

The cashier who actually cashed the check for SIL is an African American female from Oxford/Lafayette County who in fact knows SIL and other members of her family. The difference between the two establishments is the perception of the positions of power and place of the individuals cashing the check. The relationship of the cashier handling the check to ownership and thus to the dominant society is closer to that of SIL. It is SIL's perception that this cashier does not have a vested interest in the White-owned store and feels as exploited by the system as she does; therefore, this shared history makes the cashier less likely to question her about the check than the Black store owner would be. Here again, the concept of matter out of place can be employed. White businesses are perceived as dealing with checks, while Black businesses generally are not.

Influences on social behavior related to the value and power connected with material culture were revealed again in the gold-necklace conversation. The first example provides an understanding of how certain behavior becomes stigmatized and racialized by members of the Black community who are seeking to define the meaning of that behavior. The conversation about the necklace provides an understanding of an individual seeking

built? Was it built simply for convenience or to eliminate the need to pass through the Black communities? Finally, what are the perceptions of the Black community as to why the road was built? Unfortunately for this analysis, I do not have the answers to these questions.

to acquire the material culture (participate in the behavior) that is considered matter out of place both by the young boy and his mother. Although the particular material culture items discussed by both are influenced by generational views, the underlying assumptions about material culture acquisition are based on race and class. "Rich," to poor people, means wearing gold, according to the child's interpretation of social class. While rich to PWC, a working-class adult, means wearing diamonds. Both P'sS and his mother associate "rich" with Whiteness and "poor" with Blackness.

The acquisition of gold is viewed by P'sS not only as a sign requiring respect from youth but as an appropriation of power, which is of primary importance to youth who witness daily the stigma attached to both their race and their class. It is evident by the necklace conversation that P'sS recognizes that within his community *how* one is perceived by others influences social interaction and subsequently one's place within that community. Among P'sS intimate culture group, having money is valued, and the more you have, the more prominent your position within the group. The acquisition of gold (which unlike a car, food, or sneakers has no practical use) is vicariously associated by Black youth with the conspicuous consumption identified with the ideology of Whiteness. Both SIL and P'sS resent and envy the privilege accorded Whiteness, but their own particular understanding of what it means to be Black influences the reactions to that privilege. To SIL, to be Black means that one must construct an identity against Whiteness and make every effort to stay within the borders of that identity. To P'sS, to be Black means to exist in a place of varying degrees of powerlessness and thus he seeks to be a big fish in a small pond. P'sS realizes that he is not, like his schoolmates, viewed as being equal to Whites, but because his schoolmates are "blind" in the sense that they do not know the difference between quality gold and that which Wal-Mart sells, he is able to be a "king fish" in his intimate culture group. As P'sS gets older and his group becomes more knowledgeable, this tactic will not work.

Other conversations with both PWC and P'sS provided the source for the connections made between the state of being rich and being seen as rich by consuming material culture. The consumption connection formed by P'sS is heavily influenced by Black entertainers, particularly music video artists, and his understanding of the image of drug dealers. Both his mother and father commenting on people who wear gold jewelry looking like or being drug dealers have mostly influenced this latter understanding. However, it is perhaps the association of "rich" with power among

Black youth that blurs negative images of drug dealers and highlights their position in society as one of power.

PWC, with whom I have maintained a friendship since 1983, has always equated my own lifestyle with being more White than Black.[7] She commented one day after seeing a diamond ring I had purchased as a reward for finishing my undergraduate degree that having that kind of ring was what rich folks could do. PWC and her husband often tease me about being "the Blackest White person they know." This comment is not about skin tone but relates to my own cultural practices and lifestyle. I am considered by them (and many others) to talk like White folks. I also interact socially with Whites; studied and taught at the White university; and eat, dress, and drink like White folks. This last reference is to the fact that occasionally I like a good bottle of wine and "Black folks just don't pay that kind of money for no wine." Yet, I sing and dance like, and associate more with, Black folks. I wear my hair naturally in braids with no extensions, am known for my efforts to develop a pride in and respect for Blackness among both Blacks and Whites, and was married to, according to PWC and her husband, "the Blackest acting home boy" with whom they associate.

This mixture of cultural markers and practices is problematic for many members of the community who do not know me as well as PWC and her husband. In fact, one African American student from the community who visualizes himself as a Black militant called me an Aunt Thomasina because I was expected to favor my African American students in teaching a class and I did not.

It is this type of juxtaposition of the everyday activities labeled as Black against those viewed as White by members of the African American community who define Blackness against Whiteness that informs people's perceptions of one's relationship to the community and influences the culture of social relations.[8] The localist ideologies of Blackness shared by PWC's intimate culture group point to areas where class clashes with ethnic identity and affect the culture of social relations. Various intimate culture groups within the Black community interpret social practices

---

[7] She always makes comments whenever I say I like collard greens or that I used to eat chitterlings, squirrel, and possum.

[8] This reframing of the level of intraethnic interaction along lines of the perception of an individual's relationship to the community is indicative of Lomnitz-Adler's (1991) "localist ideologies." Lomnitz-Adler sees the act of adopting a particular level of interaction along lines that distinguish different intimate culture groups as shaping "localist ideologies" (1991:206–8).

and material culture symbols of class differently.[9] The interpretations of these symbols directly affect decisions as to who interacts with whom, to what degree, and on what occasion. Since the intragroup culture of social relations is affected by varying localist ideologies such as those described earlier, the larger Black community remains fragmented as a social force.

I digress in the building of this argument to discuss parallels between my own lifestyle practices, and hence my place in the hierarchy of racial and ethnic identity, and that of SIL to emphasize how the level of my operation in the community is defined by "localist ideologies." I have often been asked why SIL allowed me, a person who obviously travels in both Black and White society and who is not a member of her intimate culture group, to observe the underground economy aspect of her life. The answer is fairly simplistic on the surface. Although SIL and I belong to different intimate culture groups, we are both getting over. A number of the intimate culture groups I observed expressed ideas that support that conclusion. In their eyes, I make the very system that tries to oppress me and my people work for me, and my use of my position in the university community to uplift the image of Blacks is considered subversive to the hegemonic structure of White society. In either example, the benefit does not have to be for the larger African American community; I'm a "sistuh" as long as I'm getting over and not hurting anybody Black. The example of the student who wanted me to make concessions for him because he is Black reveals why who gets hurt, in terms of racial or ethnic identity, is relative to the classification.

I am connected to SIL because she and her family exploit a system and government that has historically exploited them, and my activities are viewed in the same manner. As one informant remarked about another similar act of deception, "White folks have been getting over on us all along. It's time for us to take over." When I was first introduced to SIL at her home, a few simple comments made by her brother placed me. After describing my social connection to the community, he commented, "She's okay. She knows we got to do what we got to do." This way of thinking explains both how it was possible for SIL to feel comfortable enough around me to expose her personal business and why she was confident that the Black cashier at the White business would not expose

---

[9] Lomnitz-Adler's Cuernavaca peripheral neighborhoods reflect shared ideologies that contribute to the institutionalization of shared social practices. These shared ideologies create a constellation of classes that result in a node of regional culture.

"her business." This understanding also speaks to the situational nature of the identity of Blackness.[10]

The era of Jim Crow has had a lasting impact on the identity and coherence of the Black community. Membership in the Black race, the externally constructed identity, does not automatically accord an individual membership in the Black ethnic group from the internal perspective. Membership in the group is divided along two lines, "card-carrying" members and those who obtain membership by default. One family member's membership in the ethnic group does not guarantee that same group recognition to another family member. Card-carrying members of the Black ethnic group are entitled to prestige, respect, and a representative voice, while default membership, which comes as a result of birth, is acknowledged by members – both card-carrying and default – on a situational basis. Situations in which these default members "act Black" are the times when they are acknowledged. At the same time, default members are not expected to act Black all the time. Individuals in both ideological groups – card-carrying and default – occupy a constellation of classes, neighborhoods, and families that form the varied intimate culture groups of the community. From an external point of view, these various groups among the African American population of Oxford/Lafayette County are often perceived as *the* African American ethnic group of that region. However, actual membership in the ethnic group (from an internal perspective) is not inclusive of all members of each intimate culture group. Instead it cuts across intimate culture groups and is defined by individual levels of interaction, intimate culture behavior, and allegiance to a particular ideological perspective. The father who maintains an antagonistic relationship to both White society and law enforcement is an excellent example of how the situationality of interaction defines ethnic group membership. He is considered neither a snitch nor an Uncle Tom when he calls the police about a drug sale taking place across the street from his house. He makes it clear through his "loud-talking" that he calls in order to remove a nuisance from his neighborhood and control the cultural environment to

---

[10] As a scientist who is a member of the community of study, I am very concerned about revealing this story although considerable effort has been made to disguise the identity of both PWC and SIL. In some ways, although SIL agreed to the telling of this incident, I feel the "push–pull" of my own ethnic identity and feel as if I have done what was expected of the Black-owned business – exposed SIL's "business" to the people/system she's trying to beat. As I cross this line, I hope to see the emergence of a greater understanding between the ways in which African Americans categorize themselves and the development of cultural coherence influence mobilization.

which his household or private intimate culture group is exposed. However, a fellow member of an intimate drug culture group who voluntarily or involuntarily provides information related to the sale of drugs in order to garner favors later from law enforcement officials is labeled "a snitch," "an Uncle Tom," or "an Oreo." These labels are not only conferred by members of that intimate drug culture group but by members of other intimate culture groups as well. Since the first resident has nothing to gain in terms of prestige or patronage from the dominant society and the second does, the former is thought of more highly. Condemning the member of the drug culture group as a snitch by other intimate culture groups occurs in spite of their opposition to the behavior of the offended drug culture group. More specifically, members of religious groups who avoid and alienate drug sellers and users, particularly those who hang out on the streets in communities, are among the first to criticize an individual who reports these illegal activities to the police or the Drug Enforcement Administration (DEA).

The assertion of an ethnic identity is both a process of resistance – to a discriminatory hegemonic structure – and a process of insistence – displaying one's identity as an act of defiance of the dominant culture. However, these two processes are not necessarily utilized in each display of ethnic identity. In addition, the value placed on either process can fluctuate depending on the specific occasion where identity is being asserted. The wearing of braids, particularly by males, is one example that comes to mind. In other words, the assertion of Blackness as an ethnic identity is both a process of resistance to the tenets, practices, and ideology of the dominant society and a process of insistence that one's ethnic and individual differences are recognized, respected, and legitimized. It becomes a matter, in the language of today's youth, of "profiling" – the adoption and assertion of particular cultural codes often in association with style of dress, the way one walks and talks, and the insistence that others acknowledge the value placed on that image. As Sutton's explanation of the New York West Indian experience reveals, in order to resist the categorization and stigmatization of the dominant society, emigrants from the Caribbean refused to accept the cultural codes being assigned to them and, at the same time, established stronger ties to their past and heritage (Sutton 1992).

For a variety of reasons, African Americans in Oxford/Lafayette County rarely resist or insist as a concerted group. Instead, they handle their predicaments individually, often masking their feelings and thoughts. "Mask wearing" has traditionally been a form of African American resistance, constructed during the slave period and carried out by such behavior as foot dragging, feigning ignorance, or pilfering. No doubt during extremely repressive times in the history of African Americans, this form of resistance was the most effective available means of social action. The practice continues to have significance even for teenagers.

On weekends (particularly Friday evenings), White teenagers gather on the town square to sit in their cars with the doors open and music playing and generally horse around. Blacks generally see the practice as a "White thing." Young Blacks generally hang out at the projects or the community center. However, there is one Black teenager, HR, who hangs out with the White youth. He is small-framed, short, and unassuming. Nothing about his looks or general behavior would instill fear or distrust from Whites. HR is a fairly clean-cut teenager whose clothes are neat – with very little about his outward appearance and manners indicative of his poverty-level background. In this small town where almost everyone knows everyone else, he is clearly "the other." On the surface, his behavior could be considered matter out of place and labeled "acting White" by members of the Black community. Yet HR holds a position of prestige among his peer group and most of his intimate culture groups. This is not because he hangs with Whites but because Black youth see him as being skilled at getting over and masking. HR makes it clear to his intimate culture groups and peers that he hangs with the White youth for the money. He is a highly skilled pool player, and he uses his relationship with Whites to earn what he considers "real" money. According to his sister, HR has maintained this practice for a couple of years without having any backlash from the White community, the pool hall owner, or the police. Black youth believe that what HR does, "playing the White folks," is dangerous. But because he has been successful for what is considered a long time he is respected for his ability to beat Whites out of their money – over and over again.

Wearing masks is problematic for any group of people in spite of the fact that the practice is a form of resistance. Counteractions are often put into place by the dominant society that turn these acts into reasons that validate subjugation. Therefore, mask wearing can either enhance or deny the opportunity to resist domination and establish autonomy. This is a particularly important point when we consider the way in which the dominant society used the wearing of masks as a means of legitimizing further degradation of the cultural, intellectual, and social identity of African Americans.[11] For example, the acts of resistance known as

[11] An interesting parallel exists in contemporary society where performing artists who have created the "gangsta rap" genre are currently shaping the image of young Black youths.

foot dragging, feigning ignorance, and pilfering used by slaves to balance the power exerted over their bodies by the masters have been used by White society to justify their treatment of Blacks and define African Americans as lazy, less intelligent, and thieving. A more contemporary example is the lifestyle and image perpetuated by "gangsta rap." This style is rarely indicative of the actual life or social behavior of those individuals who imitate the style through dress and language; however, the "gangsta" image is associated with all Blacks who imitate that image. Members of the dominant society preserve the power to define identities, particularly identities of the marginalized groups they traditionally control.

Not only is wearing the mask problematic for marginalized groups who struggle daily with stigmatized identities, but years of wearing the mask could lead to reification of one's outward appearance and eventually to self-mystification. I suggest that the possibility of believing and falling prey to the projected image is increased with the frequency and length of time the mask is worn. As an example, the elderly gentleman in his car at the stoplight, described in the Introduction, provided my first experience of the extent to which the colonial experience becomes embedded in the everyday experiences of the colonized and continues to manifest itself more than a century later.

The significance of the preceding conversations and assertions is their relationship to the ambivalence experienced by African Americans as they negotiate the use of cultural codes and markers in their day-to-day existence. African American Lafayette County residents are caught between stigmatized perceptions of their own identity and the construction of new positive codes symbolic of a history of resistance. Oxford/Lafayette County's African American community is today at a point where decisions must be made to change or exchange old codes for new ones. They are still unable, at this ethnographic moment, to reconcile these different symbols of the same group identity, and the boundaries of that identity continue to change according to varying levels of social interaction.

A recent exercise in identity building has begun to take place in Oxford. The use of memory and family mythology, as mentioned earlier, is one way the residents have begun to construct and reconstruct their histories of resistance. In many ways, these practices are becoming the one space around which the varying intimate cultures are beginning to institutionalize shared practices. The documentation of church histories that reflect postbellum breaks from White churches, efforts to establish historical markers designating Freedmen Town as the first Black community in the area, and attempts to publish a book entitled *The History of Black Lafayette County* are all symbolic means of constructing a local history of shared resistance.

On the other hand, the construction of these local histories creates images that in many ways contest present-day reality and continue to contribute to hegemonic White control of the social structure and political processes. Older residents become nostalgic and romanticize the past in their reconstruction of a history that views the present as worse than the past in terms of social consciousness. NT, an 80-year-old retired teacher, points out, "We seemed to want more than these young people today. They don't seem to want to do nothing. They think everything is just going to be given to them." Thus we see the construction of an identity that, in its effort to redefine and reinterpret stereotypes of the past and establish what by some are considered "proper" communal values, stigmatizes the present. This internal criticism of community and stigmatization of the identity of the younger generation is detrimental in practice, particularly in the way in which organizational structures, including the church, are ordered. Members of the younger generation are passive participants in the functions of the church. They do only what is expected of them – come to Sunday School and worship service, join the choir or the junior usher board, and attend Baptist training union. Only recently have they been allowed to suggest songs their own choir sings.

How does this contribute to sustaining hegemonic control? Like the operation of the church, little effort is given to incorporating members of the community who are under 50 into active roles within the civic, social, and political organizations. Little attention is given to the younger generation's perspective on problems and even less to suggested solutions. The use of outdated methods for dealing with social issues is a turnoff for those younger members who attempt to be active and productive members of the organizations. This is particularly problematic for the post–Civil Rights generations of African American residents who are experiencing a different type of identity crisis. Products of a highly consumer-oriented, capitalist culture, the youngest of the younger generation find little coherence between the prayers of the older generation and their own consumer-oriented goals. They are – unlike the member of the development association who prayed to members of the community to stop complaining and be thankful for what they have or the housekeeper who cleans her boss's new $250,000 home and is content in her rented three-room shotgun where she barely makes ends meet – looking for salvation *now*. Unprepared for dealing with the newer forms of discrimination, many of them find salvation in the underground economy, a bottle, or indiscriminate sex, which accounts for the high crime rate, the high percentage of African Americans incarcerated annually, and the increasing numbers of drug addicts, teenage pregnancies, and AIDS cases that plague the community. In this sense, the devaluation of the potential of the younger generation, which increases the lack of respect of that generation for the older generation, eliminates a significant number of potential social actors from participating in the efforts to establish appropriate communal values and cultural coherence.

The complexity of constructing identity in Oxford's African American community is obscured further by the national assertion of difference among Black youth evident in today's hip-hop culture. This assertion of Blackness is viewed as both a setback of and a roadblock to positive images of Blacks, particularly in the Oxford White world. Although there are not a significant number of youth in Oxford who dress, talk, walk, or wear their hair in that particular popular culture style, older adults often comment about its negative influences on White perceptions and the inevitable ramifications on employment. The realization for their offspring of the economic and social advancement[12] that Hughes proposes in his poem that introduces this chapter is seen as the practical benefit of the efforts of the Civil Rights Movement by older Black Oxonians. Although they may shun certain consumption aspects of those benefits, they desire full access to economic security and social acceptance in American society. They see the new youthful assertion of identity as a hindrance to that access and acceptance; however, they do not draw parallel conclusions about their own assertions of Blackness that connect certain interracial relationships and particular types of cultural consumption as "selling out." Again, as DuBois has vividly pointed out, it is the American-ness of their African American identity that makes the assertion of Blackness problematic. I suggest that the difference between the assertion of Blackness by the youth (through hip-hop) and that of the older community members (through earlier cultural and racial markers) is a result of a duality of consciousness among the older generation accustomed to masking, which permits a kind of "identity" code switching – one image for Whites and a different one among Blacks. In other words, the culture asserted by the

---

[12] Reference line: "Tomorrow I'll be at the table / when company comes. / And no one will dare say to me / eat in the kitchen then. / Besides they'll see how beautiful I am / and be ashamed."

hip-hop generation is "a Black thang" and should not be exposed for White consumption.[13]

The African American community as a whole is caught up in issues of identity that segment the community, in ways other than class, that seriously impair the development of a coherent collective. The varying ideas of what constitutes Blackness and the Black experience create intimate culture tensions that cut across generational differentiation and severely limit the number of individuals who share ideas.

[13] The author acknowledges that since 1994 and 1995 hip-hop has crossed cultural boundaries. This crossover and its impact have not been studied in Oxford.

7

The Final (Af)front

Space and the Black Public Sphere

Before examining the function of the Black public sphere and its relationship to use of space by Blacks in Oxford/Lafayette County, I want to address more generally the practices of subordinate groups for instituting change in stratified societies. This discussion sheds light on examples of getting over provided in previous chapters. The chapter goes on to describe what constitutes the Black public sphere in Oxford/Lafayette County and then addresses the use-of-space problems that become impediments to the operation of that sphere.

The general concern of this chapter is social change. Social scientists recognize that social change is often brought about through two distinct methods – either as a result of the deliberate attempt of a group to solve some perceived problem or as a result of forced subordination during especially intense contact between two societies. Despite this awareness, we rarely acknowledge that, in addition to the expected changes, unintended consequences often accompany these two methods. In stratified systems, the model for change is influenced and constructed by the ideology of the dominant society. This is largely the result of its control over the necessary resources and the means of production – both economic and cultural. The dominant society constructs the major institutions, such as churches, schools, and newspapers. These institutions in turn legitimate the position of the dominant society. They enforce and maintain changes made through political and social repression. Even in a "democratic" society such as the United States, citizens who occupy the lower rungs of the economic, political, and social ladders do not have, or at the very least, do not perceive that they have power to institute change. They are limited by the hegemonic structure that makes the rules, elects or chooses representatives who pass laws that serve its interests, and encourages the ruled masses to believe social stratification is natural. Seldom are those members who occupy the lower rungs of the stratification ladder consulted, nor are they a part of any discussion of the structural production of that society. This has been the fate of colonized people, including African Americans. The ability to institute change from this position in society is severely limited, which is why African Americans have used a myriad of methods in order to try to chip away at the structure that has oppressed them as a people for more than three hundred years.

A key interest of mine in the study of social movements is an understanding of the means through which oppressed people can institute or resist social change.[1] The contributions that are offered by Scott (1985) from his work on Southeast Asia and de Certeau (1984) on France are key to an understanding of the ways in which "the weak make use of the strong." We know that in the past African Americans were unable to take advantage of traditional methods of instituting change in this society and used many of the methods Scott and others describe to gain some relief from their oppression. The stories about the young pool player and the check-cashing incident, and even the underground economy stories told about The Hole and The Yard, can be viewed as methods for bringing about change.[2] However, the question becomes: What morally appropriate methods of instituting social change are available to African Americans in contemporary society, particularly in the South, and how are these processes played out?

This chapter examines one form of social change – the deliberate attempt of people, specifically grassroots or peasant societies, to solve their perceived problems by effecting change. A number of theories address ways in which people become social actors and institute change; however, theories on the operation of the public sphere provide a base from which to examine how structural changes are brought about in Oxford. We are able to observe from the data the way in which the particular

---

[1] James C. Scott in *Weapons of the Weak* (1985), Eric R. Wolf in *Europe and the People Without History* (1982), Michel de Certeau in *The Practice of Everyday Life* (1984), and Brackette F. Williams in *Stains On My Name, War in My Veins* (1991) investigate the means through which oppressed people are able to institute or resist social change.

[2] It is noted that among scholars such acts are contested as being acts of resistance. However, because institutions, laws, and practices are put into place to counter underground economy venues and the activity of that economy raises the economic status of a number of people, I suggest here that such acts are also "weapons of the weak." Also, from the point of view of those involved in the acts, they see themselves as initiating change and balancing power.

spatial circumstances of Oxford/Lafayette County make the use of public opinion to institute change problematic.[3]

Theories on the operation of the public sphere are particularly important given earlier and more radical ones regarding the conditions under which change is instituted under social and/or political repression.[4] Habermas, in contradiction to Marx's and Engels's theory of *violent* revolution, states that the public sphere (developed during the eighteenth century) was, at its inception, a forum in which private persons could conduct rational debate that would result in solutions to problems that served the public good.

Habermas's (1994) work on the public sphere has become significant for contemporary anthropological theory as we work to define what we mean by "the public" and as we interpret its role as a social category. So, what is the public sphere? Generally defined, it is an arena in which issues that are of concern to the public are rationally debated and social changes are implemented. Habermas describes the character of the public sphere as being constituted by private people putting reason to use. Put simply, it is the use of public opinion to make changes in society. For democratic societies, it encompasses the world of politics but also operates outside formal institutions. Eighteenth-century ideology, according to Harbermas, suggested there should exist a difference between affairs that private persons pursued individually – each in the interests of the reproduction of his or her own life – and the interaction that *united* private people into a public. This interaction during that period was based on the world of letters. It was in the salons, clubs, and reading societies that private people expressed their double roles as bourgeois and human (Habermas 1994:160).[5]

Habermas suggests that it was believed to be possible to resolve problems regarding the public good in this sphere. Of course, this sphere was composed of a specific socioeconomic group that garnered sufficient leisure time to pursue public interests, and one that was literate enough to be able to produce rational and informed discussion. In his description of

---

[3] I have chosen this process – the use of the public sphere – because of its significance in the Civil Rights Movement. A discussion of that use was presented in an invited paper I delivered at the University of Mississippi's Department of Southern Studies 1994 Sesquicentennial Celebration (Thomas-Houston 1999).

[4] See Farganis (1993) for discussions of theories of change ranging from the classic tradition to the post-modern era.

[5] See Richard Sennett's (1995) *The Fall of Public Man* for his version of what has happened since this period.

the transformation, however, Habermas idealizes the eighteenth-century public sphere as actually functioning for the good of the entire public, a critical point raised in the 1990s by many contemporary theorists.[6]

The question of how such notions of the common good reflected actual problems of the general public during the eighteenth century is also salient for our understanding of that which is deemed "the common good" in today's societies. Habermas's reference to the transformation of the public sphere illustrates that members of the public who occupy the lower socioeconomic stratum do not have and, I add, never had public outlets for the issues they deemed pertinent to *their* good, particularly if those issues in any way threatened the balance of power. I suggest that, historically, African Americans have recognized this predicament as far back as slavery and, as such, after freedom instituted "counterpublics" by using church pulpits, local and national African American publications, barbershop waiting rooms, porches, and community street corners in many American communities to discuss issues important to the Black experience.[7]

From a broader view, these numerous "counterpublics" constitute a "Black public sphere" that addresses the interests of Black Americans. I believe that the seed for the constitution of a Black public sphere began with what E. Franklin Frazier (1964) calls "the invisible institution," the underground church that emerged when plantation owners did not allow religious organizations to develop openly. This is a highly significant point in the analysis of the operation of the Black public sphere in Oxford/Lafayette County.

Historically speaking, the church can be viewed as a key forum for the Black public sphere, and spirituals, as its mass media mechanisms. For example, Alkalimat et al. (1986) remind us that the "sweet chariot" that was to "swing low" referred to the underground railroad and was a way of conveying to those who wanted to escape slavery that the train would be arriving and leaving from a particular location at a particular time. The singing of various spirituals carried different messages from plantation to plantation. By stretching the imagination only slightly, we could certainly consider this form of coded communication as a forum designed to address issues important for the good of the Black public.

---

[6] See Fraser (1990), *Rethinking the Public Sphere: A Contribution to the Critique of Actually Existing Democracy*; Mann (1990), *Unifying Discourse: City College As a Post-Modern Public Sphere*; and Polan (1990), *The Public's Fear, or Media as Monster in Habermas, Negt, and Kluge*, all included in a special, 1990 issue of the journal *Public Culture*.

[7] Outside of the bush arbor meetings of the "invisible institution," these other public uses of space for discussion of problems related to the Black public are postslavery phenomena.

The invisible institution and its spirituals can be seen as an "information highway" for a people who were severely punished if found gathering in groups outside the presence of Whites. This highway also provided data with which Blacks resisted slavery. Later we will see the importance of this developed dependence on the church for communicating ideas of importance to the larger African American community and its crippling effect for social action efforts.

After slavery, the invisible institution merged with churches founded by free Blacks and led to the formation of the National Baptist Convention, USA, in 1880 as well as other independent denominations. These institutions created offshoot institutions such as schools, mutual aid societies, and sickness and burial societies. Alkalimat states: "These early efforts at capital accumulation also helped to lay the basis for church-supported businesses, newspapers, banks, and insurance companies" (1986:196).

By the early 1920s a number of Black journals and newspapers augmented discussions and debates that were topics of sermons and meetings of Black organizations. These forums coincide with what Mann refers to as "a community-based public sphere" (1990). Possibly the most famous debate – that between W. E. B. DuBois and Booker T. Washington – took place in the Black public sphere and can be seen to have grown out of the many directions (or counterpublics) Blacks were headed toward. I suggest that the varying counterpublics are the result of the numerous intimate culture groups that formed Black society then and now. On a broader base, local chapters of the Urban League, the NAACP, the Masons, and the Eastern Star constitute intimate culture groups within Black American society as do groups formed by religion, wealth, and educational status. I also suggest that the era called the Harlem Renaissance was born out of such a counterpublic.[8] However, in spite of the role this era played in bringing Black issues before a particular aspect of America's White public, most of the actions of the Black public sphere were segregated from Whites, and many of the vigorous debates that took place were *unknown* to Whites until Blacks took their ideas to the general public sphere.

There is more than ample proof that during slavery African Americans used "the invisible institution" as a base for developing counterpublics, and later, leaders of the Civil Rights Movement took advantage of both

---

[8] For the sake of brevity, I include within this era the age of "the New Negro" when Black intellectual thought became a matter of public record and motivated dialogue within White intimate culture groups and between Black and White private persons, such as DuBois's relationship with Boas.

the Black and the general public sphere of the dominant society in their quest for justice and equality. An evaluation of the Black public sphere's operation not only is beneficial for understanding one of the processes involved in a significant event in the history of African American struggles here in the United States but also will provide understanding of the value of such an option for the voiceless minorities, including African Americans, here and in other democratic and authoritarian societies.

Public opinion is a major influence in contemporary public sphere debates. While public opinion generally helps to maintain the status quo, the Civil Rights Movement provides a brilliant example of African Americans influencing public opinion and as such bringing about changes in social environments and political structures without the oppressed rising up in violent revolution.

In the plantation South, the old system's organizational structure created separate pockets of slave communities or neighborhoods – as the old slave quarter might now be called. This structure aided the agenda of plantation society because it spatially limited significant numbers of Blacks from meeting and hence organizing. Without those rare opportunities when slaves were able to steal away to meet, communication in the form of public debate with the larger slave community would have been nonexistent. Therefore, as previously suggested, the invisible institution played a major role in providing a Black public space for rational debate and organized communication among the slaves.

In Oxford/Lafayette County, the church, as we have seen, continues to be the key instrument through which information is passed between neighborhoods on a regular basis. One of the principal reasons for relying on this venue is that no newspaper publishes issues that affect the African American community from the Black perspective. The local radio stations also do not carry programming that addresses these issues, although, as in the local newspaper, announcements of events and meetings are provided as a public service. However, access and actual readership and listenership limit the effect of these announcements. In terms of programming, the radio stations in Oxford cater to the predominantly White student body of the university campus. The university's television station consists mostly of programs that are produced and directed by students about campus issues or issues important to the university community. On rare occasions, a story may highlight "local color." These stories never address counterpublic issues. The local newspaper, like most instruments of the dominant society's general public sphere, rarely addresses concerns of the local Black community. The paper itself serves more as a society page, devoting a considerable amount of space to weddings and engagements, deaths and burials, and awards and honors.

What then are the avenues of communication among African Americans in Lafayette County? The main ones are the churches and a Black-oriented monthly (*Soul Force*), which was established during the early 1970s by one of the community organizers mentioned in Chapter 2. This monthly, a project of the development association, has generally served also as a "Black society page" and has from time to time in more recent years begun to address issues for the good of the Black public. A more interesting occurrence is that the publication has begun to include varying controversial ideological perspectives on the same issues, thus constituting itself as a forum for debate on the Black public good.[9] However, this publication is published only monthly, and because of this and the limited staff – a husband and wife – much of the information is reported after the fact. However, they make a substantial effort to present a calendar of events. Given the lack of other media, the traditional methods for communicating, such as word of mouth and announcements made in church, bear a tremendous burden trying to overcome this problem.

Churches are the primary source of communication because these facilities are places where significant numbers of African Americans come together at least twice a week (for Sunday services and Wednesday prayer meetings). The dependence on the church for communicating ideas of importance to the larger African American community has had a crippling effect on recent social action efforts in Lafayette County. These religious gatherings are not used as forums for debate of secular issues; however, because the order of service at these gatherings includes announcements, those who attend are kept somewhat abreast of other meetings that are designed to address more secular concerns. Announcements of regular monthly meetings of such organizations as the NAACP, ODA, and the Sewing and Savings Club and specially called meetings are accommodated at these gatherings.

Using this forum as the primary instrument for communication presents a number of problems; however, the most central obstacle is that this method includes only certain intimate culture groups of the Oxford/Lafayette County African American population – those who are

---

[9] The debates are generally included in the column "Hull's View." James Hull's commentaries have carried such titles as "Assaults On Affirmative Action Are Hypocritical, Unjustified" (April 1995) and "Louis Farrakhan, Patrick Buchanan Have Something Other Public Figures Do Not Have" (April 1996).

churchgoers. Additional problems are created by the structure of church scheduling in the community. The earlier descriptions of religious institutions in the community revealed that only a handful of churches meet every Sunday in a month; most meet bimonthly. This scheduling eliminates a considerable number of people from a gathering every other Sunday, although a good number visit other churches that meet when theirs do not.

Another problem concerns the method of distributing announcements to churches. Most churches are located in the county and do not have addresses. If an organization or individual has an announcement, it must be hand delivered to either the individual who makes the announcements or to a responsible member of each of the churches. Under the best of circumstances, this is a tremendous accomplishment. In addition to the difficulties of travel (to which the spatial layout of the county contributes), announcements get misplaced, are forgotten by children who accept them for their parents, and are blown away after being left at the door. Any changes in the content of these announcements after they have been delivered depend upon word of mouth and, as such, are subject to misinformation. During many Sunday services, I observed announcements being made from the floor by one member of an organization or club that was unable to get a typed announcement or revision delivered, and then another member of that same organization would make a correction in the time, day, or location. I have also observed such contradictions left unresolved, leaving the responsibility for getting the correct information up to the listeners, who must contact other members for clarification. Usually this type of confusion results in extremely low turnout at secular meetings. These observations reveal that although the contemporary church continues to serve as a major space for the dissemination of information to the Black community, its operational structure and dependability seriously compromise the Black community's organizational efforts.

This spatialized structuring of the larger Oxford/Lafayette County African American community has had an impact on the development and operation of the Black public sphere. In order for a public sphere to develop, a consistent group of concerned citizens must regularly come together to discuss their concerns. (The question of the use of technology rather than face-to-face communication as possible outlets for the operation of public concerns will be discussed later in this chapter.) The Black community of Oxford/Lafayette County does indeed have regularly scheduled public meetings. But the problem with the formation of the Black public sphere is the inconsistency of its membership.

Starting with the churches where the announcements of the secular-oriented meetings are publicized, the system of gathering is such that a consistently significant number of people do not meet. Some Sundays, churches are full, and on others only a handful attend. I am reminded of one church in particular. This church, which is located in the county, meets, like most, every other Sunday. On the first Sunday of the month when they meet, the youth choir sings, and the church is fairly full. However, on the third Sunday of the month, the senior choir sings, and the congregation is small. Speculation among members is that this is the result of the senior choir's less enthusiastic singing. On one senior choir Sunday, only one member was seated in the congregation; therefore the choir, consisting of seven people, had to march down and be seated in the pews in order for the minister to have an audience.[10] If an announcement of a meeting is delivered on a Sunday when only a handful of members attend, the value of the church as a forum for communicating information is severely limited.

A number of other issues are also connected to the use of space. The most problematic for the development of a representative body of residents of which the public sphere is composed is the fact that most meetings are held in churches. There are a number of potentially active concerned citizens who do not attend church and who do not wish to be subjected to the religious aspects of organizational meetings that occur in church or are conducted by ministers. Other Black-owned public facilities, such as a civic club building and "juke joints" have dubious reputations and therefore are deemed inappropriate for meetings.

As mentioned previously, with the exception of the churches located within the city limits, most of the churches in Lafayette County are community-based institutions. This means that they are actually located in or on the border of an enclave and therefore serve members of that neighborhood and their families. Several use-of-space problems are connected with this phenomenon. Meetings held in county churches are often considered too far away for members who do not live in that particular area and therefore attendance is limited (see Maps, *http://formypeopleprods.info* for location of churches in the county and town). Quite often meetings are not scheduled at those churches again. Some church members, offended because meetings are not held in their church, either drop their

---

[10] Ministers of the churches in Oxford/Lafayette County are salaried and thus not dependent upon the offering for the day. This is in no way considered a message to the minister, but it does present a problem for intraracial communication.

membership in the organization or, at the least, maintain membership but stop attending meetings. "Let them...do what they want to, I ain't got time to be bothered with their foolishness" is a typical response to this perceived act of alienation.

Another issue related to use of space is connected to the factionalism that exists among churches. Some members of organizations do not attend meetings scheduled at different churches because they don't like a particular church's minister or the perceived attitudes of its congregation.

The limitations of the African Americans' communication system severely hamper the ability to form a fully operational Black public sphere. What then is the structure and operation of Oxford/Lafayette County's Black public life? Approximately ten people from the community consistently meet to discuss community issues and problems. Unfortunately, these same people are members of most of the community organizations in addition to their commitment to church groups. They are the most socially conscious residents of the community. This is not to be confused with being the most highly educated because this core group of residents is approximately evenly divided between college, high school, and non-high school graduates. The larger body of members fluctuates around this core.

Even with these limitations, good ideas and sparks of good ideas related to the common good are generated. However, difficulty occurs in a number of ways in the effort to put these ideas into practice. More often than not, the president of one organization is the vice president of another organization. The secretaries and treasurers of a number of organizations are the same. Committee chairs for one organization end up being committee chairs for another. Burnout is a perpetual hazard for the operation of organizations that attempt to address public concerns. When "new blood" joins the core, they are quickly swept up and given leadership responsibilities often against their own desires and occasionally even counter to their actual capabilities. This practice often prevents the introduction of new ideas or plans because the person who introduces an idea generally gets assigned the responsibility of carrying it out.[11] I have observed this process in action at a number of meetings. Quite often, the individual, particularly if he or she is attending for the first time, is frightened off and never returns. Two of my informants, fairly high-level university employees, who attempted to become involved in community activities and were immediately swept into the top levels of the organization,

[11] The introduction of migrated new blood is more problematic because their actions are usually suspect until proven otherwise.

never returned because they felt that too many assumptions had been made about how they should fit in. Their intention was to attend meetings for a while and find out where they thought they could best be of service as well as if this was an organization with which they wanted to be associated. Thus, members and former members of organizations often create and discuss ideas in private spaces that could be of benefit to the common good, but the ideas are never implemented because they are introduced in an environment not designed to carry them out. Frequently, good ideas are dropped because potential members fear that they will be asked to lead the effort to carry out the idea.

Black activism in Oxford/Lafayette County, because of poor communication networks complicated by spatial dispersion, limits on the use of space, and the perpetually changing body of residents who attend community organization meetings, regularly starts with a bang and ends with a fizzle. This is why such organizations as the NAACP periodically become defunct, which was the state of the local chapter for about a six-month period in 1996 in spite of the tremendous efforts the organization put forth and its accomplishments in the 1995 election.[12] Burnout, character assassination, and poor communication have contributed once again to the slowing down of the association's momentum.

The question of the use of technology rather than face-to-face communication as a possible outlet for the operation of public concerns is an issue of theoretical debate. Habermas sees mass media outlets such as newspapers and television as being corrupted by consumerism and therefore problematic for rational discussion. A recent perusal of the Internet revealed that although Web sites are supporting free speech, some of them also are using that freedom to suppress the speech of others. For example, WOTAN, a site sponsored by the Aryan Nation, has a page for training interested people in methods of hacking Web sites.[13] In other words, (WOTAN) exercises its free speech rights in order to teach would-be hackers how to prevent others from exercising their rights. Unlike the public sphere envisioned by Habermas, the Internet can be used to suppress debate because of its anonymity and the ease with which one may exclude the opinions and voices of those with whom they disagree.

---

[12] The president of the NAACP resigned unexpectedly from all of his community positions including his assistant pastor's position. Since that time, he has been unavailable for discussion of his reason. However, as has been noted in previous chapters, a cloud of gossip hovers over the resignation. A recent visit to Oxford in 2004 revealed that the NAACP local chapter is again inactive.

[13] WOTAN is an acronym for will of the Aryan Nation.

Other problems with the use of technology as a substitute for face-to-face communication are economically and culturally based. Few Blacks in Oxford/Lafayette County are able to afford outlets other than television and the telephone. So not only is the Internet suspect as a public sphere arena to begin with in the United States, but it is also, to a large extent, unavailable to the underclass in U.S. society, thus reinforcing its role as a support network of the status quo.

During the Civil Rights Movement, commercial television and radio in Mississippi often used censorship in the form of blackouts and technical difficulties to prevent residents outside the area of a demonstration from knowing about it. The use of television as entertainment also limits its authority as a voice of the people. Another phenomenon that is spatially oriented in terms of its regionality is the preponderance of religious-oriented shows aired in the South, particularly Mississippi. The main focus of many of the shows is the individual, not the community. Although a show may be dedicated to addressing economics, the primary emphasis is on what the individual must do to be "blessed" in that manner. However, the majority of the shows focus on preparation for the afterlife. This otherworldly theme addresses the behavior of the individual not the behavior of the society and how that society treats the individual. Even when such issues as abortion rights are discussed, community involvement is not a topic of discussion. Finally, most television shows that address issues related to the good of the Black public are televised on Sunday – usually Sunday morning when a major portion of Oxford/Lafayette County's activist Black public is in church.

What does all this mean for social change? Without the ability to construct a forum through which issues of the common good can be discussed and solutions to those issues implemented, social change in Oxford/Lafayette County stands to be constructed more by accident and force than by the deliberate attempt of a people to solve their perceived problems.

Conclusion

African Americans struggle among themselves for the limited resources allocated to them under the systemic stratification of American society. As a result of these daily struggles, intraethnic interaction is negotiated on an event-by-event basis using varying cultural markers to control the level and effectiveness of that interaction. More often than not, this power-oriented process, a consequence of being on the lower end of American capitalism, not only perpetuates individualism and fragmentation but also contributes to varying forms of intraethnic division that support the hegemonic structure of the larger society.

The structure of African American society, however, does not require group homogeneity to operate as a unit. In times of need, varying segments of the larger group concerned with a specific issue will come together and form a social action unit. The degree to which they are successful depends not only upon the magnitude of cultural coherence but also upon the level of resistance exerted by elements of society responsible for producing and reproducing the social process or institution they are seeking to change.[1] As for those who do not participate, I am reminded of a title from one of the first contemporary Black Broadway musicals (written, produced, and directed by African Americans), which pleads, "Don't Bother Me I Can't Cope." One segment of nonparticipants perceives the specific goal of change as beyond their place and often envisions themselves as powerless against the larger society. Other nonparticipants are often caught up in the immediate needs of subsistence or personal advancement and

---

[1] The most recent election in Oxford/Lafayette County is a prime example.

neither envision themselves as part of a larger unit nor see their individual concerns as part of a larger problem.

The shared experiences of struggle among Oxford's Black residents, in the past, helped to construct institutions and ways of being that connected intimate culture groups into larger more interdependent social groups. These groups shared established mutual aid societies, created gardens, took turns babysitting, provided transportation for those without it, and in general extended the realm of family far beyond the borders of blood. The incident regarding the movement of the sales of drugs to intimate culture areas occupied by TIM's children in Chapter 5 is strong evidence that these practices are waning. West (1996) suggests that a market culture creates a market morality that produces a market mentality of "I want...now." He emphasizes that nonmarket values such as love, care, and concern are pushed to the periphery and produce spiritual impoverishment. Members of Oxford/Lafayette County's African American community show, at times, characteristics of this spiritual impoverishment as they struggle among themselves for prestige and power. In spite of their peripheralization by the dominant society (which in theory should foster a form of cultural coherence), a particular market mentality, developing among some of Oxford's Black young adults and university-based intellectuals, is replacing the community concern and the "nonmarket values" that existed in earlier periods. This market mentality produces individualism, which justifies the further alienating intragroup process of placing. Although I did not find evidence of the actual formation of an intimate culture group shaped by this market-driven ideology, some are likely to develop as the numbers of this generation increase. (The few Black faculty members of the university are less likely to form a cohesive group that will have an impact on the culture of social relations of Oxford's native Black population.)

In Chapter 2, MDJ (who migrated to Oxford/Lafayette County in the early 1970s) provides an understanding of the role individual economic status plays among the Black middle class and Black professionals. His story clarifies how individualism and fragmentation directly support hegemony. MDJ's observations – that the Black elites' efforts to subvert social action aids the organizational instability of the local NAACP – support West's theory on how nonmarket values come to be pushed aside. The social cohesion necessary for social movements becomes increasingly difficult as the individualism driven by market mentalities is sustained among privileged Blacks. Because insider/outsider and old leader/new leader tensions are interconnected with the culture of interethnic interaction such as patronage and prestige, the enthusiasm for action often dissipates among members of the NAACP, the only organization that has been reasonably successful at mobilizing large numbers of people from the Black community in Lafayette County. The inaction caused by the individualism and fragmentation not only helps to maintain the status quo but allows the development of new processes and structures that contribute further to economic and social disparities in Oxford/Lafayette County such as the inappropriate use of block grant funds and neglect of services to Black communities.

Religion within the African American community also enables the hegemonic structure's division and stratification of the population. For example, recreational activities are limited both in affordability and availability. African Americans in Oxford have limited funds for these activities, and competition for those scarce funds can be described as a struggle between the sacred and the secular. Persons who spend their recreational time and money in church-sponsored activities garner more credibility within the larger African American community than those who do not.[2] As a result, ideas, projects, or suggestions that come from members of the community who are perceived as being more secularized bear little weight and receive little support, regardless of the potential benefits for the larger community. This is one of the problematic results of placing. Identifying African American people in Oxford/Lafayette County as a "religious" people often overrides other criteria for membership in the ethnic group, such as a shared history of oppression and efforts to improve conditions in the region for the group. This is particularly important since one's church membership or association is the first criteria of placing used in the construction of the identity of a newcomer.

Individualism and fragmentation contribute to the development of processes within the African American community that also indirectly support the hegemonic structure. The position of pastor in the region carries prestige and power in both White and Black communities of Oxford/Lafayette County, and in spite of the economic difficulties incurred in choosing that vocation, schoolteachers, factory workers, manual laborers, housewives, and people of all ages attend local seminary classes with the hope of being ordained. As a result, there is intense competition

---

[2] Whites are obviously aware of the role of church affiliation as validation for representation and recommendations in Black communities. This knowledge is revealed by the appointment of ministers and deacons to community boards and other civic organizations and by the use of a minister to represent a White candidate at Black events.

among preachers for assistant pastorships and competition among churches regarding which pastor carries the most prestige.[3] The competitive aspect of Oxford/Lafayette County's religious intimate culture groups often influences cooperation among congregations and support of sponsored events on the church level and character assassination on an individual level. This severely limits the development of coherence between leadership and intimate culture groups.

Ministers who initiate programs or activities are often attacked by members of their own congregations who compete for power in the area of decision making for the church and by community people (including other ministers) who compete on a broader scale for prestige in the community in one of three ways. These attacks take the form of (1) up-front rejection of ideas, (2) uncooperativeness in the form of foot dragging, and (3) spreading gossip that is indefensible.

However problematic the church's influence is on the culture of social relations, it remains the primary source for the development of Black leadership in Oxford/Lafayette County. The buildings themselves continue to provide centralized locations for the exchange of ideas among members of that community. Church organizations recognize the talents and contributions of individuals who ordinarily go unrecognized by the dominant society. The spiritual comfort the church provides holds the community together by remaining a stabilizing force for the emotional and psychological needs of this marginalized group of African Americans.

DuBois's (1903) "dual consciousness" theory helps explain issues of identity maintenance and structure of Oxford/Lafayette County's Black community from a number of perspectives. An individual's value to this specific region's Black ethnic group is directly related to how much his or her behavior reflects a White worldview or a Black one. The perceived degree of Blackness or Whiteness of an individual affects interaction with that person because it influences the degree to which the community gives or withholds support. This has important implications for elections on every level.[4] It also affects the level on which an individual chooses to interact with the dominant society. In addition, each level of interaction differs according to an individual's degree of Blackness/Whiteness. Interaction between Blacks and Whites is generally spoken of in vague terms

---

[3] Unlike the internal struggles of Smith's Peruvian community, where the arguments between strata contribute to the construction "not just of notions of 'leadership' but also of what is to be fought over and possibly killed for" (1991:182).

[4] This helps to explain the support Blacks gave Bill Clinton on a national basis and the lack of strong support for the Black running in the local sheriff's election.

when the conversation relates to a third party whose acceptance or lack thereof by the dominant society is the result of an unknown degree of Blackness/Whiteness. If, however, the reason for acceptance is presumptively known, the conversation usually follows the line of perception of the dominant society in spite of that individual's standing within the Black community. From an intragroup perspective, the degree of an individual's Blackness/Whiteness determines the internal group support or lack thereof. In addition, it continues to define the parameters of Blackness on an event-by-event basis. In events of interethnic public sphere interaction, the degree of an individual member's Blackness/Whiteness never becomes an issue even if, in the Black public sphere, that individual's allegiance to the ethnic group is seriously in question.

We must understand that the election of the Black officials discussed in Chapter 4 was not simply an effort to elect Black officials. It was a concerted effort to establish a cohesive front. Support for the candidates of the Black race was more of a strategy to convince members of the White race that all is well among Blacks as an ethnic group than it was a strategic plan to position Blacks in key political areas that could benefit that community.[5] A brilliant example of this was the conflict that existed within the Black community over the African American who was running for office on the Republican ticket because it indicated that Blacks in the area were divided along ideological party lines. This is a tremendous infraction of the parameters of Blackness in the local African American community, which only discusses the Democratic primary. The perception by the dominant society of a unified Black community is valued by the Black community as a whole, in spite of internal allegations of "our people just *won't* [their emphasis] stick together." This valued component of the outward image of the ethnic group is articulated often in the Black public spheres constituted in all intimate culture groups.

How do the preceding explanations clarify the problems of political participation among Oxford/Lafayette County's African American population? The politics of stratification is such that diversity among African Americans constructs various intimate culture publics. These intimate culture groups produce distrust among members of the community who historically share a particular patriarchal level of interaction with members of the dominant society. The distrust produces either additional stratification or envy within the culture of social relations of intraethnic

---

[5] An intragroup statement was made as well by family members who rallied around blood and marital connections.

interaction. This envy often forms as a result of the appropriation of symbols and behavior that are historically and traditionally viewed as aspects of the dominant society.

Jim Crow practices of segregation also have had a spatial impact beyond the use of public facilities. Oxford/Lafayette County's particular form of de facto residential segregation plays a tremendous role in obstructing the development of a collective and conscious social movement among African American residents in several ways. The numerous cul de sacs in Oxford/Lafayette County form neighborhoods that physically separate Blacks from each other. This spatial isolation is a remnant of plantation life and the limited access to property during the Reconstruction period. Notwithstanding that physical influence, consisting of more than fifteen enclaves of Blacks from various socioeconomic and intimate culture backgrounds, there exists a psychological spatial distancing in terms of one's perceived place within the larger society that generates different ideological understandings.

These differences at the level of practice constitute variation in behavior. The variations range from the kinds of food one eats and the way one talks and dresses to the people one associates with and the reason for one's association with members of White society – all contributing to a determination of one's degree of Blackness. For example, the Black pool player in Chapter 5 who associates with youths from the White community on a regular basis carries a great amount of prestige among his peers. Beating the man or getting over becomes a valuable asset for those members of the African American community whose economic, educational, family, or religious standing is not viewed as traditional grounds for interethnic interaction. In other words, the action of simply associating with Whites does not constitute trying to be White. The culture of those social relations determines the degree to which that individual has sacrificed some of his or her standing within the ethnic group. Expressing a preference for White company over Black with no material benefits is cause for group alienation. Distancing oneself from the material and social world of Whites for the establishment of closeness to the Black world validates an individual's card-carrying membership.

Group membership and identity are constructed by shared historical, spatial, social, and ideological circumstances. Because of the element of difference often referred to as the race of African Americans, some social scientists and often African Americans themselves conceive of themselves as one ethnic group. I suggest that the ethnic group of a people who were forced immigrants leans heavily upon *specific* shared experiences; domination, oppression, and even slavery are not sufficient for establishing ethnic attachments. These experiences of colonization manifest themselves in numerous forms; therefore, the varying degrees and combinations impact the colonized differently. For example, the plantation system of Mississippi cotton planters differs greatly from that of the tobacco growers of Virginia, just as the system in the Mississippi Delta differs from that of Oxford/Lafayette County. When these differences are combined with others such as national origin of the planter, religious orientation, and individual planter perceptions of the humanity of the forced immigrants, it becomes clearer why one needs to understand the more common day-to-day lived experiences as they shape the generally shared experiences of domination, oppression, and even slavery to form ethnic identities among Blacks. This most often can be viewed in the conflicting ideologies of Black West Indians and Black Americans born in the United States and those differences that exist among peoples of the Caribbean.[6] All are the sons and daughters of former slaves, but their experiences in terms of the culture of social relations with the dominant society have shaped different worldviews and understandings of place within those societies. Each region can be divided into smaller regions, and intimate culture groups consist of members who belong to other intimate culture groups. Therefore, the social construct of ethnic identity should be treated as cultural and political phenomena that change according to the needs and intents of the defining parties. In other words, the individual who is considered Black today by both Blacks and Whites may not be considered Black tomorrow; and vice versa.

How does this situational group identity affect political participation? Many who aspire to the attainment of equal rights consider voting to be the end-all.[7] Although participation in the Civil Rights Movement demonstrations by Black Oxonians was for all practical purposes nonexistent, after the Voting Rights Act of 1965 there was a significant increase in the number of African Americans in this area who first became registered voters and then actually voted. Those who voted represented a high percentage of the registered voters. In recent years, the fervor of a movement that never quite caught fire in Oxford has cooled, and there is an increasing withdrawal from publicly asserting one's rights as a citizen – particularly the right to vote. The 1995 election in Oxford is an exception.

---

[6] See Sutton (1987) for an understanding of diversity among peoples from the Caribbean.

[7] On a national scale, an emphasis on voter registration became the primary thrust of the Civil Rights Movement.

The statistical evidence of voting practices by African Americans in Oxford/Lafayette County reveals a decrease in the number of voters participating in both local and national elections. The 1995 election, which for the first time in the history of the community provided opportunities for a significant number of African Americans to be elected to public office, showed that other African Americans often looked upon those candidates with suspicion and mistrust, much of which was based on negative perceptions of the relationship of the candidates to locally prescribed definitions of Blackness.

In situations of public policy or elections where issues can clearly be defined in racial conflict terms, African Americans are more inclined to operate as a unit. However, when issues are not easily defined along racial lines and cannot be couched in terms that inspire us against them dialogue within the Black community (although the consequences have a significant impact on the Black community), interest in the political process generally wanes. When such an issue arises, the differing worldviews structured by specific histories of shared experiences and intimate culture memberships influence intragroup interaction and fragment the community. This segmentation of the Black community presents tremendous problems for mobilization around nonracialized issues.

Developing strategies for offsetting such problems of mobilization are primary concerns facing Black leadership in Oxford/Lafayette County. The various combinations of shared experiences that shape the worldviews of the community's African American population are extremely complex. This complexity complicates efforts to educate the groups so that they associate the interconnectedness of political processes, economic structures, and public policy with their own personal social, economic, educational, and quality-of-life experiences. Making these social connections is further hampered by African Americans' own perceptions of the relationship of life chances and lifestyle to Blackness or Whiteness. According to Cornell West, the crisis of Black leadership "is a matter of grasping the structural and institutional processes that have disfigured, deformed, and devastated Black America such that the resources for nurturing collective and critical consciousness, moral commitment, and courageous engagement are vastly underdeveloped" (1994:69).

The underdevelopment of a collective and critical consciousness is evident in the state of the Black public sphere in Oxford/Lafayette County. The Black public sphere is virtually nonexistent as a tool for raising the level of social consciousness among the African American community and for instituting social action. A complicated pattern of alienation divides the community along ideological, intellectual, and spatial lines preventing mobilization for "the good" of the Black public. Although having the type of grasp on the situation that West calls for is important to an intellectual understanding of the underdevelopment of social consciousness, the ways in which structural and institutional processes *within* Black America influence intraethnic and intraracial interaction are important to understanding the situation at the level of practice. As pointed out in the description of the African American intelligentsia, for the most part and with the passing of time, they have become increasingly less involved with the grassroots population, and today fewer than a handful enter into coalition with that population. Those who do eventually drop out of coalitions for two reasons: (1) They are overburdened by organizational leadership tasks because there are too few participants for the enormous size and number of organizational needs, or (2) they are forced out by those members whose personal agenda is not group oriented but individually driven in the larger scheme of competition for prestige and power.

Attempts at leadership by members of the community illustrate the two problems mentioned here as well as other problems unique to that particular social position. If individuals who are not natives are willing to try their hand at leadership within the community, they face a constant battle for validation. Their commitment to service, education, past experience, or common background are insufficient for eliminating suspicion, mistrust, and outright subversive activity in the majority of cases. Thirty years of residence are not sufficient for eliminating insider/outsider divisions. Natives who attempt leadership also encounter suspicion, mistrust, and subversive action but never to a degree equal to that of the outsider. For example, LT, the native who interacts with the larger community in a number of ways, is a member of the board of several of the larger society organizations. He is admired for his ranking within that larger society but is also regarded with suspicion as to his motives whenever he attempts to introduce social plans within the community. However, the community preferred having him as the president of one of the political organizations to the current president who is from another area of the state. As one of the would-be outsider leaders remarked, they questioned the outsider's right to come to their town and tell them how to run things. I strongly suspect that the organization's current president, being an outsider, would not hold that position had it not been for his position as minister and his willingness to do a great deal of the work needed himself.

Local perceptions of self explain the Black community's past and present responses to mobilization. Definitions of self acted as a double-edged sword for participation both in the 1960s Civil Rights Movement and in present-day enjoyment of its benefits or assertion of one's rights. The value applied to specific goals of the movement, which include the decision to participate or not, was directly related to local definitions of self and ideas of place that are influenced by individual and local intimate culture experiences. The traditional behavior associated with the intimate culture of an individual's experiences, including stories associated with those experiences, greatly influences the value placed on premovement, movement, and postmovement activities.

If Black leadership is to be successful in mobilizing African Americans around particular social issues, Black leaders must recognize and appeal to what Cohen refers to as "the discreteness of *local* experience" (1982). These local experiences are most significant where communities see themselves as peripheral or marginal; therefore, connections between the specificity of their own personal experience and the goals of mobilization must be clarified. This connectedness on the level of experience rather than racial identity provides an opportunity for the creation of a sense of "belonging," and for the development of trust, and for delegitimizing perceptions of intragroup peripherality. Theoretically, this sense of belonging should produce the needed coherence to institute social action.

A major part of mobilization is compatibility of ideology. As is evidenced in the lack of a liberation theology within the intimate culture of local Oxford/Lafayette County religion, the political (read as secular) interest of the more aggressive, self-empowering NAACP creates conflict for those community residents who are members of both intimate cultures. This conflict is also compounded by educational levels, which in this particular instance are conflated with an ideology associated with the dominant society.

The effort to organize around issues of a nonreligious nature creates a breakdown within the Oxford African American community that produces a relatively incoherent space similar to Lomnitz-Adler's "space of mestizaje" (1991:209).[8] In a sense, in Oxford, two poles are created, the

---

[8] The structure and process of mestizaje address the phenomenon that occurs in Oxford/Lafayette County when leadership attempts to organize around political issues that cannot be directly connected to religious understandings. The term "the space of mestizaje" itself is problematic only in its language specificity. However, at the time of this writing, there appears to be no existing terminology related to the African American experience that parallels the term "mestizaje" as used by Lomnitz-Adler.

culture of the dominant society (which is the category most political activities fall into) and the cultures of the various, primarily religious, intimate culture groups of African Americans that are separated from the larger group. The institutions or leaders or any of the members of the intimate culture groups who attempt to organize efforts around nonreligious issues fall into the incoherent space between the two poles. They are separated from the African American cultural group because the issue is nonreligious and from the dominant society because the issue focuses on the interest of the African American community. This process, of course, is devastating for political action among Oxford/Lafayette County African Americans because the organizers/leaders of nonreligious movements are symbolically extracted from their cultures of origin without being assimilated into the dominant society. Therefore, they lack power to generate a sufficient committed following and are not able to reproduce themselves culturally. The dominant society often takes advantage of this state of incoherence by exacting negative sanctions on those members who occupy the space between the poles. The ridicule and firing of the Ayers case attorney is an excellent example of leaders who occupy this space.

Lafayette County's African American community believes that the rights the Civil Rights Movement promotes are the rights of all human beings. These rights coincide with what the community equates with Christian values, but this coincidence creates ambivalence in responses among most of the community's population. On the one hand, through lived experiences they observe inequities, abuses, and repression by the dominant society and recognize that the action of the movement is designed to remedy those social (read as sinful) wrongs. Yet, on the other hand, divine intervention is perceived as the only real solution to the problems; therefore, prayer becomes the work in which the community should involve itself. If those stones that have been placed in their way are not removed, an analysis of the problem renders the conclusion that the community needs to be "getting closer" to God, that their prayers will not be answered if they are not "right" with the Almighty.

This becomes a double-edged sword when the leaders of the social movement are the leadership of the church as well. Perceptions of being consumed with earthly matters present leadership problems for them both inside and outside the realm of religion. They are perceived as having self-aggrandizing motives and are often categorized along with other members of the population as "trying to be White."

What this latter conclusion says about the goals of the movement and localists' goals are that some goals are not deemed as having a positive meaning for the expected recipients of the benefits. Through their own experiences, they conclude that the benefits are either not a needed or desired part of their lifestyle (read as culture) or that the negative ramifications of achieving the goals outweigh the benefits. "Ideology is accepted only if the appeal to the principles in question lends meaning to the receiver's experiences" (Lomnitz-Adler 1991:206). Those activities viewed as White folks' business are viewed with skepticism and doubt based on African American understandings of the disparities in power relations. In spite of being allowed to participate, they reason that the balance of power will continue to be uneven in favor of the White society because, regardless of how much White folks give up, they have some underlying reason for the concession that continues to allow them to remain on top. Racial integration is viewed as one of those activities. Participation in the political arena is another activity viewed with skepticism. Political office is deemed as being corrupted and corrupting as are any other activities of the state. They believe that, in spite of the promises and the hopes based upon them, nothing really changes; Blacks will still get the short end of the stick.

The Civil Rights Movement attempted to appeal ideologically to the various intimate culture groups through rhetoric that emphasized the goals of overcoming shared oppression. This type of mobilization effort works, and there are many examples throughout the South and Mississippi that support the efficacy of this type of effort. *So why did the movement not have the same impact in Lafayette County?* We have observed the problems faced in practice. Theoretically, it is possible for cultures that develop independently to be brought together through the expansion of socially constructed means, which in the Civil Rights Movement's case is the creation of a single cultural region through political expansion. The single cultural region for the movement was not a specific location but a specific ideology. This ideology united, for a brief moment in African American history, the NAACP, Congress of Racial Equality (CORE), Student Non-violent Coordinating Committee (SNCC), Southern Christian Leadership Conference (SCLC), and other local-based organizations that shared the belief that African American oppression must end.[9] The presence of these larger national organizations through regional, state, and community chapters developed a culture of social relations among the numerous intimate culture groups throughout the larger national African

---

[9] In Mississippi the coalition was structured under COFO, the Council of Federated Organizations.

American community through the common elements it shared with localist ideologies. Clayborne Carson (1986) suggests that local grassroots
goals helped to shape and chart the course of the national organizations. I suggest that local community leaders, such as those described
in Chapter 2, inspired by the shared understanding and goals of the various national organizations, aligned themselves with or instituted local
branches of those national organizations for the purpose of carrying out
their specific local agendas. Therefore, rather than the mobilization being
defined as a top-to-bottom or bottom-up structure, it should be viewed
as a collaborative process.

What does the study of Oxford/Lafayette County offer to the study
of mobilization and political participation during the 1960s? This study
suggests that communities resembling Oxford/Lafayette County did not
have the goals, spatial organization, and economic integration that corre-
sponded with communities that attached themselves, collaboratively, to
various national civil rights organizations, and therefore, saw no need
to align themselves with those organizations or institute local branches.
Their specific local agendas were best carried out by traditional local methods. Those small African American communities, like Lafayette County,
point to those contested spaces between intimate culture groups and larger
regional cultures. Ideologies were not created to ease such tensions between the diverse and particular lived experiences of the smaller cultural
groups and the larger generalized bounded ethnic group. No national, regional, or state representative of any of the national organizations came
to Oxford to develop an understanding of the specific needs of that community. As a result, local leadership had no voice in the national agenda,
which very much resembled the culture of their relations to the dominant
society. The Civil Rights Movement became "their [other folks] thing."
Any efforts to bind various intimate cultures into coherent larger groups
require addressing the strongest shared experiences of each group rather
than the most common shared experience. The rallying cry of shared oppression and the need for a new integrated social structure constituted
the understanding of shared experiences and *a* perspective on the solution to the problems of that shared experience. However, an understanding of the need for a readily available replacement of the system
of patronage to which so many members of the Lafayette County Black
population were dependent was neither addressed in the solution nor
evident in the stating of shared oppression. A coherent cultural or ethnic rather than racial identity (in the eyes of Black Lafayette County)
of the intended beneficiaries of the movement was not fully developed.

As a result, they stood on the sidelines and observed as the movement passed by.

Unlike the earlier theoretical assertion that "the process of binding an intimate culture and transforming it into an 'ethnic group' contributes to the institutionalization of shared social practices within an intimate culture" (Lomnitz-Adler, 1991:207), my research suggests the contrary. Shared social practices among the various intimate culture groups of the larger African American society do not constitute the formation of an ethnic group. The data from this research suggest that the tensions between religious and social organizations prevent the institutionalization of a socially active religion. These unresolved tensions for local African Americans render the socially constructed category, race, as the only shared experience or point of reference around which they can mobilize. Therefore, Oxford/Lafayette County leadership often invokes "racial solidarity" as the common ground for coming together. However, efforts around racial solidarity are limited to actions that are deemed fairly safe or least likely to bring White backlash because of the economic vulnerability of members of this area's larger African American community. As such, mobilization energies are sapped by such projects as historical markers, museum exhibits, church homecomings, and various "appreciation" programs.

The study of African Americans of this small rural community also provides a different understanding of identity construction. As was pointed out earlier, what it means to be Black varies according to the particular histories of members of the Oxford/Lafayette County community. The only binding aspect of the description of what Blackness is becomes not Whiteness, which is as ambiguous as Blackness. This is because the definition is influenced by the particular history of the member of that community invoking the category at the moment. African American history in general, and that of Lafayette County in particular, points to the realization that even within the smallest communities, African Americans have been stratified in such ways as to constitute classes among that group of diverse people as far back as slavery. Furthermore, these classes have significance for intraethnic interaction because they influence the culture of social relations between Blacks and Whites as well as among Blacks. Given the penchant for oral narratives and storytelling within the population, the contemporary meanings applied to Whiteness are embedded in understandings informed by history, tradition, and lived experience. Therefore, any connection of Blackness to Whiteness is evaluated from those historical, traditional, and lived experience perspectives.

What does this mean in the case of practice? Various intimate culture groups among African Americans are able to mobilize around issues related to race that are clear-cut in terms of benefits for the group, as long as those benefits do not in any way constitute a base for negative reprisals. That is how the Black community of Lafayette County could rally around efforts to elect a Black sheriff and Black supervisors in spite of believing that there would be no real benefit from the move; in fact, other than occupying the space formerly held by a White, they believed that nothing would change. It is also important to point out here that a few of the African Americans who withheld their support from the Black running for office of sheriff took that position because they believed that he would be worse than the White incumbent. This perception was based on the belief that Blacks in positions of power in the dominant society often wield their power more indiscriminately than Whites for three reasons: (1) They use every opportunity to exert power because they are not accustomed to having it; (2) they feel impelled to prove to White folks that they can do a better job; and (3) they do not want to appear biased in their dealings with other Blacks. A prime example is the alderman who was first appointed and then elected. Although no benefits could be credited to his first term in office, he was perceived as not doing any harm and elected to a second term. However, during his second term, he was perceived as having established allegiance (through his voting practices) with the dominant society and inflicting harm on certain sectors of the African American community. Many discussed his removal from office and have categorized the official in a much more problematic category than acting White. He has been branded with the labels "Tom" and "Sambo." It can be concluded that the crisis of identity within the African American community, complicated by historical, economic, educational, and associational differences, interacts with varied historically influenced ideological positions to fragment this body of people as a political force. The shared experience of discrimination often leads to concerted efforts based around the socially constructed concept of racial identity; however, their momentum is short-lived.

My experiences with Oxonians suggest that some segments of the African American community are less concerned with, equipped to handle, or less desirous of change. Some of the members of this latter group are most adamant about not changing ideology. For others, it is economic dependence, material culture consumerism, or a myriad of cultural codes that construct identity; therefore, they constantly create and recreate ways of being that reinforce those positions and shun change.

That is why, for example, in the area of language, a college graduate who reads the announcements in church pronounces "usher" with an additional "r" – *ur-sher* – and why a member of a development association commented in his prayer that God wants us to be where we are. For him, the degree to which selfishness and individuality (spiritual and community conscious faux pas) are intricate parts of participating in the capitalist system (interpreted by him as greed and power) makes the desire to participate in that cultural environment sacrilegious and destructive to the moral climate of the community. As such, it is detrimental to a people whose very existence depend on extended family networks and a strong sense of community.

The Oxford/Lafayette County community has proven to be a rich source of ethnographic data for understanding the connections between tradition, identity, memory, and social action. It reveals many ways in which the meanings attached to varying levels of intraethnic interaction construct differences and fragment the African American segment of the community, thus preventing effective mobilization and concerted social action. The election of Black officials that occurred in 1995 constitutes a change in the operation of local government in Oxford/Lafayette County and African American political participation. Moreover, that change has significance for the African American community in areas other than public policy and social action in two ways: (1) For a period in time, Blacks in the community showed Whites they could pull together and, (2) Blacks were able at this specific time to "outsmart" Whites and beat them at their own game. That game, of course, is the election process itself, not the power associated with being an elected official. They have assumed that the power inherent in the elected offices will, in fact, be used against them. This is not to say that all Blacks in Oxford/Lafayette County were driven by those motives. Indeed many of the community leaders described in the section in Chapter 2 entitled, "From the Mouths of Those Who Would Be King" had hopes that the 1995 election would lead to further social action and public policy changes. However, even they had doubts based on their own particular histories.

A final lesson to be learned from the Civil Rights Movement is not about whether it was able to weave African Americans more intricately into the fabric of American society. The movement should instead be remembered for its moral stance for all Americans and its intraethnic accomplishment. The movement, made up of activists from a constellation of classes, found and stressed the shared elements of various intimate culture groups. For more than twenty years, this transclass/transideological ethnic group made up a node of regional culture that was able to influence political and social change. Those who were ready, willing, and able to participate in the change did, and those who were not did not. Perhaps this degree of involvement is what the struggle for freedom is all about – the right to choose.

However, while ethnicity and nationalism have been considered processes through which movements of social change are carried out, Oxford/ Lafayette County's African American population reveals conditions under which those processes are limited and rendered ineffective. This study has shed light on a number of contemporary social issues being addressed by anthropologists as well as other social science and humanities scholars, public policy makers, and community and national leaders. In the areas of race and ethnicity, the study provides a new way of looking at these categories. It interprets the ways in which race is constructed from within the African American community and confirms that the meanings and identities associated with that construction continue to be primary for that particular group. It distinguishes between race and ethnicity among an American-born population, a distinction usually made when people come from different places. It provides an understanding of how these analytical categories aid in clarifying issues of mobilization within African American communities and help to explain the diverse reactions not only to the Civil Rights Movement but also to the goals the movement attained. It illustrates some of the reasons segments of the larger Black community stood on the sidelines of the movement and why some continue to limit their participation in those perceived gains for the masses of Blacks. In addition, this study provides an understanding of questions related to the Black intraethnic experience that are not often asked in studies of African Americans as a group. In the area of identity construction, this study highlights and reiterates the important role history, interconnected with shared experiences, plays in the construction of a coherent ethnic identity. It also addresses the larger issue of race and the importance it continues to play in the lives of African Americans, even in intraethnic interaction. By addressing intragroup structures and processes other than those associated only with religion and family, we are able to isolate some of the origins of the different ideological perspectives that exist among African Americans. The examination of the Black public sphere in this community provides another view of the value of that arena as a space for instituting social change, an issue that anthropologists are currently debating. It also illuminates the value of a well-developed communication system for social organization, mobilization, social action, and cultural coherence and the development of a public sphere. In addition, intra-group interaction, particularly that of public culture groups, sheds light on the processes and structures within the African American community that operate as "stones in the road" of social action. Finally, the study suggests a need for further inquiry and comparative analyses in order to strengthen our understandings about the social conditions that influence social change.

Appendix A

Lafayette County Population Chart

Lafayette County Population Chart, 1840–80

	1840	1850	1860	1870	1880
Whites	3,676	8,346	8,989	10,819	11,385
Free Coloreds	13	4	7	7,983	10,286
Slaves	2,842	5,719	7,129	–	–

Source: A History of Lafayette County Mississippi and U.S. 1880 Census Report.

Appendix B

Proclamation Honoring Ole Miss Demonstrators

To All To Whom These Presents Shall Come: Greetings

Whereas, the Afro-American Studies Program at the University of Mississippi is dedicated to educational opportunity and education quality for all citizens of the State of Mississippi, and

Whereas, black students enrolled in the University of Mississippi in the Spring of 1970 proved to be equally dedicated to educational opportunity and quality education for all students at the University of Mississippi; and

Whereas, their commitment was manifested in actions to increase minority enrollment, diversify the faculty and staff and acknowledge the contributions of Blacks; and

Whereas, in the Spring 1970, black students at the University of Mississippi put forth demands for the "incorporation of Black Studies programs highlighting the contributions of Black people in the fields of literature, history, the fine arts, etc." and "the employment of Black instructors in all schools of the university"; and

Whereas, after several campus protests 97 students were arrested, 40 of whom were sent to Parchman Prison, 8 of whom were suspended from the University; and

Whereas, by the Fall Semester 1970, the Black Studies Program and courses had been approved and the first black faculty member appointed, the process of building an Afro-American Studies Program and recruitment of black faculty had begun, Therefore be it

Resolved that the University of Mississippi's Afro-American Studies Program hereby recognizes the positive contributions and sacrifices of those students in their efforts to expand educational access, opportunity, and a diversity of understanding and knowledge.

Date

James F. Payne, Director
Afro-American Studies Program

Payne dated and signed this proclamation.

Appendix C

Chancellor's Statement of Commendation

The University of Mississippi is dedicated to equal educational opportunity and a high quality of life for all of the citizens of the State of Mississippi. The current representation of African Americans within all levels of responsibility among faculty, staff, and students has reflected significant changes across time as the University continues to work toward the realization of our goals of equal opportunity. The receipt of national awards for the Minority Graduate Program acknowledges the visibility of our diversity efforts.

These achievements have been built on the foundation laid by the diligent efforts of many courageous Mississippians who have been committed to ensuring the accessibility of The University of Mississippi and other higher education institutions in our state of all citizens. One such important instance occurred during the spring of 1970 when black students at the University put forth demands for the incorporation of a Black Studies Program and underscored the need for the administration, faculty, and staff at the University to be reflective of the diversity within our state. One participant in these events, Dr. Don Cole, now serves as the Assistant Dean of the Graduate School and Associate Professor of Mathematics. His achievements underscore the positive contributions that he and his fellow students from that time have made to the University. In saluting Dr. Cole we recognize the contributions that he and his fellow students who helped establish in fact, as well as theory, that The University of Mississippi exists for the development of all our citizens.

– R. Gerald Turner, Chancellor   2/24/95

Appendix D

Speech by Susie Marshall for Second Baptist Church Honoring Rev. Blind Jim Ivy

This is how the story is told in the words of Rev. Blind Jim Ivy.

The son of Matilda Ivy, James Ivy, was brought to Oxford, Lafayette County, with his mother in early childhood. His mother, Matilda, was one of the ex-slave women who formed the nucleus of the first Colored Baptist Church, now Second Baptist, in 1869. He was brought up in this church and ordained to preach the gospel. In a whirlwind courtship he married Blind Rosa Sanders and lived across the street from Second Baptist Church. Blind Jim as he was called said that he was blinded while working [. . .] on the Tallahatchie Bridge when he was a teenager.

Being members of Second Baptist, Rev. Blind Jim would always lead the opening of the worship on Sunday at eleven o'clock services by singing "Let the Heaven Light Shine on Me."

Blind Jim became a part of the University of Mississippi in 1896. It is said that while selling peanuts at one of the football games he loudly cheered, "Hey! We're gonna beat 'em." After that event the students honored him as mascot of the football team and also honored him as Dean of the freshmen class. Blind Jim was loved by the students who took him with them to all the out of town football games where he cheered for the team and sold peanuts. He often would comically say, "I've never seen Ole Miss lose a football game." In his 60 years of selling peanuts, Blind Jim Ivy was never short changed.

Blind Jim Ivy was honored by the administration. He was the only individual ever to be allowed to drag his cane and his vendor with peanuts inside the halls of the Lyceum.

Blind Jim Ivy was thought of as being "grace" of the Ole Miss campus for 69 years before his death in 1955. His funeral services were attended at Second Baptist Church, the church which he supported spiritually and financially.

Appendix E

Susie Marshall's Unpublished Draft of Freedmen Town Marker Dedication Speech Recounting July 4, 1867, Speech of Oxford Ex-slave

Freemen Town 1869

We spend our lives as a tale that is told from word of mouth by our ancestors[;] nothing was recorded in the Oxford History of Lafayette County or Mississippi. After the Emancipation Proclamation was issued Jan. 3, 1863 hundreds of slaves were freed. These destitute people depended on the US Freedmen Bureau that made its appearance in Oxford December 27, 1866; a lieutenant of the union Army with a small band of troops to support him was responsible for furnishing food, clothing, shelter and security for 17,000 freedmen in Lafayette County during the period of 1865–1872.

Jim Nelson a colored man of about 35 years old was the principle Marshall of the 4th of July Celebration 1867. He said with a low bow, my colored friends, we are all free now, as the white folks are. I don't know why I am free, nor who made me free. The Yankees said they did and I suppose it's so. (But the white folks are our friends.) We have known them all our lives, but who ever made us free I thank them, and we all thank them for it, although it made many of us a heap worse off than we were before. (The speech is taken from the Oxford Falcon July 13, 1867) of Oxford Historical Society after freedom was declared, the first flush of freed slaves continued to worship as they had in day of bondage in white churches. (They had no homes or [blank space]) [S]oon eight ex-slaves women (write names) got permission from First Baptist Church minister to build their

Note: Typed from original handwritten version. Some punctuation, capitalization, and spelling have been inserted in order to clarify this document, which was not written to be read but heard.

own bush arbor so they could worship God in their own way. Baptist and Methodist enslaved worshiped together until March 20[. A] group of the Methodist faith purchased from Harrison Stern a fraction of lot No. 472 which borders Jackson Avenue, and established a small frame service chapel church building: the original building was replaced in 1910 by a red brick structure the church was renamed Burn Methodist Episcopal after Bishop Burn. Political meetings [were held in the] frame church during reconstruction (John Grisham, the writer owns the brick building).

Four years later, April 21, 1873 the Colored Baptist congregation purchased a fraction of lot No. 69 from Richard Burke a black man for $65 and built a small frame church. [This] church building was mysteriously destroyed by fire. Blind Jim Ivy helped to put the roof on the second frame church building.

Additional land was acquired from Taylor Robinson and wife Edmonia. In 1895 Lot No. 69 was entered again when property with a house on the Westside was purchased from Hattie Anderson. The deed is acknowledged by trustees George Harvey[, and] J. W. and Charles Avant.

[In] 1911 a stone church structure was built and named Second Baptist Church (located on the southeast edge of Freedmen Town[. S]chool was taught in Second Baptist Church for several years by the Minister H . . . W. Ber . . . [illegible].

By the turn of the century small houses dotted the neighborhood north of the maker to Price St. between Gulf . . . [illegible] and N. 7th Street. Around each house there were small gardens and often livestock, such as pigs, chicken and cows. [W]ater was furnished from cistern and wells dug by the residents. Second Baptist Church is located on the Southeast edge of Freedmen Town not far away at that time was Odd Fellows Hall, a Funeral home, a store and [illegible] Rosenwald School, built in 1917. Near by Bud Kirkwood ran his black[smith] shop, shoeing horses and firing wagons. Increasing numbers of Black families moved into the vicinity for work and educational purposes.

When Urban Renewal came, the subdivision was enlarged and improved the area under this urban renewal grant by the federal government in 1974. The head of the Oxford Housing Authority, Walter Rogers, an African American, was asked to name the area embraced in the renewal project. Mr. Rogers revived the old name of Freedmen Town. The residents of the refurbished beautiful neighborhood proudly refer to their community as Freedmen Town. And requested the authorization of the Board of Trustees of the Mississippi Department to erect a marker designating the neighborhood as Freedmen Town.

Bibliography

Abu-Lughod, Lila. 1990. The Romance of Resistance: Tracing Transformations of Power through Bedouin Women. *American Ethnologist* 17:41–55.

Alkalimat, Abdul et al. 1986. *Introduction to African American Studies*. Chicago: Twenty-First Century Books and Publications.

Anderson, Elijah. 1990. *Street Wise: Race, Class, and Change in an Urban Community*. Chicago: University of Chicago Press.

Barrett, Russell H. 1965. *Integration at Ole Miss*. Chicago: Quadrangle Books.

Bass, Jack. 1986. *The American South Comes of Age*. New York: Alfred A. Knopf.

Blu, Karen I. 1979. Race and Ethnicity: Changing Symbols of Dominance and Hierarchy. *Anthropological Quarterly* 2(2):77–85.

    1980. *The Lumbee Problem: The Making of an American Indian People*. Cambridge: Cambridge University Press.

Brightman, Robert. 1995. Forget Culture: Replacement, Transcendence, Relexification. *Cultural Anthropology* 10:509–46.

Carson, Clayborne. 1986. Civil Rights Reform and the Black Freedom Struggle. In *The Civil Rights Movement in America*, Charles W. Eagles, ed. Jackson: University Press of Mississippi.

Chafe, William H. 1980. *Civilities and Civil Rights: Greensboro, North Carolina, and the Black Struggle for Freedom*. New York: Oxford University Press.

Chapman, Abraham, ed. 1968. *Black Voices: An Anthology of Afro-American Literature*. New York: St. Martin's Press.

Coffey, Walker. 1995. Unpublished. Genealogy of Freedmen Town, Ms. in possession of author.

Cohen, Anthony P. 1985a. *The Symbolic Construction of Community*. New York: Tavistock Publications.

    1985b. Symbolism and Social Change: Matters of Life and Death in Whalsay, Shetland. *Man* 20:307–24.

    1987. *Whalsay: Symbol, Segment, and Boundary in a Shetland Island Community*. Wolfeboro, NH: Manchester University Press.

1994. *Self Consciousness: An Alternative Anthropology of Identity.* New York: Routledge.

Cohen, Anthony P., ed. 1982. *Belonging: Identity and Social Organisation in British Rural Cultures.* Manchester, England: Manchester University Press.

Cox, Oliver Cromwell. 1970. *Caste, Class, and Race: A Study in Social Dynamics.* New York: Modern Reader Paperbacks.

Davis, Allison et al. 1965. *Deep South: A Social Anthropological Study of Caste and Class.* Chicago: University of Chicago Press.

de Certeau, Michel. 1980. On the Oppositional Practices of Everyday Life. *Social Text* IE:3–43.

1984. *The Practice of Everyday Life.* Berkeley: University of California Press.

Dirks, Nicholas, Geoff Eley, and Sherry B. Ortner, eds. 1994. *Culture/ Power/ History: A Reader in Contemporary Social Theory.* Princeton, NJ: Princeton University Press.

Dollard, John. 1957 (1937). *Caste and Class in a Southern Town.* New York: Doubleday Anchor Books.

Douglas, Mary. 1991. *Purity and Danger: An Analysis of the Concepts of Pollution and Taboo.* New York: Routledge.

DuBois, W. E. B. 1903. *The Souls of Black Folk: Essays and Sketches.* Chicago: A. C. McClurg and Company.

Dunbar, Paul Laurence. 1968. We Wear the Mask. In *Black Voices: An Anthology of Afro-American Literature*, Abraham Chapman, ed. New York: St. Martin's Press, p. 355.

Durr, Virginia. 1985. *Outside the Magic Circle.* University, Alabama: University of Alabama Press.

Eagles, Charles W., ed. 1986. *The Civil Rights Movement in America.* Jackson, MS: University Press of Mississippi.

Emmett, Isabel. 1982. Fe Godwn Ni Eto: Stasis and Change in a Welsh Industrial Town. In *Belonging: Identity and Social Organisation in British Rural Cultures*, Anthony P. Cohen, ed. Manchester, England: Manchester University Press, pp. 165–97.

Evers, Myrlie. 1967. *For Us, The Living.* Garden City: Doubleday.

Fanon, Frantz. 1967. *Black Skin White Masks.* New York: Grove Press.

Farganis, James. 1993. *Readings in Social Theory: The Classic Tradition to Post-Modernism.* New York: MacGraw-Hill.

Fields, Karen. 1994. What One Cannot Remember Mistakenly. In *History and Memory in African-American Culture*, Genevieve Fabre and Robert O'Meally, eds. New York: Oxford University Press, pp. 150–63.

Foley, Douglas E., Clarice Mota, Donald E. Post, and Ignacio Lozano. 1988. *From Peones to Politicos: Class and Ethnicity in a South Texas Town: 1900–1987.* Austin: University of Texas Press.

Fraser, Nancy. 1990. Rethinking the Public Sphere: A Contribution to the Critique of Actually Existing Democracy. *Social Text: Theory/Culture/Ideology* 8(3)–9(1):56–80.

Frazier, E. Franklin. 1964. *The Negro Church in America.* New York: Schocken Books.

Friedman, Jonathan. 1992a. *Modernity and Identity.* Oxford: Blackwell.

1992b. The Past in the Future: History and the Politics of Identity. *American Anthropologist* 94:837–59.

1994. On Perilous Ideas. *Current Anthropology* 35:173–4.

Geertz, Clifford. 1973. *The Interpretation of Cultures.* New York: Basic Book.

1980. *Negara: The Theatre State in Nineteenth-Century Bali.* Princeton, NJ: Princeton University Press.

1983. *Local Knowledge: Further Essays in Interpretive Anthropology.* New York: Basic Books.

Giddens, Anthony. 1986 (1984). *The Constitution of Society: Outline of the Theory of Structuration.* Berkeley: University of California Press.

Ginsburg, Faye. 1989. *Contested Lives: The Abortion Debate in an American Community.* Berkeley: University of California Press.

Glick-Shiller, Nina. 1994. Introducing Identities: Global Studies in Culture and Power. *Identities* 1:1–6.

Gordone, Charles. 1969. *No Place to Be Somebody.* New York: French.

Grayson, J. Paul. 1980. Introduction. In *Class, State, Ideology and Change: Marxist Perspectives on Canada*, Paul Grayson, ed. Toronto, Canada: Holt, Rinehart & Winston of Canada Limited.

Gregory, Steven. 1992. The Changing Significance of Race and Class in an African-American Community. *American Ethnologist* 19(2):255–74.

1994. Race, Identity and Political Activism: The Shifting Contours of the African American Public Sphere. 7(1).

1996. We've Been Down This Road Already. In *Race*, Steven Gregory and Roger Sanjek, eds. New Brunswick, NJ: Rutgers University Press, pp. 18–38.

Gregory, Steven and Roger Sanjek, eds. 1996. *Race.* New Brunswick, NJ: Rutgers University Press.

Gwaltney, John L., ed. 1981. *Drylongso: A Self-portrait of Black America.* New York: Random House.

Habermas, Jürgen. 1994. *The Structural Transformation of the Public Sphere: An Inquiry into a Category of Bourgeois Society.* Cambridge: MIT Press.

Harrison, Faye V. 1998. Introduction: Expanding the Discourse on "Race." *American Anthropologist.* 100(3):609–10.

1995a. The Persistent Power of "Race" in the Cultural and Political Economy of Racism. In *Annual Review of Anthropology* 24:47–74.

1995b. "Give Me That Old-Time Religion": The Genealogy and Cultural Politics of an African-Christian Celebration in Halifax County, North Carolina. In *Religion in the Contemporary South: Diversity, Community, and Identity*, O. Kendall White, Jr. and Daryl White, eds. Athens: The University of Georgia Press, pp. 34–45.

Hawkins, Denise B. 1995. Four Decades After Brown, Southern Higher Education Remains Separate,..., *Black Issues in Higher Education* 6, 12(7):12.

Hemenway, Robert E. 1977. *Zora Neale Hurston: A Literary Biography.* Urbana: University of Illinois Press.

Hollman, Kenneth W. 1976. *A Study of the Economic Impact of the University of Mississippi on Oxford and Lafayette County.* University, MS: University of Mississippi Bureau of Business and Economic Research.

Holt, Len. 1965. *The Summer That Didn't End.* New York: Wm. Morrow.

Hughes, Langston. 1968. I, too, Sing America. In *Black Voices: An Anthology of Afro-American Literature*, Abraham Chapman, ed. New York: St. Martin's Press.

Hurston, Zora Neale. 1978. *Their Eyes Were Watching God*. Urbana: University of Illinois Press.

Johnson, Hildegard Binder. 1976. *Order Upon the Land: The U.S. Rectangular Land Survey and the Upper Mississippi Country*. New York: Oxford University Press.

Joint Center for Political and Economic Studies. 1990. *Black Elected Officials*. Washington, DC: Joint Center for Political and Economic Studies Press.

Jordan, June. 1972. *Fannie Lou Hamer*. New York: Crowell.

Kasinitz, Philip. 1991. *Caribbean New York: Black Immigrants and the Politics of Race*. Ithaca, NY: Cornell University Press.

Kennedy, Theodore R. 1980. *You Gotta Deal with It*. New York: Oxford University Press.

King, Martin Luther, Jr. 1996. I Have a Dream. In *Negro Protest Thought in the Twentieth Century*, Francis L. Broderick and August Meier, eds. New York: Bobbs-Merrill.

Kingsolver, Ann E. 1992. Contested Livelihood: "Placing" One Another in "Cedar," Kentucky. *Anthropological Quarterly* 65(3):128–36.

Kunkel, Peter and Sara Sue Kennard. 1971. *Spout Spring; A Black Community*. New York: Holt, Rinehart and Winston.

Krüger-Kahloula, Angelika. 1994. On the Wrong Side of the Fence: Racial Segregation in American Cemeteries. In *History and Memory in African-American Culture*, Genevieve Fabre and Robert O'Maelly, eds. New York: Oxford University Press.

Lewis, Hyland. 1955. *Blackways of Kent*. Chapel Hill: University of North Carolina Press.

Lomnitz-Adler, Claudio. 1991. Concepts for the Study of Regional Culture. *American Ethnologist* 18:195–214.

1992. *Exits from the Labyrinth: Culture and Ideology in the Mexican National Space*. Berkeley: University of California Press.

Mann, Patricia. 1990. Unifying Discourse: City College as a Post-Modern Public Sphere. *Social Text: Theory/Culture/Ideology* 8(3)–9(1):81–102.

Marshall, Susie. 1994–1995. Speech by Susie Marshall for Second Baptist Church Honoring Rev. Blind Jim Ivy.

1995. History of Second Missionary Baptist Church. *Soul Force*. March, pp. 14–15.

1996. Susie Marshall's Unpublished Draft of Freedmen Town Marker Dedication Recounting July 4, 1867, Speech of Oxford Ex-slave. Speech Photocopy in author's possession. Reprinted in Appendix E.

Meier, August and Elliott M. Rudwick. 1973. *CORE: A Study in the Civil Rights Movement, 1942–1968*. New York: Oxford University Press.

Meredith, James. 1966. *Three Years in Mississippi*. Bloomington: Indiana University Press.

Mississippi State University (Web site). 1999. *http://msuinfo.ur.msstate.edu/hot_news/ayers*

Molpus, Nash. 2002. *http://www.olemiss.edu/depts/south/register/fall02/cover.htm*

Moody, Anne. 1968. *Coming of Age in Mississippi*. New York: Dell Books.

Morley, David and Kevin Robins. 1995. *Spaces of Identity: Global Media, Electronic Landscapes and Cultural Boundaries*. New York: Routledge.

Morrison, Minion K. C. 1987. *Black Political Mobilization: Leadership, Power, and Mass Behavior*. Albany: State University of New York Press.

Myerhoff, Barbara G. 1980. *Number Our Days*. New York: Simon and Schuster.

Ogbu, John and Margaret Gibson, eds. 1991. *Minority Strategies and Schooling: Immigrant vs. Involuntary Minorities*. New York: Garland.

Orum, Anthony M. 1972. *Black Students in Protest: A Study of the Origins of the Black Student Movement*. Washington, DC: American Sociological Association.

Peters, John Durham and Kenneth Cmiel. 1991. Media Ethics and the Public Sphere. *Communication* 12:197–215.

Piven, Frances Fox and Richard A. Cloward. 1979. *Poor People's Movements: Why They Succeed, How They Fail*. New York: Vintage Books.

Polan, Dana. 1990. The Public's Fear, or Media as Monster in Habermas, Negt, and Kluge. *Social Text: Theory/Culture/Ideology* 8(3)–9(1):56–80.

Powdermaker, Hortense. 1966. *Stranger and Friend: The Way of an Anthropologist*. New York: W. W. Norton.

   1993. *After Freedom: A Cultural Study in the Deep South*. Madison: University of Wisconsin Press.

Priest, Kersten Bayt. 1998. Disharmony in the 11:00 AM Worship Hours: A case study of an abandoned interethnic church merger. Master's Thesis, University of South Carolina.

Rubin, Morton. 1951. *Plantation County*. Chapel Hill: University of North Carolina Press.

Scott, James C. 1985. *Weapons of the Weak*. New Haven, CT: Yale University Press.

Sennett, Richard. 1995. *The Fall of Public Man*. New York: Vintage Books.

Sewell, George Alexander. 1977. *Mississippi Black History Makers*. Jackson: University Press of Mississippi.

Shanklin, Eugenia. 1994. *Anthropology and Race*. Belmont, CA: Wadsworth.

Silver, James. 1964. *Mississippi: The Closed Society*. New York: Harcourt, Brace & World.

Smith, Gavin. 1991. The Production of Culture in Local Rebellion. In *Golden Ages, Dark Ages*, Jay O'Brien and William Roseberry, eds. Berkeley: University of California Press.

Smitherman, Geneva. 1986. *Talkin and Testifyin: The Language of Black America*. Detroit: Wayne State University Press.

Sobotka, C. John, Jr. 1976. *A History of Lafayette County, Mississippi*. Oxford, MS: Rebel Press.

Sutton, Constance. 1987. *Caribbean Life in New York City: Sociocultural Dimensions*. New York: New York Center for Migration Studies of New York.

   1992. Transnational Identities and Cultures. In *Immigration and Ethnicity*, Michael D'Innocenzo and Josef P. Sirefman, eds. Westport, CT: Greenwood Press.

Thomas-Houston, Marilyn M. 1995. Drawing On the Past Fifty Years To "Create Our Future." *Soul Force*, March.

    1998. Creating a New Perspective for the Interpretation of the African American Experience. Unpublished Master's Thesis, New York University.

    1999. What's Black and White and Read All Over?: The Use of the Public Sphere during the Civil Rights Movement. Paper delivered at the University of Mississippi for the Center of Southern Studies Sesquicentennial Celebration.

U.S. Department of Commerce. 1995. *County Business Patterns 1993 Mississippi*. Washington, D.C.: Bureau of the Census.

Walker, Clarence E. 1991. *Deromanticizing Black History: Critical Essays and Reappraisals*. Knoxville: University of Tennessee Press.

West, Cornel. 1996. SC United Action Presents: An Evening with Dr. Cornel West (Lecture). Orangeburg, SC.

    1994. *Race Matters*. New York: Vintage Books.

Williams, Brackette F. 1989. A Class Act: Anthropology and the Race to Nation Across Ethnic Terrain. *Annual Review of Anthropology* 18:401–44.

    1991. *Stains on My Name, War in My Veins*. Durham, NC: Duke University Press.

Williams, Robin M. Jr., and Gerald David Jaynes, eds. 1989. *A Common Destiny: Blacks and American Society*. Washington, DC: National Academy Press.

Willis, Susan. 1994. Memory and Mass Culture. In *History and Memory in African-American Culture*, Genevieve Fabre and Robert O'Maelly, eds. New York: Oxford University Press.

Wolf, Eric R. 1982. *Europe and the People Without History*. Berkeley: University of California Press.

Index